The Man Who Saved the Whooping Crane

UNIVERSITY PRESS OF FLORIDA

Florida A&M University, Tallahassee
Florida Atlantic University, Boca Raton
Florida Gulf Coast University, Ft. Myers
Florida International University, Miami
Florida State University, Tallahassee
New College of Florida, Sarasota
University of Central Florida, Orlando
University of Florida, Gainesville
University of North Florida, Jacksonville
University of South Florida, Tampa
University of West Florida, Pensacola

The Man Who Saved the
WHOOPING CRANE

The
Robert
Porter
Allen
Story

Kathleen Kaska

University Press of Florida

Gainesville / Tallahassee / Tampa / Boca Raton / Pensacola

Orlando / Miami / Jacksonville / Ft. Myers / Sarasota

Printed in the United States of America. This book is printed on Glatfelter
Natures Book, a paper certified under the standards of the Forestry
Stewardship Council (FSC). It is a recycled stock that contains 30 percent
post-consumer waste and is acid-free.

This book may be available in an electronic edition.

Frontispiece: Robert Porter Allen on the Grand Detour Portage, May 24, 1955.
Photo by Robert C. Stewart. Courtesy of Alice Allen.

17 16 15 14 13 12   6 5 4 3 2 1

Library of Congress Cataloging-in-Publication Data
Kaska, Kathleen.
The man who saved the whooping crane : the Robert Porter Allen story /
Kathleen Kaska.
p. cm.
Includes bibliographical references and index.
ISBN 978-0-8130-4024-0 (alk. paper) — ISBN 0-8130-4024-8 (alk. paper)
1. Allen, Robert Porter. 2. Whooping crane—Conservation—North
America. 3. Cranes (Birds)—Conservation—Florida. 4. Wetland birds—
Conservation—North America. 5. Cranes (Birds)—Conservation—North
America. I. Title.
QL696.G84K384 2012
639.9'7832—dc23   2012009838

The University Press of Florida is the scholarly publishing agency for the
State University System of Florida, comprising Florida A&M University,
Florida Atlantic University, Florida Gulf Coast University, Florida
International University, Florida State University, New College of Florida,
University of Central Florida, University of Florida, University of North
Florida, University of South Florida, and University of West Florida.

University Press of Florida
15 Northwest 15th Street
Gainesville, FL 32611-2079
http://www.upf.com

To Alice Allen,

without whose assistance

this book

would not have been possible

Contents

Foreword

In 1939, Bob Allen left New York City with his wife and their two young children and moved to the tiny backwater fishing village of Tavernier, in the Florida Keys. The National Audubon Society had sent the ornithologist into the wilds of Florida to solve the mystery of the roseate spoonbill's decline. Most other species of wading birds had rebounded after the cessation of the "plume wars" a few years earlier. What Allen discovered in his research was that most locals were more interested in cooking the local birds than in preserving their numbers. As a result, Allen took on the added position of wildlife ambassador.

Shortly after his arrival in Tavernier, Allen set up camp on Bottlepoint Key in Florida Bay, where the only known spoonbill nesting colony existed. While conducting his research, he lived as a hermit, returning home to his family every few weeks. Sleeping in a tent, running tests in a makeshift laboratory, and cooking over a wood fire was the lifestyle Allen relished. The result of his work on the spoonbills led to the publication of one of the most comprehensive and authoritative narratives on spoonbill biology and ecology we have today.

Allen followed his spoonbill work with similar in-depth studies of the severely endangered flamingo, eventually taking on his most dangerous and challenging project: saving the whooping crane. As you read Kathleen Kaska's account of Allen's North American adventures, most of which threw him into inhospitable habitats, you will understand the dedication of one man's desire to make a difference in saving birds.

As the current director of Tavernier Science Center, a position created for Bob Allen more than seventy years ago, I have been able to carry

Allen's work into the twenty-first century. After earning my master's degree, I first came to the Science Center to undertake an eighteen-month field study of spoonbill food resources. Up to this point, my field of study had been fish behavior. A fieldwork program in Costa Rica resulted in a life-changing experience, and my interest shifted to tropical ecology. That project resulted in a Ph.D., a satisfying career, and a strong devotion to the welfare of our "pinks" (local term for the spoonbills). Twenty-two years later, I'm still carrying on Bob Allen's work. As the great ornithologist said, "My plans have given way before the magic of its appeal."

So I was genuinely thrilled when Kathleen told me of her intention to write Bob Allen's biography. I had fervently wanted to write the story myself one day, albeit from the standpoint of his work in conserving Florida's wildlife and wild places. After all, it was Allen's work that helped establish Florida's Everglades National Park.

As I sit writing these words, I look around my office and see many reminders of a man I feel I know even though he died only days before I was born. On top of the bookcase is the antique hygrometer that he used to measure salinity. Sitting on a shelf is a flamingo skull that he collected. My computer monitor sits on a handmade pine box Allen built to hold spoonbill eggshells, for which it's still used today. The file drawer of my desk is full of Allen's handwritten and typed notes, letters, and reports. I find myself frequently looking through this file drawer for insights into spoonbill behavior or to gain a perspective on what life was like in Florida Bay in the 1940s and 1950s. Sometimes my intention is simply to commune with an old friend I never had the pleasure of meeting. Having Allen's research material and personal possessions close at hand is a testament to how important his work was to me. I stand on the shoulders of a giant; and for this, I am humble and forever proud.

Jerry Lorenz
Director, Tavernier Science Center

Preface

In the fall of 1885, two families of six whooping cranes sailed across the Dakota Territory on their way to the marshes along San Antonio Bay in Texas. The day's flight had been a long one, and the juveniles who were migrating for the first time struggled to keep up with their parents. As the flock approached the Missouri River, the birds detected a momentary slack in the warm air current on which they had been gliding; the lead adults spiraled down and landed on the mud banks. The shallow waters would provide a generous banquet of fish and frogs, and the open flats would allow the adults to spot predators during the night. A female wasted no time and high-stepped into the reeds to spear a frog. The youngsters, still sporting their rust-colored plumage, probed for snails. Suddenly, a snap of dry brush scattered the flock. The next sound split the air, bringing down two birds. The adult died before it hit the ground. The juvenile fluttered into the brush.

Young S. W. Oliver and his brother rushed to claim their prize, hoping for two birds to throw into the family cooking pot. The boys peered through the brush at the crane chick: and the chick peered back, wild-eyed and frightened. Seeing the bird's injuries were slight, they brought it home to nurse its wounds. The Oliver brothers ended their hunting of whooping cranes. They named the bird Bill and raised it as a pet. That first winter, as Bill grew into a graceful, lanky bird, the boys learned to appreciate Bill's prowess as he stalked food along the ponds. They listened as he sent out his crane calls in the early morning. They watched as Bill danced the crane dance of his species. One morning, the Oliver boys rushed from the house at the sound of a shotgun blast and found Bill dead in his pen. A hunter, visiting from the East and finding an easy target, had shot the captive bird and walked away.

In 1948, more than sixty years later, S. W. Oliver opened a copy of *Life* magazine, saw a whooping crane photo, and read the article about the endangered birds. Oliver wrote to the National Audubon Society and told his story. Ornithologist Robert Porter Allen read Oliver's account and responded in an editorial in *Audubon Magazine*:

"I imagine that these are the fellows who have killed most of our lost whooping cranes. They are without knowledge, without understanding and without purpose. Now we are without Bill and nearly all of his kind. Mr. Oliver's story will convince you that we are much poorer because of this loss. Much poorer than most of us seem to know."

In the last chapter of Allen's book *On the Trail of Vanishing Birds*, he relates many such chilling accounts of blatant disregard for endangered birds. Bill's story was just one of the many inspirations that fueled Allen's desire to make a difference in the world of avian conservation.

Allen's story, and seeing the whooping cranes myself on numerous occasions at the Aransas National Wildlife Refuge, inspired me to bring attention to Allen's work preserving these magnificent birds. In 1984, I had the opportunity, while studying marine biology at the University of Texas Marine Science Institute, to observe dozens of shorebird species along the Texas coast. I returned one December to take my first whooping crane tour at the Aransas Refuge. Learning of the cranes' endangerment, I immediately knew I wanted to make a difference in the species' survival. As a middle-school science teacher, I included a bird unit in my environmental curriculum. I was determined to instill in my students a passion for any environmental cause.

Years later when I began freelance writing, I realized I had another outlet for spreading the word. In researching an article about whooping cranes for *Texas Highways* magazine, I learned that few people had ever heard of Robert Porter Allen or the work he did to save the species. This was when I decided to continue my research and turn the project into a book. Robert Porter Allen's story needed to be told.

I

The Making
of an Ornithologist,
1905–1946

I don't wish to be didactic,
But there's something enigmatic
In the little game the Pink Bird plays with Time.
So I've cast my lot with his 'un,
In this mangrove-studded prison
And I'm looking for the reason and the rhyme.

Robert Porter Allen, *The Flame Birds*

1 ~

By Some Strange Miracle

It was April 17, 1948, in the early hours of a muggy Texas morning on the Gulf Coast. The sun at last burned away the thick fog that had settled over Blackjack Peninsula. The world's last flock of wild whooping cranes had spent the winter feeding on blue crab and killifish in the vast salt flats they called home. During the night, all three members of the Slough Family had moved to feed on higher ground about 2 miles away from their usual haunt. The cool, crisp winter was giving way to a warm balmy spring, the days were growing longer, and territorial boundaries were no longer defended. Restlessness had spread throughout the flock.

As Robert Porter Allen drove along East Shore Road near Carlos Field in his government-issued beat-to-hell pickup, he spotted the four cranes now spiraling 1,000 feet above the marsh. He pulled his truck over to the roadside and watched, hoping to witness, for the first time, a migration takeoff. One adult crane pulled away from the family and flew northward, whooping as it rose on an air current. When the others lagged behind, the crane returned, the family regrouped, circled a few times, and landed in the cordgrass in the shallows of San Antonio Bay. It was Allen's second year at the Aransas National Wildlife Refuge. He had learned to read the nuances of his subjects almost as well as they read the changing of the seasons.

In the days preceding, twenty-four cranes left for their summer home somewhere in western Canada, possibly as far north as the Arctic Circle. This annual event, which had been occurring for at least ten thousand years, might be one of the last unless Allen could accomplish what no one else had.

The next morning when Allen parked his truck near Mullet Bay, the Slough Family was gone, having departed sometime during the night. That afternoon, he threw his gear into the back of his station wagon and followed.

Robert Porter Allen's colleagues often joked that the charismatic ornithologist could walk into a room of adversaries and have them questioning their lifelong beliefs in less than five minutes. He stood solid and strong, yet there was a pleasant and easy air behind the deep-tanned face. A no-nonsense sort of man who couldn't be bothered with excuses or the idea of defeat, Allen possessed a subtle self-confidence that did not come only with experience; it was clear from the get-go that Bob Allen was born with the drive, tenacity, and ability to change minds. In a community where many locals cared nothing for the protection of a few birds, Allen could turn the hostile tides, gain sympathy, and have ardent adversaries pledge their support to his cause. And that cause was inevitably . . . saving birds.

Bob Allen's story began long before his quest to follow the whooping cranes north. At the train station in South Williamsport, Pennsylvania, Allen pushed his way to the front of the crowd as the local National Guard unit boarded a troop train bound for the Mexican border. An officer stood on the rear platform as the train left the station and raising his rifle, proclaimed his weapon would be the one to kill the bandit Pancho Villa. For Allen, a boy of eleven, it was an exciting moment. A deep desire for adventure had taken hold. The year was 1916, and it proved to be a turning point in Robert Porter Allen's life. Five years later, he enlisted in the local guard, having fudged his age. The experience was not much more than Friday-evening drill practice and two weeks of artillery training in the summer. After six months, his first check of $26.67 arrived. The money went to buy a pair of field glasses for the sole purpose of studying the local bird population.

Growing up in Pennsylvania, shortly after the turn of the twentieth century, Allen and his younger brother, Johnny, spent their early years exploring the wilderness of Bald Eagle Mountain, stalking bears and cougars, fishing the mountain streams, and identifying every bird that flew. Accompanying them on their traipses through the woods was a copy of Ernest Thompson Seton's *Two Little Savages*, a tale of two young boys determined to learn the life of American Indians and live it with gusto.

More than a survival guide, Seton's pages were laced with a high regard and respect for wildlife and nature's beauty. The Allen boys used it as their wilderness bible. By the time Allen was ten years old, he had read the book so many times that the pages had turned soft with wear. Many years later, the knowledge gained from Seton's experience in the wilderness would save Bob Allen's life.

—

Allen came from a family of outspoken and dedicated enthusiasts. His father, grandfather, and great-grandfather were lawyers. His grandfather, after whom Allen was named, also served a term in the Pennsylvania State Senate in 1874. Allen's maternal grandfather was a Methodist circuit rider. His mother, Edith Allen, a schoolteacher, marched with the suffragettes down Fifth Avenue in New York City. After Allen's father died, she married Renshaw C. "Tommy" DeWitt, a church musician. She later became an at-large delegate to the 1936 and 1940 National Democratic Conventions held in Philadelphia and Chicago, respectively. Needless to say, from a young age, Allen was not without candid, charismatic role models.

By the time he was in high school, Allen's desire to study ornithology had crystallized. Recognizing his potential, his biology teacher encouraged Allen to join the Junior Audubon Club. Through this organization, he was to meet notable ornithologists who would eventually direct and shape his career. Finding a university that offered a degree in ornithology was not easy. Enrolling in Lafayette College in Easton, Pennsylvania, the alma mater of his father, grandfather, and numerous other relatives, seemed like the best place to start. However, for a young man who had spent his youth hiking the mountain trails of the Susquehanna, canoeing river rapids, and tracking black bear, life at Lafayette proved tedious. Allen found it impossible to shed his outmoded Norfolk jacket and join the ranks of the coat-and-tie echelon.

Johnny Allen had adapted to college life much more easily and eventually graduated and moved to New York City. Bob Allen remained at Lafayette for two long, unsatisfying years, a time he later described as "wasted" as far as advancing his career. In his *On the Trail of Vanishing Birds*, Allen wrote of his college years: "I did learn a few things about the rest of the world that lay beyond the shadow of Bald Eagle Mountain. But I remained an undisciplined nonconformist, incapable of learning many of the graces and determined to find a way of life wherein the kind of shoes you wore and the sort of knot you tied in your tie were of no importance whatever."[1]

During his time at Lafayette, Allen corresponded frequently with ornithologist and avian artist Louis Fuertes, who encouraged Allen to enroll at Cornell University. Soon after the transfer, Allen's father died suddenly. His mother, now needing work, accepted a teaching job at a girl's school in New York. Feeling that ornithology was not in the stars, Allen dropped out of school after three months. To satisfy his restless spirit and assist his mother financially, he joined the Merchant Marine and hopped a freighter bound for Singapore. In the next four years, he circumnavigated the world twice and survived a shipwreck in the Sulu Sea. During this time, he read every adventure book he could get his hands on.

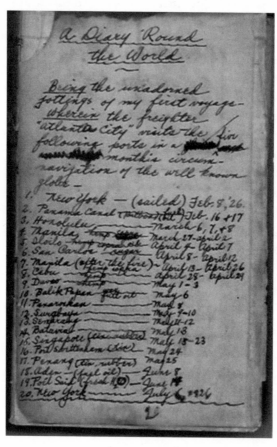

A page from the personal diary of Robert Porter Allen while he was in the U.S. Merchant Marine in the 1920s. Courtesy of Alice Allen.

Allen returned to New York in 1929. He was twenty-four years old. His experience at sea had toughened him but did nothing to quell his restless nature. The forty-eight cents in his pocket wasn't going to get him far. Allen planned to reenlist for another stint with the Merchant Marine. Then one evening that December, as winter settled in, Bob Allen's life took an unexpected turn. At the party of a friend, he met a young woman.

Evelyn Sedgwick was living in New York City. She had just graduated in piano from the Institute of Musical Art of the City of New York (later renamed the Juilliard School of Music) and was preparing for her début recital at Steinway Hall. The promising young pianist had been born and raised in south central Iowa. Her father, Tom Sedgwick, a hard-core Republican, was a telegrapher for the railroad and her mother, Effie, a housewife. While living in Mystic, Iowa, Effie Sedgwick often strolled by the small music shop in town. In the window was a piano. She would pray that the child she carried would one day learn to play. At the age of eight, Evelyn took her first lesson and fell in love with the instrument.

That winter evening after Bob Allen and Evelyn Sedgwick left the party, they wandered into Washington Square Park and talked well into the morning, paying no attention to the snow dusting the streets, unconcerned that their futures lay in totally different directions. "We talked and talked, on and on, endlessly," Allen wrote. "By some strange miracle each of us seemed to have things to say that the other wanted very much to hear, and although we had met purely by chance the lives of both of us were changed from that moment on."[2]

Allen now had a reason to stay in New York. All he needed was a job— and not just any job. Romance had not squelched his desire for adventure; whatever work he found would have to keep the spark alive. During his time at sea, Allen had corresponded with an ornithologist he'd met at a Junior Audubon Club lecture in Pennsylvania. Dr. Frank Chapman was now the director of the Bird Department of the American Museum of Natural History. Hoping the ornithologist might be able to find him a job with the museum, Allen paid Chapman a visit. The best Chapman could do was offer Allen volunteer work with the possibility of a paying position in the future. With only enough money in his pocket for one subway ticket, Allen couldn't wait for an opening. Chapman sent him to the Audubon House to see T. Gilbert Pearson, a man Allen had met while in high school. Pearson was now president of the National Association of

Audubon Societies (later renamed the National Audubon Society) and was delighted to see Allen. But Audubon was not hiring. The two men visited, catching up on the past few years. Pearson was not immune to Allen's charm, and after a long congenial conversation about the wonders of the outdoor life, Allen left the Audubon office as the new library cataloguer. The work involved unpacking and sorting through mountains of dusty documents stored in the basement, not quite the adventure he had hoped for, but it promised a paycheck and opportunity. Allen rushed to a friend's apartment and wrote to Evelyn, who was staying with her parents, now living in St. Louis. Soon the young couple began to plan their wedding.

In the meantime, Allen made quick work of his cataloguing job, and Pearson promptly promoted his young enthusiastic employee to Audubon librarian. With the Depression putting millions of people out of work, Allen was grateful for the opportunity. However, he had no intention of remaining among Audubon's books and papers. Early in 1931, Audubon got word of a colony of great black-backed gulls nesting on some islands off the coast of Maine. Allen convinced Pearson to allow him to survey the colony. This expedition and survey became Robert Porter Allen's ticket out of Audubon's library and into the field.

At this time, the Linnaean Society of New York, a group of scientists and amateurs dedicated to the observation and study of birds in New York City, was gathering force. With a membership of ornithologists that read like a Who's Who in the birding world—Aldo Leopold, Allan Cruickshank, Bill Vogt, and Joe Hickey (who became a close friend of the Allens and later, godfather of their children)—Allen jumped at the opportunity to join. Working with Hickey and on the Field Work Committee, Allen studied every facet of ornithology: taxonomy and classification, ecology and migration, avian evolution, and a new growing interest—the study of bird territories and bird behavior.

In March of that year, not long after her début, Evelyn broke the news to her parents of her plans to marry Bob Allen. A concert tour had been in the planning, and Evelyn's becoming the wife of an ornithologist had not been part of that plan. Tom Sedgwick had spent a great deal of time and money on Evelyn's education and was no doubt concerned about her marrying a man with a meager income. But the Sedgwicks had raised a strong-willed, independent-minded, young woman. On January 14, 1933, with Allen's Audubon mentor Ernest Golsan Holt and his wife, Margaret, as witnesses, and with Allen's mother and brother, Johnny, attending, Bob and Evelyn were married in a quiet service in the Presbyterian Church on Fifth Avenue.

—

In earlier years, while Bob and Johnny Allen explored the wilderness in northern Pennsylvania, the Industrial Revolution was in full swing, marching its way across the country. Grasslands were plowed under and turned into farmland, loggers were destroying thousands of acres of old-growth forests, and the country's wetlands, swamps, river bottoms, and bottomland forests were drained for development. Avian habitats were disappearing as fast as loggers could fell the trees. The recent laws passed to protect wildlife and establish sanctuaries were not enough to stem the flow of destruction.

Unrestrained hunting caused the disappearance of the Carolina parakeet in the early 1900s. Ornithologist C. J. Maynard writes of the bird's demise in his book *The Birds of Eastern North America* (1881): "In Florida their enemies are legion; bird catchers trap them by the hundreds for the northern markets, sportsmen shoot them for food, planters kill them because they eat their fruit, and tourists slaughter them simply because they presented a favorable mark."[3] Teddy Roosevelt, in his letter to the editor of *Bird-Lore* magazine in June 1899, described their loss as being as "severe as if the Catskills or the Palisades were taken away."[4] Farther south in the woodlands of the United States, the ivory-billed woodpecker had slipped beyond hope. Its last two footholds disappeared when the Singer Tract in Louisiana was cut for timber and the Santee River marshes in South Carolina were flooded after the construction of a dam for hydroelectric power. There was a concerted effort by conservationists to set aside a few acres for a preserve, but the areas were destroyed before any action could be taken. Only a few decades earlier, the passenger pigeon, an elegant bird with a 16-inch-long tail and iridescent plumage, had numbered in the billions. Between 1866 and 1876, more than 12 million brooding pigeons were killed, which resulted in the starvation of 6 million nestlings. No mercy was shown in man's effort to capture the bird. They were shot, trapped, and burned. Sulfur pots were ignited underneath the birds' roost to suffocate them, after which they were knocked from their nests with long poles. Why the interest in pigeons? Food—squab had found its way to restaurants and dinner tables in the midwestern and eastern states. The birds were sold for fifty cents a dozen. The last passenger pigeon, Martha, died in the Cincinnati Zoological Garden at 1:00 p.m. on September 1, 1914.

Immediate measures had to be taken to keep the American flamingo, roseate spoonbill, California condor, and the whooping crane from following suit.

By the early 1900s, 95 percent of the country's bird population had disappeared, and habitat loss was only a part of the problem. A new fashion trend was growing in the United States and Europe. Bird feathers were being used to adorn ladies' hats. As the fad caught on, the designs became more outrageous. Women could be seen strolling down the street with stuffed hummingbirds, sparrow wings, bald eagle feathers, and even owl heads perched on their hats. Due to the high demand for plumage, commercial bird hunting had become a lucrative business. Milliners offered big money to plume hunters for killing and plucking the birds for their feathers. These feathers were then shipped to hat makers in New York, Boston, Philadelphia, and Europe. Since the slaughtered adult birds were taken in such great numbers and their young left to starve, many populations were unable to recover. Several bird species in the wetlands along the Atlantic coast were almost wiped out. Two of the most sought-after birds were the great white and snowy egrets. One ounce of their willowy white feathers was worth twice as much as an ounce of gold.

News of the avian destruction and disappearance found its way into the media. In 1896, Harriet Hemenway, a wealthy socialite from Boston, read an article about the bird slaughter. Outraged, Hemenway began an unprecedented environmental campaign to stop the practice. She enlisted the help of her cousin Minna Hall, and the two women went directly to the source of the problem. They invited their friends, ladies of society, to tea and challenged them to cease participating in the devastation by pledging not to buy plume-decorated hats. Not long after, their small group grew to more than nine hundred strong. They called the organization the Massachusetts Audubon Society. The organization was not the first to go toe-to-toe with the millinery trade. Ten years prior, George Bird Grinnell, game hunter and creator of *Forest and Stream* magazine, formed the original Audubon Society in an attempt to discourage the reckless killing of wild birds and the use of bird feathers for fashion. Although his membership reached almost forty thousand, Grinnell disbanded his organization after two years when he failed to stop the destruction. Hemenway, fortunately, had the financial means and political connections to succeed where Grinnell had failed.

The American Ornithologists' Union (AOU), active in bird conservation since 1883, joined the fight in what became known as the Plume Wars. Although most of the organization's work was centered in New England, its focus had turned to the battle stronghold in Florida. In 1902, the AOU hired Guy Bradley as Florida's first game warden. His assignment was to protect birds from plume hunters and to identify the culprits. Bradley went undercover to battle some of the most notorious plume hunters of South Florida. Less than three years into his assignment he was murdered. Plume hunter Walter Smith was arrested for Bradley's murder. Although evidence of murder was strong, Smith claimed self-defense, and the grand jury did not return an indictment.

Bradley's case, however, caught the attention of the public. AOU associate member and later Audubon Association president William Dutcher, who was responsible for Bradley's hiring, made sure of that. Dutcher wrote the following editorial in *Bird-Lore* magazine: "A home broken up, children left fatherless, a woman widowed and sorrowing, a faithful and devoted warden, who was a young and sturdy man, cut off in a moment, and for what? That a few more plume birds might be secured to adorn heartless women's bonnets. Heretofore the price has been the life of birds, now is added human blood."[5] The backlash from the grand jury's failure to indict Smith for Bradley's murder resulted in more women's clubs campaigning against the millinery trade's use of bird feathers. The plume hunters struck back, and in 1908, Florida warden Columbus G. McLeod disappeared and was presumed murdered after his efforts to protect birds from the hunters in Charlotte Harbor. Less than a year later in September 1909, L. P. Reeves, warden from Branchville, South Carolina, was shot and killed outside his home. Both of these murders went unsolved. The AOU continued to press for legislative reform. But help did not come until President Woodrow Wilson signed into law the Migratory Bird Treaty Act on July 3, 1918, ending the Plume Wars, with victory finally going to the birds.

By 1920, nature lovers were growing in force. A decade earlier, Teddy Roosevelt had traveled across America touting the country's newly designated national parks. Bird-watching had risen to a popular pastime with amateur ornithologists taking to the outdoors with camera and check-lists in hand. Bird-watching clubs flourished. The circulation of *Bird-Lore* magazine, created by Allen's mentor, Frank Chapman, and first published in 1899, was rapidly increasing.

In 1905, the year Robert Porter Allen was born, new chapters of Audu-bon had spread across the country. The state chapters eventually united and became the National Association of Audubon Societies, which was renamed the National Audubon Society (NAS) in 1940. By the time Bob Allen began his career with Audubon, a new, more salient danger loomed, one that could not be stopped no matter how many influential citizens jumped on the environmental bandwagon.

Since the time when Audubon fought to save the birds from ending up on stylish hats, the organization's emphasis had become educational. Audubon realized that if it were to stay in the game and remain a viable force for bird conservation, it would have to alter its focus. The Migratory Bird Treaty Act of 1918 had done its job to project waterfowl by regulating hunting, but new, more imposing issues had arisen. Wetlands across the northern United States were being drained for farm and ranch land, caus-ing waterfowl nesting and breeding habitats to disappear. The govern-ment needed to tighten hunting restrictions to keep from exacerbating the problem even further. An immediate transformation of Audubon's modus operandi was required.

In 1934, a new executive director of the National Association of Audu-bon Societies for the Protection of Wild Birds and Animals, investment banker and one-time World War I fighter pilot John Baker, was fast in making changes. T. Gilbert Pearson, who had hired Allen and reigned over the organization since its inception, was stepping down. One by one the old board of directors was edged out by a younger group of activists who felt the need to shake up the status quo. Pearson did not want to make waves with Congress and felt that future legislative action was not the answer. The waterfowl situation reached crisis level. Birds crowded in small ponds on the few refuges available. Water became polluted with bacteria, which in turn caused the birds to die of various diseases.

Other organizations were speaking out and challenging Congress to act. The General Federation of Women's Clubs was responsible for a new law that reduced daily bag limits on waterfowl. A new organization formed by Rosalie Edge, Emergency Conservation Committee, openly attacked Pearson and Audubon for their politics and lack of action. As word spread, Audubon members joined Edge's organization and did not renew their Audubon membership. As a result of Edge's attacks, Pearson was called on the carpet for his management of Audubon's first sanctuary, the Paul J. Rainey Wildlife Sanctuary in Louisiana, and his handling of the organization's finances. Although an investigation had proven Pearson innocent of all accusations, the damage was irreversible. As the number of waterfowl species continued to decline, so did Audubon membership. In fewer than four years, enrollment dropped from 8,400 to 3,400. John Baker called for Pearson's resignation on October 30, 1934.

Baker's vision for Audubon was now directed specifically toward saving threatened or endangered species. His plan contained three strategies: continue to educate the public through the schools and publications; focus on protecting nesting colonies; and beef up the research department. Baker believed that the knowledge gained from the study of bird behavior and ecology could be used to develop policies to ensure species' survival. He filled the office with innovative people who could make his vision a reality.

Baker had also taken notice of Bob Allen and was impressed with the young man's drive and tenacious attitude toward his work. In 1934, when it came time for Baker to appoint a director of Audubon sanctuaries, the decision was a no-brainer. At the age of twenty-nine, Allen became one of the youngest Audubon sanctuaries directors ever appointed.

Baker was not an easy person to work for. He was all business and expected his staff to make the most of every minute. While most of the offices in Manhattan were closed on Saturday, the Audubon House was open, its employees still at work. Meeting Baker's expectations was not a problem for Allen nor was staying out of office politics. Allen's job kept him in the field, and besides, Allen was not the type of person to buckle under to intimidation. His self-assurance and strong work ethic resulted in a smooth working relationship between the two men.

In those early years, Bob and Evelyn were living in an apartment in the Village. Like many young couples, they were busy adjusting to life in the city. Next to Allen's office at Audubon, Roger Tory Peterson, then the organization's artistic director, was designing covers for *Audubon Magazine*.

The two men became friends, and before long Peterson was dropping by the Allens' apartment for an occasional meal. At such times, Peterson, still a bachelor, usually had his laundry in tow.

Also living in Manhattan was Allen's brother, Johnny, who was working as an artist for the newly formed *Fortune* magazine. Just as when they were boys exploring the woods in Pennsylvania, Bob and Johnny were inseparable. Those were happy days. Bob and Evelyn Allen were now blessed with two sons, Bobby and Tommy. Although Evelyn had given up on her plans to tour, music was still an important part of their lives. Johnny, a musician in his own right, bought a piano. Many evenings found Johnny and Evelyn playing Gilbert and Sullivan songs while the music-loving Bob Allen sang along at the top of his lungs.

Allen was busy working his way up the Audubon ranks when tragically, early in 1935, Johnny was diagnosed with lung cancer and given a few months to live. He was twenty-seven years old. Suddenly, living in the city became confining. Allen moved his young family and Johnny to Freeport, Long Island. Being near the water and the woods gave the Allen brothers comfort. On Johnny's good days, they sailed along the south shore of Long Island, enjoying the bird life along the way. When he was too weak for outings, Johnny would open the window and listen to the shorebirds. As the year came to a close, Johnny lost his fight with cancer. A few months later, Bob and Evelyn's younger son Tommy became ill and died of pneumonia. Later, Evelyn would bemoan how during that dreadful winter, "keeping the drafty, old house warm was impossible."[6]

More important than anything in Allen's life was his family. Losing his brother and his son devastated Allen; living at the house in Freeport held too many memories. Bob and Evelyn moved to the village of Amityville on the South Shore of Long Island. Allen continued his daily rail commutes into the city, while Evelyn and Bobby began to enjoy the surroundings of their new home. They spent time outdoors when the weather permitted. Evelyn, using Johnny's piano, also kept busy with her piano practice.

It wasn't long before another professional opportunity came Allen's way. When the Linnaean Society began looking for someone to conduct a study of a black-crowned night-heron colony nesting on Long Island, Allen was selected. He arranged with John Baker, who was also a member of the Linnaean Society, to adjust his work schedule with Audubon.

"It was my plan to get up at 4 a.m. and pedal my bicycle some three miles west to Massapequa where a colony of black-crowned night herons was established each season in a cedar swamp," Allen wrote in *Trail*. "I felt that the result might justify all the trouble involved and perhaps increase my ultimate value to the Society."[7]

John Baker immediately agreed to the plan.

Then, in the fall of 1937, Bob Allen came home from work one afternoon to find Evelyn eagerly awaiting his arrival. She told him she was carrying their third child. Though he'd been delighted with his success with Audubon, he was elated upon hearing the news that he was to again become a father. In the spring of 1938, Evelyn gave birth to their daughter Alice.

For the next three years during nesting season, Allen and his partner, Frank Mangles, worked well before dawn banding young herons and documenting their activity. The work in the field had proven invaluable in honing Allen's research skills and giving his work credibility. In October 1940, Allen and Mangles published their findings in the Linnaean Society's *Proceedings*. For Allen, it was one of many scientific publications to follow.

Things were moving along at Audubon as well. Field fellowships for research had been established through Cornell University and assigned to various members. Graduate student James T. Tanner had been awarded the ivory-billed woodpecker project in Louisiana. Carl B. Koford, another graduate student from the University of California, had been assigned the much-coveted job of studying the California condor. Because of limited funds, a decision had to be made between two other species. Not necessarily more critical, but possibly more savable, the roseate spoonbill was selected. The whooping crane, for the time being, was on its own.

Although Allen's university credentials were limited, he had gained respect and proven himself in the world of ornithology through his field research. When it came time to assign the spoonbill research position, Baker asked Allen to give up the directorship and move to Florida. In October, Bob and Evelyn packed whatever they could into an old 18-foot-long travel trailer, hooked it behind a new Ford, and with their two small children in tow, set out for the Keys. Evelyn's piano remained behind.

Up to this point, Allen had commuted to the city by train, as did most people who lived on Long Island. It was the most efficient way of getting to the city. For Allen, however, this mode of transportation was not only convenient, but necessary. The day the Allens left Manhattan, Evelyn drove. Pulling a two-wheeled trailer behind their car was no easy task. In an oral history interview years later, Evelyn recounted that the car and trailer swerved from one side of the Holland Tunnel to the other, coming dangerously close to sideswiping vehicles in the oncoming lane. The best Allen could do to help his wife on the drive to Florida was to offer words of encouragement, for at the age of thirty-five, Bob Allen had not yet learned to drive.

Just south of Miami, Evelyn had a sense of foreboding. As she drove through Homestead and watched the last vestiges of civilization disappear in the rearview mirror, her heart sank. The area south of the city was a virtual wilderness. "There were no people, no nothing, just miles and miles of trees which I later learned were mangroves," Evelyn related in 1988. "I thought what in the name of common sense are we doing here?"[8]

In 1939, the small town of Tavernier, Florida, was not much more than mangrove swamps, mosquitoes, and rattlesnakes. The Overseas Highway, U.S. 1, had just been completed the year before. About 10 miles south of Key Largo, Tavernier sits on a narrow finger of land; a mere 500 yards separate Florida Bay from the Atlantic Ocean. In the early twentieth century, the area was home to the Conchs, descendants of Bahamian immigrants who had settled in Key West in the 1800s, and the few folks who had come to Florida to scratch out a living from fishing, turtling, sponging, woodcutting, and charcoal burning. Many of these Conch families, including the Alburys, Russells, Lowes, and Parkers, had moved north and settled in the Upper Keys from the Matecumbes to Key Largo to homestead the land after the passage of the 1862 Federal Homestead Act. Robert Albury, Amos Lowe, and Sam Johnson settled what eventually became the town of Tavernier, in the 1880s. There were also those who had settled after flocking to the Keys to work on the construction of Henry Flagler's railroad in 1905. The 1920s saw a new influx of people arrive in Florida. Much of the acreage in the Upper Keys had yielded to agriculture with limes, tomatoes, and onions as major crops. More than 60,000 crates of limes were shipped north each year. A three-story packinghouse was built in Tavernier to store and process the products before shipping them off to market.

H. S. "Mac" McKenzie, an opportunist and entrepreneur, and his wife,

Hazel, drove into Tavernier in 1928. Seeing opportunities abound, they immediately put down stakes. In no time, McKenzie built what had become the core of a town. He owned and operated the Tavernier Standard Oil Station (a gas station and automobile repair shop), the local grocery and hardware, icehouse, lumber company, and movie theater. After working out a deal with Florida Power and Light, McKenzie installed a fifty-horsepower diesel generator behind his drugstore and ran wiring to homes requesting his services. His generators, depending on the time of year and the weather, operated between 5:00 and 10:00 a.m. and 5:00 and 10:00 p.m. except on Saturday, when he would occasionally accommodate the local beer joints with extended hours. Citizens relied on oil lamps during blackout hours. Indoor plumbing was a luxury; most people had to pump their own water from cisterns. Even so, the infrastructure for a budding town was finally in place.

The Allens parked their trailer under a mangrove stand on a small plot of land on the highest ground available. It was the home of an Audubon warden who had agreed to allow Allen to hook up in the front yard. In 1939, "hook up" did not refer to plugging into an outlet and connecting to a water source; it meant unhitching the trailer and securing it to the ground. Evelyn surveyed their new homesite and sighed; at least they had a water view. Later that day she wrote in her diary: "I cannot do this. No water, no electricity, no phone."[9]

Audubon had sent word to the community through the local warden that a man from their New York office would be moving to Tavernier to study the spoonbills. He was bringing his family. A community sit-around-and-chat social had been arranged for the Allens at the local gathering place near the McKenzie grocery store on the first evening of their arrival. October in New York was already ushering in the cold season with paper-dry leaves scattering the ground in Central Park. The only way to recognize autumn in Tavernier was the early sunset. The mangrove trees stayed green, and the humidity hung like a wool coat until the first cold front. Even then, the coldest temperatures were brief, rarely dipping below 40 degrees.

That evening in Tavernier could best be described as hot, damp, and downright oppressive. The Allens donned their coolest, most comfortable clothes—Evelyn dressing one-year-old Alice in little more than the bare necessities—and strolled across the street to meet the members of the community. When they arrived, Evelyn looked down at her daughter. Alice's rosy, pink skin had turned black with mosquitoes. Bob grabbed their two children and ran inside the dark building. Before their eyes adjusted, a foul, poisonous-smelling mist coated them. Roger Albury, the Methodist Church deacon and grandson of the original settler, armed with a flit gun (a hand-pump insecticide sprayer), had doused them with insecticide. Smoke from a dozen smudge pots, another mosquito deterrent, clouded the air and stung their eyes. At first glance the room, little more than a roof with screened walls and drop shutters, appeared empty. Then soft voices and laughter drifted across the room. When Evelyn's eyes grew accustomed to the dark, the dozen warm, smiling faces looking back melted her heart and made her rethink the misgivings she had had earlier in the day. That evening, Evelyn fell in love with the local Conch people. Years later, while reflecting on that first day in Tavernier, Evelyn recalled: "We dashed into the building and spent the entire evening visiting with these lovely people, all native Conchs, not being able to see them or breathe because of the smoke and smudge pots. It was quite an experience for a city gal."[10]

Allen wasted no time in beginning his search for the spoonbills. With meager funds from Audubon, he bought an old skiff, plugged the leaks, and set up his field research camp on Bottlepoint Key, a small mangrove island located in Florida Bay. Evelyn set about making a home for her family in the tiny community, and it wasn't long before they fit right in. Unlike New York with its sophistication and opportunity, the unpretentious Tavernier was all about the type of person you were and how hard you worked. Evelyn had located a piano before her husband had located the spoonbills.

Allen's assignment was to study and produce a report with recommendations to restore the spoonbill to its natural habitat. Before he could begin, he had to discover what had caused the *Ajaia ajaja*'s numbers to dwindle, not an easy task since the decrease in population was worldwide and had begun centuries earlier. Edward I of England commissioned the first study into the bird's decline during his reign in the late 1200s. His concern was not so much for the bird, but for his larder. Seems the king had a taste for roasted spoonbill. The hunting of spoonbills continued,

Bob Allen at the research station on Bottlepoint Key in Florida Bay. Courtesy of Alice Allen.

and by the seventeenth century, the bird had disappeared from England. Thus, Allen suspected that the spoonbills in Florida remained only because they hadn't yet found their way into the "local cooking pots."[11]

Early explorers reported spoonbills nesting in abundance along the Gulf coast from Texas to Florida until 1860. By the turn of the century, the population had decreased considerably. W.E.D. Scott, ornithologist with Princeton University, reported seeing hundreds of spoonbills near Cape Romano on the west coast of Florida as late as 1880. Locals boasted of large rookeries where, at one time, thousands of young spoonbills were easy targets for hunters. These rookeries were now abandoned. One shotgun might find only one target, but that single blast proved fatal to dozens of birds. When nesting sites were repeatedly disturbed by gunfire, the surviving birds failed to return to incubate the eggs, and in many cases, did not procreate if another suitable site was not found. Several local residents Scott spoke with also admitted hunting the birds for their feathers.

For the next forty years, spoonbill sightings along the Gulf coast were rare. Many believed the bird had disappeared from North America entirely. It was a surprise when, for some unknown reason, a few spoonbills reappeared. That small colony nesting on the southern end of Bottlepoint Key in Florida Bay became Allen's focus. He needed to figure out how to keep them there and, hopefully, increase their numbers.

On his first outing to the key, Allen met with problems as soon as he pulled his skiff ashore. The narrow slit of sandy beach disappeared under a tangle of red mangroves. Allen climbed over and through gnarly branches that had woven a thick mat across most of the key. Where the vegetation had thinned, small pools of water fed by a brine creek created soggy ground. Within a short time, Allen was knee-deep in mud and covered with a layer of gritty crust, a mixture of sand, salt, and sweat. By the time the sun was deep in the western sky, mosquitoes had done their work over every inch of Allen's exposed skin. He was more than ready to call it a day.

With a cot, mosquito netting, gasoline lantern, notebooks, reference books, binoculars, canned beans, coffee, and a tin of pipe tobacco, Allen set up camp among the twisted mangroves a few hundred yards away from the colony. It didn't take long to become personally acquainted with the other more active life forms on the key. After dark on his first night's stay, he learned that mosquito netting was no deterrent against the sand flies. In desperation, he poured insect repellent into his hands and doused his scalp, hair, and skin. The sand flies fled, only to return, and the battle continued through the night.

Later in the evening, after the sand flies had settled, he was awakened by scratching and clawing at his grub box just outside the tent. Allen stirred, and the sound stopped. He settled in once more, and the scratching began again. The game continued until he gave in and emerged from his tent. His flashlight beam hit the box, and two huge eyes, dangling on the ends of rubbery antennae, gaped back. Then without warning, jets of liquid shot upward from the creature's head before it sidled back into the brush. Feeling sure the crab had retreated, Allen settled back inside and filled his pipe. Within ten minutes, the crab was back with reinforcements, and this time no amount of shouting and kicking sand would discourage the crustaceans to move on. Defeated, Allen moved his equipment inside the tent. He left the flap open to allow a breeze in the now crowded, stuffy enclosure. Along with the breeze came the mosquitoes, which whined and hovered on the netting, performing their high-pitched buzzing recital throughout the night. The sleep that finally overtook him was short.

A blood-chilling howl jolted him awake. Allen was sure he'd camped on a mangrove island inhabited by prehistoric creatures. Another bellow echoed farther away, sending a second animal in pursuit toward the call. Allen waited until the sound grew faint, reminded himself that he *was* a scientist, and left the safety of his tent to investigate. The beam of his flashlight illuminated deep tracks just inches from his tent. From there, they led to the beach, confirming his suspicions. Allen recalled a colleague with the National Park Service espousing that American crocodiles had been discovered living on the Upper Keys in Florida Bay. These were not the alligators of the Gulf coast freshwater swamps, but the elusive, fierce, savage crocodile, reputed to attack humans without warning. Since the tracks disappeared into the water, Allen felt somewhat safer. Then he discovered a second trail leading into the sandy marl. Reluctantly, he followed. As he stepped into the brush, the noises of the night ceased; it was as if every living thing knew better than to make a sound and give away its presence. When the silence was broken by a faint rattle, Allen took heed and backtracked to his camp, climbed into his tent, zipped the flap, and suffered through a steamy night.

The next morning, the sun pierced sharply through the mangroves. The vibrant sounds of birds and insects had returned. Allen shook the sand from his clothes and boots and left camp to move closer toward his quarry. As he approached to within 50 yards, the spoonbills flushed from their nests. Allen watched the birds disappear over the bay, realizing he needed to reconsider his situation. It had taken him almost an hour to reach Bottlepoint Key by skiff. Trudging through mangroves and slogging through swampy mud took another couple of hours. Until he could figure out how to get close enough without sending the birds fleeing Bottlepoint Key for good, he decided to study the habitat and ecology and find out what grew, crawled, swam, burrowed, slithered, and flew on the keys of Florida Bay. The task required sifting through sand, filtering mud, seining marshes, and combing through turtle grass, then matching the larval forms with the adults to discover what ate what in the swampy food chain. A discussion of the situation with Evelyn prompted the decision that if Allen were to make a thorough search, constant surveillance would be required. The only way to accomplish that was to move to the island for extended periods of time. In the days that followed, Allen built a platform on stilts. There he set up his tent, camp stove, and laboratory on the key's northern end.

Shortly after beginning his research on Bottlepoint Key, Allen gained the assistance of Ed Moore, a warden with the local Audubon chapter. For two months, they collected specimens, wrote copious field notes, pressed plants, and identified every living thing within their grasp, all the while staying away from their main subject. In mid-January, Allen felt it was time to approach the spoonbills and figure out what was troubling the enigmatic pink bird.

Allen invited members of the Audubon field staff to help with the patrol. Joining Allen and Moore was Alexander Sprunt Jr. and Ray and Jud Barnes, both wardens with the coast patrol. The plan was for the five men to form a line and move across the key in formation. At certain points, the red mangroves formed solid walls, making for slow progress. They hadn't gone far when Allen came across crocodile tracks. His tale of finding signs of the ancient reptile on the key had become fodder for a few laughs among his colleagues. Now they proceeded with a heightened awareness. Suddenly, the spoonbills sent out their rapid warning call, and moments later, Ray Barnes was heard saying, "Ah'm standin' right under a nest with two strappin' young Pinks in it!"[12] The other four men gathered quickly and watched like proud parents as two young spoonbills ambled around their nest. Little more than fluffy white balls, the birds had not yet donned their pink feathers. The nestlings appeared to be no more than three weeks old. Allen tagged the birds, placing red and white striped celluloid bands around their legs, indicating they were part of the class of 1940. A second nest with three young spoonbills was discovered and then another with four more nestlings. By this time, the men had reached the edge of the key. The entire colony on Bottlepoint Key had consisted of only nine young.

No one spoke on the ride back to the harbor. The joviality of the afternoon had given way to the grim reality: of the hundreds of adult spoonbills Allen had counted, only a handful were reproducing. What Allen had witnessed early, now made sense. If the parents were nesting and raising young, the nestlings would have been old enough to demand enormous amounts of food from the parents, forcing them to fly back and forth from the shallows. That was not the case. The adults Allen and Moore observed would leave in the morning and not return until later in the day. Now that Allen had found his birds, he needed to figure out why so few were nesting.

When they pulled onto the dock, a man named Cap'n Bob Combs, a curious source of Allen's previous interviews, was waiting for them, eager to hear of the group's progress.

Combs asked, "How's th' chicken a-doin' out thar?"

Wanting to sound encouraging, Allen answered, "Just fine, Cap'n Bob, just fine."

"Liar," Ed Moore whispered.[13]

2

The Decision

During the weeks Allen conducted his study of the spoonbill nesting colony, Evelyn focused on finding a niche in the community. What she needed was an environment where her children could thrive, an outlet for her music, and a friend. It didn't take Evelyn long to discover that she and Bob were not the only ambitious young couple to move to the Upper Keys. While shopping at the market one afternoon, Evelyn noticed a young woman who looked as if she'd just stepped out of a chic Miami salon. Thinking the woman must be passing through, Evelyn changed her assessment when the woman greeted the store clerk in a familiar fashion. Evelyn, never one to let an opportunity pass, introduced herself. "K" Wilkinson and her husband, Jack, had just married. Jack, an MIT graduate with a degree in aeronautical engineering had come to the Keys in 1936 after quitting his job with Curtis Aviation in Miami. Three years later, he married "K" Mata, and they settled in Tavernier. As she and "K" chatted, Evelyn was shocked to learn that "K" and Jack lived in a tent near their dock. On her first visit, Evelyn was quite impressed how "K" had turned a life without modern conveniences into a neat and well-functioning home. "The tent was comfortable, you had everything you wanted, you never missed electricity or running water. "K" always looked like Mrs. Astor."[1]

"K" helped Evelyn get used to the primitive living in Tavernier. With plumbing not available until after World War II, buckets of ocean water had to be carried in to flush their toilets. Freshwater for cooking, bathing, and washing clothes was hauled from a cistern, but only after checking first to make sure a rat or frog had not met its watery demise in the reservoir the night before.

Through the Wilkinsons, Bob and Evelyn met Bud and Marty McKenney, who had arrived about the same time as the Allens, and Mac and Hazel McKenzie, who had come in 1928. Mac had been a schoolteacher in Miami but quit to go into business building petroleum storage tanks. The McKenzies eventually opened the local drugstore. It was inevitable the couples would meet. All four families had come to the Keys with a desire to accomplish something more in their lives. Jack was looking for an opportunity to be his own boss. Bud and Marty dreamed of opening a showplace aquarium. Once she settled in, Evelyn had her heart set on bringing music to Tavernier, and Bob Allen was determined to save a rare bird from disappearing. The couples offered each other encouragement and support, which fueled their passions and ignited an enthusiasm that spread through the growing community.

One morning after Evelyn had organized the trailer, creating two bedrooms, one for the kids and one for Bob and herself, she walked into the McKenzies' drugstore. Sitting in the corner was an upright piano, old and dusty, and most likely out of tune, but a piano nonetheless. Having momentarily forgotten her shopping list, Evelyn sat down on the wooden stool and began playing. A crowd gathered to listen to the lighthearted music, and that day Evelyn was added to the entertainment list for the weekly Saturday night socials.

The drugstore was also the rest stop for the bus bringing travelers from Miami to the Keys. The music circuit got word of this talented young pianist living in Tavernier, and soon jazz musicians from Key West began to arrive on Saturday nights to sit in with Evelyn. The McKenzie drugstore quickly became the hot spot in the Upper Keys. Swing, Dixieland jazz, movie tunes, you name it, could be heard every weekend. McKenzie's generator operator and Hazel's brother, Austin Reese, was given free beer to keep the electricity flowing long past the normal cutoff time, often until three or four in the morning. On those nights when Reese headed home early, candles were set out and the music continued.

The Saturday nights at the drugstore were just a beginning for Evelyn. She had no intention of having the locals enjoy music as mere spectators. That first winter, she organized a glee club, produced three musical extravaganzas at the local theater, casting almost everyone she met. Lack of talent, skill, or experience was not a deterrent, for Evelyn taught her cast how to sing, dance, and act. On production nights, the entire town gathered for what she called her "minstrel shows."[2]

While Allen floated along in Florida Bay, sketching, counting, and dissecting killifish and pot-bellied minnows, Evelyn found a second piano and another conduit for her music. The Tavernier Methodist Church welcomed her into the congregation, and before long, she organized their choir. On Saturday afternoons, Evelyn gave free music lessons to any child who wanted them. Settling in and establishing a home was becoming easier and more enjoyable by the week.

On those weekends when Allen was not in the field, he, Evelyn, and the kids spent time with the Wilkinsons on their dock. Their conversations occasionally centered on politics, teasing one another about their opposing views: the Wilkinsons were staunch Republicans, and the Democratic Allens leaned toward the liberal side. Allen helped Jack with his tent-home improvements, while "K" and Evelyn reflected on the men's endeavors. "K," being a new, young bride and ten years Evelyn's junior, turned to her for advice from time to time. Years later when "K" wanted to learn how to drive a car, Evelyn was her teacher. Alice and "K" and Jack's son, Johnny, were the same age. Those first couple of years, Evelyn and "K" used the screened-in room built on the dock as a huge playpen. While the adults lounged on the dock, their young children were safe inside with no chance of tumbling into the water. "They were comfortable and cool and happy with each other," Evelyn related. "They had everything they needed in there, toys, food, water, and we could go about our business knowing the children were as well off as we were."[3]

Allen continued his field research from his Bottlepoint Key station. By March 1940, he had yet to find a large breeding colony, the study of which was paramount in his endeavor. In April, he traveled to the Texas coast to observe a well-established breeding colony near the Second Chain of Islands in San Antonio Bay. Knowing he would be there for about three months and not wanting to be away from his family, Allen brought Evelyn, the kids, and the family dog, Cleo, along. The most logical place for the family camp was on Rattlesnake Point, a narrow finger of land that extended out into Copano Bay. From there, he could motor his skiff out to the island every morning and return to camp in the evening. That time of year, living in the great outdoors would be ideal. Allen hired some local men to build Evelyn a temporary structure to give the family a little more room. The men brought with them a butcher-block table for her to use to prepare meals. Evelyn quickly discarded it as the table deserved its name—the deep scratches in the surface appeared to be filled in with dried blood.

As the day warmed up, Rattlesnake Point also lived up it its name. Evelyn could handle the rugged condition, but having an adventurous seven-year-old son and an active two-year-old daughter living in the wilds on a Texas bay with poisonous reptiles slithering from the dens after a winter's hibernation would not work. That afternoon, Allen dismissed the hired help and moved his family to a small rented ranch house a few miles away. Cleo stayed with Allen.

With the family close by and safe, Allen set up a day camp on a nearby island in a grove of marsh elder, using his equipment and gear from his Bottlepoint Key site. The isolated area had been designated an Audubon Sanctuary in 1934, and the pink birds had been able to survive quite well, undisturbed by egg hunters. The spoonbills were so numerous that Allen could observe to his heart's content, often arriving before dawn and remaining until it was too dark to see his subjects. Over the next three months, he documented the most precise details of their feeding habits, locations, times, and sources. He concluded that the spoonbills fed mainly at night, predominantly on minnows and killifish, in shallow water less than a foot deep.

In June, after completing his research in Texas, he returned to his Audubon office in New York to conduct the type of tedious research that was not his favorite. For the next nine months, Allen buried himself in museums and libraries, studying old spoonbill skins, specimens of insects and fish that were their main food supply, and organizing his copious data. For Allen, focusing on his research was never a problem, but staying indoors while doing so was.

At the time Allen was in New York, the World's Fair was in full swing, and Brazil was exhibiting spoonbills. He made a field trip to watch the spoonbills feed, more for enjoyment than for the collection of data. He was granted permission to feed the birds himself. He offered them bits of fish, which they scooped up. Then he tried stale bread with the same results, then small chunks of chocolate, which they ate without hesitation. Apparently, his subjects were not picky eaters. Watching the captive spoonbills swing their bills side to side like they did when they fed in the wild told Allen that despite his past few months of study, both outdoors and in, he was unable to identify any conclusive reasons that their numbers were so low. He was certain, however, that food was not the limiting factor causing the spoonbill's trouble.

Allen's failure in this endeavor made him even more determined to solve the mystery. He was back in Tavernier in October for his second winter's study, and this time, he'd planned to visit every single spoonbill nesting and feeding area on record and to get as close as possible without disturbing them. The problem was that the islands in Florida Bay spread over an area of 150 miles. Paddling a skiff would allow him to get reasonably close; covering that distance every day from a base camp on shore to the vast Florida Bay was impossible. Allen then came up with an ingenious idea, one that suited his sense of adventure. He would overhaul his skiff, affectionately named the *Croc*, and turn it into a floating laboratory.

The image began to take shape in Allen's mind, and he quickly realized the construction task was beyond his ability. According to the locals, there was only one man who could do the job right, Ocean Grandease, a sun-dried, skin-charred Floridian who, as Allen found out that first morning, exuded a ripe aroma of clams and booze. Grandease's eyes lit up when Allen described his ideal spoonbill vessel. Excited by the prospect of building a one-of-a-kind launch, the boatbuilder insisted that he begin the task the very next morning.

Within the first hour, the *Croc* began to take on a completely new appearance. The hull rose 6 inches higher, and a new stem had been added. By the time Grandease called it a day, Allen liked what he saw and said he would be back early the next morning. When he turned to leave, Grandease asked if Allen would pay him for his day's work: "Would it be . . . er . . . agin yer rules t' pay me now fer t'day?"[4] Allen hesitated, then gave the man his well-earned pay for nine hours of labor.

By midmorning the following day, the sun was well above the horizon and any thought of an early start had vanished with the early-morning breeze. Allen had waited almost two hours before he found Grandease passed out drunk in the weeds behind the schoolhouse. Seemed the old guy had taken his earnings from the day before and celebrated his good fortune. Since Grandease was in no shape to work on anyone's boat, Allen hitched up his skiff, took it home, and finished the project himself. The new *Croc* was launched a week later. The stern was now closed in with a small hatch; there was storage space for charts, his compass, and reference books, a built-in watertight food locker, and planks for his bedroll. Under the planks was additional space for a portable gas stove, a 15-pound anchor, an oar, and miscellaneous boating equipment. A sturdy, waterproof tarpaulin would provide shelter against rain and sun. Finally, a spritsail was added to the new mast. Tied to the stern of the *Croc* was a smaller skiff, which contained gasoline cans, water cans, collecting gear, and a box of two-for-five cigars. Allen described his creation as looking like a floating rummage sale.

With the weather bureau predicting fair sailing, Allen launched the revamped *Croc* on the morning of April 7, 1941. He hoped to make it to East Cape Canal that evening, but strong tides prevented him from motoring faster than 3 to 4 knots. He got no farther than End Key by the time the sun set. On the second day of his venture, he had an opportunity to test the soundness of his vessel. As he pulled into East Cape Canal, dark skies toward the north signaled a brewing storm. Just after dinner, the rain fell and the wind blew in stiff gusts. He stretched out in the bottom of the *Croc*, allowing the swaying to rock him to sleep. The next morning he woke to a cerulean sky, safe and dry and ready to tackle the next phase of his spoonbill study.

Just 2 miles from the first island, he ran into trouble again. Despite his seaworthy vessel and experience in the Merchant Marine, Allen had run aground. His tide table showed that he was going nowhere for twenty hours. "I sat down and did the only thing possible under the circumstances. I made a pot of coffee. Already I had learned that a casual but undeviating perseverance and ability to drink gallons of strong coffee can be reckoned among the field ornithologist's most valuable assets."[5] It is not certain what else he did to occupy his time, but a memorandum written by his friend and successor Sandy Sprunt, and published in *Auk* magazine, included one of Allen's amusing sketches, a caricature of himself riding astraddle a crocodile, a pair of binoculars around his neck, a pipe in his mouth, and a pot of coffee on a gas stove perched on the animal's rump.

Two days later, Allen finally motored out of the East Cape Canal. He'd planned to go ashore on East Cape and pay a visit to the man who had paved the way for ornithologists like himself. Under a small grove of palm trees on an otherwise barren shore was the grave of Guy Bradley, the murdered game warden who had fought the plume hunters thirty-five years earlier. (The original grave and monument erected by the NAS was washed away by Hurricane Donna in 1960. A new monument now stands at the Everglades National Park Visitors Center in Flamingo, Florida.) The strong outgoing tide had other ideas, and Allen was forced to pay his respects at a distance. It took a few more days before Allen learned to use the tides to his advantage.

During the three months in Florida Bay, Allen developed a routine. Every ten days, he'd pull ashore and call Evelyn from the grocery store in the village of Everglades. She would gather the kids and they would make the 100-mile drive to collect their wayward husband and father. That first encounter with their father after an absence of ten days had Bobby and Alice uncertain if their mother had collected the correct fellow. He looked more like a swamp creature from a horror movie. He was unwashed, un-shaved, several shades darker than when he had left, and his clothes were covered with grime. The family would spend two to three happy days together. On those evenings at home, Allen entertained Bobby and Alice with his adventure stories, sometimes reading from Edward Lear's *The Courtship of the Yonghy Bonghy Bo*. To Alice, he'd read from *Alice's Adventures in Wonderland* (she had been named for its heroine). After catching up on life in Tavernier, Evelyn would drive him back to his floating lab and his pink birds.

By the end of his twenty-five-month study, Allen stumbled upon the spoonbill problem by accident. During his more leisurely moments on the water, either waiting out the tides or enjoying a hot cup of coffee and a cigar, Allen sketched more than three hundred spoonbills, noting that the slight color variation of their plumage darkened as the birds aged. Over time, he became skilled at telling a spoonbill's age by a mere glance, and slowly, the big picture emerged with a clear understanding of why there were no roseate spoonbill nesting colonies in Florida.

Allen knew that spoonbills molted several times before they attained their bright, pink adult plumage at about the age of thirty-three months. By this time, he had collected data on the plumage of 305 spoonbills, more than half of the approximate 500 total that flew to Florida in the summer. His plumage analysis concluded that less than 1 percent of the

Florida flock was more than three years old. In other words, 99 percent of the Florida birds had not yet reached breeding age. In his second year's report to Baker, Allen summarized what was, without a doubt, the spoonbill's problem: "The chief reason the Roseate Spoonbill does not increase in Florida is the failure of breeding adults to reach the mainland in large numbers in a spring migration."[6] Unfortunately, as with most scientific discoveries and viable postulations, new answers led to new questions.

—

In the three years since Bob Allen's arrival in Florida, he was winning the battle to change the minds and attitudes of many locals who had, for so many years, viewed the area birds, including the spoonbills, as food for the taking. A descendent of one of the Conch settlers, a man known as Uncle Leonard Lowe, told Allen that since turkeys weren't available, wild birds were hunted and served on Thanksgiving and Christmas. Realizing the scarcity of numerous birds, Uncle Leonard agreed with Allen that the birds deserved protecting. Even the fisherman, using illegal stop nets, befriended Allen and respected his efforts in trying to save the spoonbills. Although they held opposite views on nature conservation, they often shared their provisions while out in the bay conducting their business.

Allen continued his spoonbill research for four more seasons. He published his findings in a monograph entitled *The Spoonbills Research Report No. 2 of the National Audubon Society, 1942.* The document was well received internationally and held up as a model for future research projects of this type. John Baker approached his enthusiastic ornithologist with the idea of turning his scientific report into a book. Allen liked the idea. He'd proven himself an acclaimed researcher, his career had taken off, and for the first time, he had begun to put down roots.

Fate, however, had other plans, and events on another battlefront were looming. Allen's time in paradise would be short.

On July 19, 1941, Allen was in the Audubon patrol boat, the *Spoonbill,* cruising the bay with friend and Audubon warden Les Karcher. Suddenly, nine spoonbills flew over in the direction of Sandy Key, the same key where, a century before, John James Audubon saw his first and possibly only spoonbill. The birds were on a path toward the edge of the

Straits of Florida in line with the coast of Cuba only 100 miles away. Allen knew that the survival of the spoonbills pointed toward Cuba and South America.

The next morning before sunup, Allen and Karcher raced south along the Overseas Highway toward Marathon. They rented a skiff and headed to Boot Key, where they flushed seven spoonbills from the mangroves, most likely the birds they had seen the day before. Looking at a map, the most viable stopover between the Straits of Florida and the coast of Cuba was an atoll called the Cay Sal Bank. Allen referred to his well-used copy of *Sailing Directions for the West Indies* and learned that Cay Sal Bank was a fringed reef of several small, shallow sandbanks. Shell beaches covered the larger cays. Stunted palms and wild guava trees grew in abundance. Rabbits had established a thriving colony, and sea turtles came ashore to dig nests. A natural spring provided freshwater on one cay, another had a saltwater pond, and on the Anguilla Isles, the largest group of cays, the entire southern side was covered in swamp—a virtual spoonbill paradise.

Fairly certain of their migratory route, Allen longed to be on Cay Sal Bank in March to see the spoonbills glide in from the north, and to watch their crimson plumage flash across a china-blue sky as they spiraled down for a final rest before their 25-mile push to Cuba. At another time and under different conditions, he would come close to having his wish. But on this sunny morning in July, Allen stood on the shore of Boot Key looking south, pondering a decision he knew he'd have to face when the time came. That moment arrived fewer than five months later, when Japan attacked Pearl Harbor.

Allen possessed a strong sense of patriotism born from his early days in the Guard. Nevertheless, the decision was not an easy one. Despite his accomplishment with the spoonbills, he knew it was not enough to guarantee their protection indefinitely. The solution to the problem lay far beyond the Florida Keys. There was more work to be done, but for now, it would have to wait.

Allen attempted to enlist in military service and was surprised to learn that most armed forces would not take him. However, when the Army recruiting officer learned of Allen's service with the Merchant Marine, his age of thirty-six was no longer an issue.

What started out as a research site quickly became home. The Allens had fallen in love with the community, its people, and the natural beauty of their unspoiled paradise. When Allen first arrived, this small burg, located near the only remaining spoonbill colony in Florida, intrigued him. Years later, he reflected on his move to Tavernier, wondering what it would be like sharing the exotic paradise with the spoonbills and wondering why the locals kept the presence of this magnificent bird a secret. After a short time, the answer was obvious. "Now, I too have lived in this enchanted place; I have glanced up from my breakfast table to see zebra butterflies against a background of fern-like leaves and heavily-clustered flowers of a royal poinciana, trembling wings of yellow and jet black moving across a gently swaying curtain of tender green and violent scarlet and the deepest tangerine. I have looked from my window at sunrise to see a man-o'-war bird, his great seven-foot spread of dark wings motionless in the quiet glory of the warm and golden air. Pink birds fit into this picture so naturally that I realized now what I took to be an unpardonable reticence was nothing of the sort."[7]

Before leaving for basic training in California, Allen had one more chance to voyage out into the bay and say good-bye to his subjects. Returning from a patrol with the Florida Bay warden Arthur Eifler, the men pulled up to the dock alongside the *Croc*. As Eifler and Allen secured the patrol boat and finished off the morning's coffee, Allen announced that he would take the *Croc* out for one more run. Understanding Allen's sentiment, Eifler responded quietly, "I'll be right here."[8] Allen maneuvered into a slough where he hoped the spoonbills would be feeding. The tide was low, and killifish swarmed the shallow water near a cluster of mangroves. Suddenly, as if a curtain of pink had been dropped from the heavens, a flock of thirty-nine spoonbills landed. Allen shut off the outboard motor and dug his hands into the mud of the bank to steady the boat. The birds fed, perched momentarily in the branches, and then took to the sky. "As I let go of my hold on the muddy bank and permitted the *Croc* to slip quietly along with the outward swirl of the ebb, I knew, with a sudden confidence, that the eloquence of the pink bird's beauty will be its ultimate salvation. It is unthinkable that so rare a treasure as the Roseate Spoonbill shall be lost to us forever."[9]

That August outing was Allen's last on the *Croc*. The vessel was lost in the wake of a hurricane in October 1944.

Allen's next trip across the water would eventually take him in another direction, away from the Straits of Florida, away from the work he loved, away from his home in Tavernier. Allen wondered when, or if, he would return.

—

After putting Evelyn and the kids on the train to St. Louis to stay with her parents, Allen left for boot camp in March 1942. Upon completion of basic training, he was assigned to navigate the *Spurgeon* mine planter in the Gulf of Mexico and the Caribbean Sea. On one of their first maneuvers, Allen was surprised to learn that a rendezvous was planned with another convoy off the coast of Florida. Allen's patrol sailed through a network of jagged reefs, and he realized the large spot of land in the distance was Cay Sal Bank. As the sky grew darker and the ship's lights were extinguished, the island faded in the distance. During the night, an alarm alerted the convoy of an enemy submarine and the patrol boats scattered. At dawn Allen found his unit sailing toward the shelter of Key West Harbor, only a few miles from his home. A detour eastward sent them through Nicholas Channel toward Cay Sal Bank. He longed to launch the ship's patrol boat and motor in and explore the area on foot. For now, though, the mystery of the spoonbills' migratory path would remain unsolved.

Army maneuvers eventually led them on an arduous journey through the Panama Canal and into San Francisco Harbor at Sausalito. Once Allen was certain he would remain in the Bay Area for the duration of his military duty, he arranged for his family to join him. Evelyn and the kids arrived by train, settled in, and in a few days Bobby and Alice were in school. Allen, however, found living in San Francisco too claustrophobic. At the end of the 1944 school year, Allen arranged to live off base and moved his family to Kentfield in Marin County.

During that time, he had not completely abandoned his life as an ornithologist. With the success of his spoonbill monograph came the opportunity to turn his research and adventures into a book as Baker had suggested. Publishers Dodd, Mead & Company signed Allen to a contract. Between days shipboard and at home, he scribbled out his manuscript in pencil on sheets of yellow writing paper. The completion of *The Flame Birds* coincided with his discharge, and plans for the future were under way. Then, on October 16, 1945, fewer than four months before he was

Bob and Evelyn Allen in Sausalito, California, 1943. Courtesy of Alice Allen.

scheduled to leave the Army, a new challenge arose. Evelyn gave birth to their second daughter, Eve, a Down syndrome child.

Evelyn had never been one to complain about her fate. She tackled every situation with headstrong gusto, but losing one child and discovering that Eve had Down syndrome called for a special kind of strength. Help came, of all places, from the National Audubon Society. Audubon vice president Carl Buchheister, a colleague of the Allens who would assist in seeing Evelyn through many difficult times in the future, set about locating a suitable home for Eve.

While the world was at war, the situation with the whooping cranes became grave. In 1942, their numbers had dwindled to a mere fifteen. A. M. Brooking with the Nebraska Ornithologists' Union reported only three whooping cranes migrating through in 1941, four in 1942; only one lone whooper was seen flying over the area in 1943. With the birds staring extinction in the face, their nesting ground in Canada had to be located and protected. The AOU alerted the United States Fish and Wildlife Service (USFWS) and the National Audubon Society and demanded immediately action. The Conservation Committee of the Wilson Ornithological Club contacted Audubon as well with the following plea, "What practical help can be given the whooping crane at the eleventh hour?"[10]

By the time Bob Allen was released from the service in April 1946, the campaign to locate the whooping cranes' nesting site was already under way. The cranes' situation had grown so desperate the Canadian Wildlife Service (CWS), the USFWS, and the National Audubon Society formed a three-way partnership to launch the Whooping Crane Project.

Almost three decades earlier when the United States and Canada passed the Migratory Bird Treaty Act, the whooping crane was legally protected from hunters along with threatened waterfowl species. Then, in 1937, those striving to keep the whoopers from extinction won another victory. Thanks to Audubon and Franklin D. Roosevelt, more than 47,200 acres of Texas coastline between Aransas and San Antonio Bays, otherwise known as the Blackjack Peninsula, were designated protected land for migratory birds. The Aransas Migratory Waterfowl Refuge, renamed the Aransas National Wildlife Refuge in 1939, was under the protection of the USFWS, giving the cranes a safe haven, at least for their time in Texas. But no matter how monumental these efforts were, unless the situation in Canada could follow similar measures, these victories were not enough to ensure the whooping cranes' survival.

To make matters more difficult, governmental agencies were having trouble winning the support they needed. For years many outspoken ornithologists and conservationists felt that saving the whooping crane was a lost cause; they believed time and money should be spent elsewhere. As far back as 1912, Edward Howe Forbush, ornithologist and founder of the Massachusetts Audubon Society, had written in his *A History of the Game Birds, Wild-Fowl and Shore-Birds of Massachusetts and Adjacent States,* "In ages to come, like the call of the Whooping Crane, they [trumpeter swans] will be locked in the silence of the past."[11] Hal G. Evarts, a writer of Westerns and frequent contributor to the *Saturday Evening Post,* published an essay in 1923 proclaiming the whooping crane extinct. "Another species [whooping crane] of our American birds has passed."[12]

All the same, the three agencies were determined to press on, despite knowing the Whooping Crane Project would be no small feat. More than 100,000 square miles of some of the most uninhabitable wilderness on the planet would have to be explored acre by acre, foot by foot. The endeavor would be limited to a few weeks in the summer when the weather was more hospitable. However, with warmer temperatures came other problems. The melting snow meant raging rivers, which created logjams the size of massive boulders. Summers in this swamp-laden area of Canada were brutal: swarms of black flies and mosquitoes could bring the toughest man to his knees.

While the ground search was being organized, a Save-the-Whooping-Crane publicity campaign was under way. Leading the charge was Charles L. Broley, a retired bank manager from Winnipeg who had taken up bird-watching and eventually earned the nickname "Eagle Bander" for his extensive work on bald eagles. He began by distributing fliers and brochures to all who lived near the most likely whooping crane habitats. He contacted the Hudson's Bay Company, Canadian Pacific Airways, the Manitoba Game and Fish Association, the Game and Fish Branch of the Manitoba government, requesting that their employees and members be on the lookout. He placed notices in the *Country Guide* and the *Prairie Farmer,* whose combined circulation was almost 500,000, urging anyone who had spotted a crane to call in their sighting. John Baker devoted his "President's Report" column in *Audubon Magazine* entirely to the whooping crane. The public's enthusiasm grew and reports flooded in.

Despite the publicity campaign's success, the search phase of the Whooping Crane Project stalled before it began. All three organizations had lost employees to the war effort, and those who remained were involved in other ongoing research projects. Word was sent out to universities and private organizations conducting field research for assistance in providing personnel. Finally, the Provincial Museum of National History in Regina agreed to allow their curator, ornithologist

Fred Bard Jr., to come on board for a couple of months in the spring of 1945 to get the ball rolling. His first task was to analyze every scrap of data and narrow the search area down to the most likely coordinates. In late April, Bard presented John Baker and the project committee with four potential sites based on the location of the last-known whooping crane nest and the most viable whooping crane habitat: southeastern Alberta near Medicine Hat, east central Saskatchewan north of Nipawin, Meadow Lake on the western boarder of Saskatchewan and Alberta, and the area west of Saskatoon, Saskatchewan. The sites were approved. The next step involved setting up base camps and organizing an air search. Once the site was located, wardens would be hired and given the authority to protect the whoopers and nests against any and all intruders.

When Bard was told that finding pilots during wartime to fly him over the selected areas would be difficult, he went directly to the military. The U.S. Air Force had set up an air station in Regina. Bard met with the U.S. commanding general, who agreed to allow Bard to fly with the Search and Rescue division. On the first day out, he hitched a ride on a transport plane leaving for Watson Lake in the Yukon. It rained during the entire trip, eliminating ground visibility. The next day, they flew to the mountain region of Dease Lake in British Columbia. Because of the topography, the pilot was restricted to altitudes between 5,000 and 7,000 feet. Seeing a white bird at that level was like looking for a speck of white dust in an overgrown vegetable garden. Bard requested they alter their route to fly over eastern Saskatchewan. His request was denied.

Bard continued his ground search while Audubon looked for a pilot. Around the first of July, the USFWS sent the veteran flyway biologist and waterfowl expert Bob Smith to join forces with Bard. Before arriving in Saskatchewan, Smith scanned the area north of Edmonton, Alberta, but found nothing.

In Smith's Grumman Widgeon, often referred to as a flying boat, Smith and Bard searched northeastern Saskatchewan, flying over farmlands, prairies, wilderness, and wetlands. They spotted a plethora of waterfowl: ducks, geese, cormorants, grebes, and almost every species of wading bird—except the whooping crane. Hoping for success with a ground search, they traveled more than 1,000 miles by car. After weeks of searching, they found nothing. Bard could spare no more time from his position at the Provincial Museum and had to return to Regina. Smith was ordered back to his station in Winona, Minnesota. The first search ended without success.

John Baker began planning the next search for the following year. Smith would be available, but Bard would not. Baker contacted Dr. Olin Sewall Pettingill Jr., a renowned ornithologist and associate professor of zoology at Carleton College in Northfield, Minnesota, to take over. Pettingill visited Fred Brad in Regina, who briefed him on the first expedition. By the time the surviving whooping cranes had arrived at their winter home in Aransas, Texas, Pettingill was there waiting.

While at the Aransas National Wildlife Refuge, Pettingill hoped to discover detailed information on the cranes' overall territorial range, which encompassed 400 acres per crane pair, on where the cranes fed and on what, and how and where they roosted. Pettingill ran into problems from the moment he arrived. Getting close enough to the skittish birds proved exasperating, and knowing where the small flocks would land was impossible. He did discover that the cranes roosted and fed in small groups in well-guarded territories rather than large flocks like their cousin the sandhill crane.

Spring came, and it was almost time for the whoopers to leave their Gulf coast refuge. Before Pettingill began the second year of searching, he decided to pursue another possible avenue for saving the cranes, one that would eventually erupt into a heated battle among ornithologists, and one that Allen would eventually oppose.

Two whooping cranes were living out their lives in captivity, one in a bird sanctuary in Nebraska, and the other in the Audubon Park Zoo in New Orleans. In case the nesting site was not located in time, Pettingill believed the birds' salvation might lie in a captive-breeding program. The sex of some bird species can easily be determined by the color of their plumage; that of others cannot. Male and female whooping cranes are indistinguishable. The two captive cranes gave no clue as to their genders. Running out of time, Pettingill put this idea on the back burner and prepared for the spring migration.

En route north, Pettingill hoped to locate the elusive birds' stopover sites, the most likely place being on the Platte River in Nebraska. He conducted ground and aerial searches. Again, the birds gave up nothing for the ornithologist. Through Oklahoma and into the Dakotas, Pettingill did not spot a single crane on their migratory corridor. He arrived in Canada more determined than ever to track down the birds.

The second hunt began with a bang, or rather a moratorium of such. With the help of the ornithologist and illustrator Dr. Walter J. Brecken-ridge, Pettingill designed a whooping crane poster that implored hunters not to shoot any large white bird for fear the target would be a whooping crane. Seven thousand posters and questionnaires were printed and dis-tributed. In the targeted area, 5,500 schools received a poster along with a questionnaire. The second massive publicity blitz was in full swing.

Although Fred Bard was back at work at the museum, in his free time, he distributed publicity mailings to radio stations, newspapers, and mem-bers of the Natural History Society, the Canadian Mounted Police, the Hudson's Bay Company, the Bureau of Indian Affairs, and a myriad of other organizations. The response was overwhelming, and hundreds of sightings began pouring in. It was impossible to track each one, and most likely many were erroneous reports by well-meaning people who had mistaken snow geese or white pelicans for whooping cranes. Even so, the campaign had people on the lookout.

After consulting Fred Bard, Pettingill selected the sites for the 1946 search. The expedition would take him as far west as Fort McMurray in Alberta, to Lake Athabasca in the northern reaches of Saskatchewan, and down to Peter Pond and Churchill Lakes. On June 6, his wife, Elea-nor, joined him in Regina. They flew by commercial plane to the small settlement of Waterways located on the Clearwater River, where a US-FWS plane was to fly them north to the first search area. As the plane ap-proached, all hopes for a hasty getaway were dashed. The aircraft was a tail dragger, a rear-wheeled craft. Someone had forgotten to mention—or the message had been misunderstood—that a floatplane was needed for wa-ter landings. Stranded in Waterways, Pettingill grew impatient. The search needed to get under way and quickly. Finally, Terry Moore, president of the New England Museum of Natural History, and his wife arrived in their private plane. Logging more than twenty hours in the air, Moore and Pettingill flew over Saskatchewan and Alberta, scanning Peter Pond, Gordon, Garson, and the Churchill Lakes. They flew northeast toward the Canadian Shield, south over Ile-a-la-Crosse, westward and then back north to the Graham Lakes area in Alberta.

Numerous species of waterfowl were abundant, but no whoopers.

Acting on a report, Pettingill and Moore flew toward Lake Athabasca only to discover that the lead was at least three years old. Moore's fuel ration was exhausted, and, like Bard, he had to return to his real job. Leaving the Pettingills in Fort Chipewyan, Moore and his wife departed for Boston.

Olin and Eleanor Pettingill set up camp in the delta region near Lake Athabasca. While waiting for one of the three organizations to send help and fly them out, they searched for the cranes on foot. After three weeks, and no word from the groups supporting the project, Pettingill wondered if they had been forgotten. Another three weeks went by before Bob Smith arrived.

Smith and Pettingill resumed the search, flying toward northwest Edmonton, the region of Calling Lakes and Lesser Slave Lake, west to British Columbia, then turning southeast to Saskatchewan. By the end of the summer of 1946, Pettingill had covered almost 15,000 square miles over marshes, grasslands, dense forests, riverbeds, and lakeshores. As the landscape began to show signs of the approaching winter, the search was again called off. Pettingill was convinced he had been searching in the right area, but couldn't help feel that he had missed something—some mysterious quirk about whooping crane behavior perhaps. Maybe the answer was back in Texas. Maybe his previous winter study in Aransas was not extensive enough. Discovering the answers called for an experienced ornithologist, one capable of digging out the fine details.

3

The Clang of a Bell

While Pettingill was completing his final research report on the whooping crane habitat along the Texas coast, Bob Allen was preparing to return to civilian life. John Baker was eager to have his star ornithologist back in service with Audubon. In a letter dated January 18, 1946, Baker expressed impatience with the discharge process: "I am distressed at the delay in your release from service. Too bad. I don't believe there is anything I can do about it that would help, but I shall be in Washington the first days of the coming week and will make inquiry to see if I can do anything constructive."[1]

Unable to get a definite release date, Bob and Evelyn decided it would be best for her to remain in Kentfield until the end of May to avoid taking Bobby and Alice out of school. When the time came to leave California, rather than return to Tavernier, Evelyn and the kids would travel to St. Louis to stay with Evelyn's parents until Allen could get things squared away with Audubon.

At this time, Bob and Evelyn made another decision, this one much more painful. In 1946, little was known about the abilities of Down syndrome children. Support programs did not yet exist, and parents were encouraged to find a facility that could adequately care for their disabled child. Giving Eve up to live in a home where she could be adequately cared for was one of the most difficult challenges Bob and Evelyn Allen faced. Yet, Evelyn began the arduous task of finding a suitable facility.

Allen was still at Fort Winfield Scott in California in March. When his discharge finally came through, he packed his bags, told Evelyn and the kids good-bye, and boarded a bus for the 3,000-mile trip from the West Coast to New York. There, Baker had arranged for Allen to continue to work with his publishers on *The Flame Birds*. Although Allen's old office was still available for him, it was uncertain where he would stay during his time in the city. With money concerns on both ends, Allen requested, possibly jokingly, that Audubon allow him to put up a cot in the Audubon House. Baker, ever the businessman, did not grant Allen his request on the grounds that Allen's stay in the office would surely arouse curious talk. Baker offered other suggestions that would not require a tug on Audubon purse strings, writing that Carl Buchheister would be glad to have Allen stay with him, or possibly another Audubon member would put Allen up during his time in the city. He went on to write that Allen might have to find a room on his own, and if he were emotionally up to it, he might consider staying at the YMCA. Baker would be happy for Allen to stay at the Baker household, but he was not sure if he'd be in town at the time.

Allen arrived in the city beaten down and weary. He missed his family and was still feeling the emotional upheaval of the decision to place Eve in a home. Being back at Audubon's headquarters among his colleagues helped ease the stress of the last few weeks. It is uncertain where he stayed during that time in New York, but his time was well spent. The routine of work allowed him to recuperate. He finished the manuscript and completed the negotiations involving his contract. Ten thousand copies were scheduled for printing, with Allen receiving a $250 advance upon signing and another upon publication. It wasn't much, even in 1946, but it was a start, and he hoped it would lead to more lucrative endeavors. The book was scheduled for release in the spring of 1947. Until then, there was more work to be done.

On April 8, Allen was in Homestead, Florida, playing catch-up with Audubon. Much was happening in the world of nature conservation in Florida in 1946. The USFWS had declared Florida Bay a federal refuge, soon to be proclaimed Everglades National Park. Allen assisted the local game wardens in the park's establishment. He was pleased to learn that the spoonbills had fared well in his absence. Their population had recovered so significantly that Audubon began taking the public on wildlife tours to see the roseate spoonbills. Allen knew there was more to discover about their migration. Like the whooping crane, the spoonbill's ultimate protection would depend upon where they migrated.

By the time Evelyn left California that May, Carl Buchheister had located a facility in Pennsylvania that specialized in teaching Down syndrome children. The waiting list was monstrously long. Allen's mother was able to pull strings, and at the age of six months, Eve was living in the facility. As soon as Evelyn was able to withdraw Bobby and Alice from school, she packed the family car and drove to St. Louis. Being with their grandparents that summer was a delight for Bobby and Alice. For Evelyn it offered a chance to cope with her separation from her youngest daughter.

Meanwhile, Allen assisted Baker in tying up loose ends on several Audubon projects. Baker was having trouble filling state game warden positions in Florida. In June, he asked Allen to accompany Edwin Stucke, a new hire for south Florida, until he became familiar with the area he was to supervise. Baker had also planned to offer Charlie Brookfield the position as contact man for all Florida game wardens as well as the supervisory position at Okeechobee. Baker told Allen to "spend a little time with him [Brookfield]"[2] until he settled in. Whenever poaching reports came in, Allen assisted the local game wardens in investigating those as well.

Around the July 1, Allen was back in Tavernier with his family. They had rented a house and purchased furniture. Since the rental home provided extra living space, Evelyn arranged to have Johnny Allen's old baby grand piano, which had been stored at a friend's house on Long Island since 1939, sent down to Florida. Evelyn was more than ready to resume her piano teaching, but she waited. She was astute enough to realize that because of her husband's uncertain future, getting too comfortable in Tavernier might not be the wisest thing to do.

Baker wrote to Allen again on July 3. This time, his letter enumerated Allen's responsibilities for the rest of the summer. The list included the following: by July 15, Allen was to spend ten days to two weeks in Lostman's River to acquaint Stucke with the area and to make sure he understood Audubon's philosophies; return to Tavernier and see to it that the Audubon cypress skiff was in good working condition for whomever might need it; work on tweaking his manuscript with *Audubon Magazine* editor Eleanor King; make preparations for a stay in Louisiana for an undetermined amount of time to help manage the state's refuge systems, which would most likely mean moving his family again for an indefinite time; prepare equipment for Brookfield and sell whatever he didn't want; and analyze and summarize all Audubon records relating to the south Florida region in preparation for his report at the Audubon convention in New York. Baker wanted the data from Allen's report made available to the USFWS, National Park Service, and Everglades National Park Commission to use as needed. Baker also planned to use the data to print promotional leaflets and pamphlets, making sure Audubon received credit for all the work the organization had done in protecting and restoring bird life in south Florida. Sometime during this hectic schedule, Baker suggested that Allen take a two-week vacation.

Although Baker was keeping Allen busy, all the projects were temporary. After sixteen years with Audubon, Allen began to wonder if it was time to steer his career in a more stable direction. Despite Allen's past accomplishments with Audubon, there was one shortcoming he could not overcome, his lack of academic credentials. This fact alone seemed to keep the big salaries from flowing south to Florida, and he feared that the lesser projects would result in a nickel-and-dime existence. For a man of forty-one, with a family to provide for, scraping to get by was getting old. There were many opportunities for men with Allen's experience. A position as a resident biologist at the Everglades Refuge had come open. Allen's friend Jack Wilkinson had also recently returned from the service and needed help with his new business, catching marine specimens for several facilities. Marineland near St. Augustine had put in a call for a large variety of mammals, fish, and reptiles. That summer, Bud and Marty McKenney had opened their aquarium, Theater of the Sea on a saltwater lagoon in Islamorada, which was once the rock quarry Flagler used when building his railroad. (Still owned and operated by the McKenney family, Theater of the Sea is the second-oldest marine-mammal facility in the world.) With numerous orders from Marineland and the McKenneys, Jack suddenly had more work than he could handle. Working with his friend meant steady employment for Allen and the chance to stay in Tavernier. It appears he did not have to ponder his employment possibilities for long.

On August 23, Allen received an urgent letter from John Baker. Except for Allen's presentation at the October conference, everything else had come to a screeching halt. He was to report to the Audubon headquarters in New York. Olin Pettingill had accepted a new assignment from Carleton College, which required him to start work on September 20. Baker needed a new director for the Whooping Crane Project immediately. Although Baker sorely needed Allen to tend to various matters in Louisiana and Florida, the Whooping Crane Project was finally given top priority. Audubon members had rallied around the whooping crane cause, feeling that the organization's reputation was at stake; after the recent failed attempts, finding the nesting site in Canada was crucial. Although Pettingill, Bard, and Smith poured their hearts into the Whooping Crane Project and laid its groundwork, their commitment was only temporary. Baker needed an ornithologist who would work on the project exclusively, someone whose research skills were well honed, someone who possessed the tenacity and resourcefulness to get the job done. Three days later, as Allen was preparing to leave for New York, he received another letter from Baker, offering Allen the position. There was one stipulation—a change of venue—Allen would have to spend much of his time in Texas.

On August 29, Allen wrote back accepting the job with enthusiasm. Birds were his passion, and the whooping cranes deserved a chance to recover their numbers: "The Society has a great deal at stake in the particular project, and we certainly don't want to spoil our good record. I, for one, would like a chance to 'show 'em' that the old N.A.S. can still deliver the goods."[3] He went on to write in earnest how he had considered looking for other work to finally put down roots in Tavernier. "You have sensed, I am sure, that all of us will be none too happy to leave our new home in Florida. It's the first thing even remotely resembling a home that we've had in years. Here we have our own—actually our own—beds and bureaus and easy chairs and piano, all the simple comforts. I want you to know, John, that I have been sorely tempted to stay here, come hell or highwater."[4]

Allen might not have had a sheepskin on his wall, but as evident in the above letter, he had no problem speaking his mind and dealing with his boss on equal terms.

After talking it over with Evelyn, their enthusiasm grew. "In the end, of course, we knew we'd have to give it all up. And gladly, too. We're like old retired fire horses when they hear the clang of a bell."[5] By the end of the summer, it was official: Bob Allen was named the new director of the Whooping Crane Project, an assignment that would occupy his life for the next nine years.

When Allen returned from the Army, he had promised Evelyn he would not leave the family for extended periods of time. Evelyn had no doubt that he would keep his promise. Yet she had to face the reality that if her husband continued his work as an ornithologist, settling down was something the family might not do, at least anytime in the near future. Having uprooted Bobby and Alice from school several times, Evelyn decided to make their education her responsibility. Once more, Carl Buchheister came to her aide. He gave Evelyn the name of Edward W. Brown, director of the Calvert Schools. In business since 1897, the Calvert system of correspondence courses for elementary school had gained a notable reputation, shipping its curricula all over the world to families of missionaries, those in the military, or those whose work took them to isolated places. Evelyn wrote to Brown and registered with Calvert to teach her children at home.

In preparation for the move to Texas, Bob and Evelyn considered subletting the house and putting their belongings in storage. Instead, they put up the shutters, locked everything down, and bought storm insurance. They left in mid-September in time for Allen to drive Evelyn and the kids to his mother's house in Muncy, Pennsylvania, before heading out to the Audubon conference in New York.

Staying at grandmother DeWitt's house rather than enrolling in school for her third-grade year was an adventure for Alice, but her enthusiasm waned on the drive north. By the time the Allens arrived in Pennsylvania, Alice had broken out with a skin rash and was feeling poorly. Evelyn assured Bob that she could handle Alice's illness and sent her husband on his way. A few days later, Alice was in the hospital with blood poisoning.

~

Baker brought to New York a cadre of whooping crane experts, which included Dr. Olin Pettingill, who had led the previous searches, and a man Baker had met a few years before, Dr. Larry Walkinshaw, a dentist and amateur ornithologist from Battle Creek, Michigan. Walkinshaw was a leading expert on sandhill cranes and was working on a sandhill monograph for the Cranbook Institute of Science in Michigan. From the moment they first met, Allen and Walkinshaw hit it off, and Allen expressed his interest to Baker in having Walkinshaw assist in the hunt if it could be arranged. Expectations for the next whooping crane nest hunt were high. Those attending the conference—ornithologists, biologists, government wildlife officials—were certain the third time would be the charm.

Once the conference was over and Allen had presented his findings, he drove to Pennsylvania. Alice had fully recovered and was ready for another family visit. Allen drove them to St. Louis to stay with Evelyn's family. He then flew to Minneapolis, where he boarded a train to Northfield for a conference with Olin Pettingill. They spent a few days reviewing notes from the two previous expeditions. While in Northfield, Allen picked up a Fish and Wildlife Service car and contacted Fred Bard to ship the camping equipment, boat, and outboard motor to Texas. He drove back to St. Louis. It was decided that Evelyn and Alice would remain with the Sedgwicks, and Bobby would accompany his father to Texas.

In 1946, life in Austwell, Texas, made Tavernier, Florida, seem like a thriving metropolis. The few residents sprinkled around Aransas County were farmers, fishermen, and a few folks who lived off the land. When Allen and Bobby arrived in Texas on November 6, the closest place to the Aransas National Wildlife Refuge to stay was Hopper's Landing, locally known as Hopperville, just off Park Road 13. A trailer park with a few clapboard rental cabins and a small general store, Hopper's was located on the shore of San Antonio Bay. Allen rented one of the small cottages fewer than 100 yards from the beach. Although the salt water lapping the shore emerged from the same source that kissed the Florida coast, the landscape couldn't have been more different. Tangles of red and black mangrove trees were replaced with dense clumps of cordgrass. In this vast openness, Allen and Bobby would begin a field study that would have them in the coastal marshes during most of the daylight hours.

When Allen was here in the early 1940s, gathering information on the spoonbills, he had the opportunity to see the cranes on their winter turf. At the time, he wondered who would be assigned the daunting task of saving the big white bird. He hadn't the slightest notion it would be him. That first night in the small cabin, listening to the gentle slap of waves in the bay, he realized that the challenges ahead made the spoonbill project seem simple. As the new director of the Whooping Crane Project, all his experience gave way to feelings of humbleness, and for Bob Allen, that was a good place to start.

The next morning, Allen and Bobby dropped by the town's gathering place, Cap Daniel's, a general store, beer joint, and garage. Covering the walls and shelves were Cap Daniel's odd collection of firearms and war relics. Also hanging in a prominent position on the wall was a

Judge Roy Bean "Law West of the Pecos" poster. Allen remembered his friend and refuge manager, Jim Stevenson, telling how the locals gathered around Cap Daniel's coal-burning stove and complained about the government's proclamation of Blackjack Peninsula as a whooping crane reserve. He often overheard comments such as, "If you can't shoot them [whooping cranes], what blankety-blank good are they?" or "They tell me they [whooping cranes] ain't bad eating but there's no open season on them."[6] Allen was surprised to see that the attitude surrounding saving the whooping cranes was changing. A new sign on Cap Daniel's front door announced the establishment as the Whooping Crane Information Center.

Cap Daniel remembered Allen and was happy to see the ornithologist. A few days later, he asked Allen to do him a favor: "Mr. Allen, I wonder if you couldn't get ahold of some whoopin' crane pitchers I could put up on my wall. People ask me about 'em every day an' I oughta have a pitcher or two."[7] When Allen brought in a large drawing of a pair of cranes, Cap Daniel removed the Judge Roy Bean poster and proudly replaced it with the whooping crane picture. He rolled up the Bean poster and presented it to Allen as a gift. Then he informed the ornithologist to be cautious about his approach. Word had spread that a new guy who was neither farmer nor fisherman had settled in the area. Not everyone in Aransas County had embraced the idea of protecting what they felt were a few useless birds. Even some folks who appreciated the whooping cranes living in their backyards were hostile toward interlopers. They did not take kindly to an outsider telling them what to do and how to protect what was clearly theirs. Allen had no intention of using that approach. Instead, he took on the role of a whooping crane novice and requested the locals teach him all they knew. The first person he visited was a remarkable lady he'd met years earlier.

While Allen was cutting his teeth on ornithology, fifty-year-old Connie Hagar had earned a reputation of being the best, most knowledgeable amateur birder in Texas. Ornithologists from all over the country had relied on Hagar's Nature Calendar, a concise daily documentation of birds living in and migrating to Rockport, Texas. Allen first met Hagar when Baker sent him to Texas in 1941 to assist her in teaching Audubon's first summer education birding camp for adults, which was headquartered at rental cottages owned by Connie and her husband, Jack. At the time, Alexander Sprunt Jr., the Audubon southern representative, was assigned to teach the classes with Connie. Sprunt had spent years traveling on behalf of Audubon, lecturing and enlightening the public on birds. Coming to Rockport, Texas, he did not expect to find someone who could match his skill and knowledge of birds tit for tat, especially a small woman who often took to the bush wearing not only binoculars around her neck, but a set of pearls. That first week, Hagar upstaged Audubon's field representative. Sprunt was formative in his delivery and information, but could not match Hagar's charm and charisma. He left Texas before the summer classes ended, and Baker sent Allen to finish the session. Aware of her notable reputation, and keeping with his propensity to put folks at ease, Allen knew exactly where he stood. In Karen Harden McCracken's biography of Connie Hagar, *The Life History of a Texas Birdwatcher: Connie Hagar of Rockport*, McCracken writes that Allen's first comment to Hagar went something like, "Connie, it's your territory, will you help me?"[8] The Hagars took to Allen immediately. Connie was happy to report Allen's success with the summer camp: "Buoyant, outgoing, avid to learn and share sights and sounds of this new region, Bob Allen soon had the camp guests happily spilling over the area in their eager studies."[9]

During that 1941 visit, Hagar showed Allen the best birding spots in Aransas County, introducing him to the myriad of migratory species that earned Rockport the moniker of the Birding Capital of North America. Arriving with the season were species of grebes, ducks, geese, wrens, rails, falcons, kites, terns, ibises, along with oystercatchers, black skimmers, peregrine and Merlin falcons, ospreys, gallinules, hummingbirds, and songbirds. Allen and Hagar extended the camp studies to include a boat trip to Grass Island in Mission Bay. At the end of Allen's stay, she asked him to postpone his departure until the next day. She had something to show him. That spring, three whooping cranes, for some unknown reason, had chosen to summer over in Texas. Although this was his second trip to the refuge, being there with a fellow birder who could teach him a thing or two left an impression on Allen.

When Hagar learned of Allen's new assignment as the Whooping Crane Project director, she was almost as thrilled as he was.

With Connie nearby ready to assist, along with his strategy of soliciting help from the locals, Allen had gathered numerous reports of crane locations. His next order of business was to confirm the reports and then conduct a crane-count to determine if the winter flock at Aransas was the only one remaining. If so, the next step would be to figure out why the cranes preferred that particular area.

On their first day out, refuge manager Charles "Bud" Keefer and state deer trapper Guy Golbath drove Allen and son Bobby through the refuge. Because of recent rain, the only vehicle able to maneuver the muddy roads was a tractor with a trailer attached. The day started out with a cold breeze blowing moisture in from the bay. By noon, the sky had grown dark and the temperature had dropped; a "norther" was settling in over the Texas coast. After covering the eastern section around Jones and Mustang Lakes, they turned down East Shore Road; the numbing wind was now stinging their eyes. Whenever Allen spotted a white bird in the distance, it took several seconds of shouting to get Keefer's attention due to the loud clanking of the tractor. Many of these first sightings, which were at least half a mile away, turned out to be pelicans or egrets. Although Allen was determined to find his subjects, the inclement weather had taken its toll. Instead of showing his usual perseverance, he decided to head back. As they made the turn toward park headquarters, forging in the marsh not 50 yards away was a pair of whoopers. Watching these tall, lanky birds pick their way through the cordgrass, Allen wondered how he could have mistaken them for anything else. Standing more than 5 feet tall, with a 7-foot wingspan and a bright-red crown, the whooping crane possessed an awe-inspiring beauty. Allen scrambled for his notebook and, disregarding the cold, wrote down every movement the pair made until they flew off toward Mullet Bay: "At the moment we saw them they were already moving, sounding off with their bugle-clear trumpet blast of warning and running with amazingly lengthy strides before getting airborne. The red skin on top of their bare heads stood out clearly, and so did the grim, almost fierce cast of their features. They seemed like great satin-white bombers, with their immense wings flicking upward in short arcs and their heavy bodies fighting for altitude."[10]

That night, Allen and Bobby camped among a stand of live oaks, which provided protection from the fierce north wind and gave them a vantage point of the salt flats. After a dinner of canned beans and coffee, father and son built a fire, watched the sun descend on the refuge, and made plans to rise with the birds in the morning to continue their observations.

The next day brought more cold rain, drenching most of their camping gear. The weather aggravated a recurring pain in Allen's shoulder and arm, an annoyance he assumed to be an early onset of arthritis. After drying off the equipment as well as he could, Allen locked the spotting scope on a family of three cranes feeding about a mile away. At that distance, observing the nuances of their behavior was difficult, but at least it was a start.

The heavy rains had washed out many of the dirt roads, but despite the sloppy conditions, Allen went ahead with his plans for an extensive ground research. By November 15, again using Golbath's tractor and trailer, he had traversed every road and trail on the refuge, confirming the crane population at only seventeen. On November 20, with assistance from a local pilot, Bob Tanner, Allen flew over the section of the refuge that included Matagorda and St. Joseph Islands. The result was disappointing—not one whooping crane was seen. It seemed the entire Texas winter flock of seventeen that lived between Copano and San Antonio Bays was all that remained, indicating a loss of eight cranes—33 percent of the population—from Pettingill's count from the previous year.

On December 1, Allen left for Louisiana to survey the refuges around Gueydan in Vermilion Parish. The outlook in the neighboring state was worse. In 1939, John Flynn of the USFWS had observed a flock of thirteen whooping cranes wintering in the area. By the winter of 1945, that number had dwindled to two. For two weeks, Allen and John Flynn conducted an extensive air search, hoping to find more. They did not.

Allen returned to Aransas in late December. For the rest of the winter he continued to study the few remaining cranes, gleaning details concerning their diet and feeding habits, territorial boundaries, family dynamics, tolerance for other wildlife, and anything that would give a clue to assist in the species' survival. The weather had not improved, nor had his arm and shoulder. Baker had received word, probably from Allen himself, of his ailment. He wrote to Allen: "Sorry to hear your shoulder and arm have been giving you a bad time. Better get them in shape now rather than later. The sooner you do so the less the period of recovery will be."[11] Although Baker's advice made sense, taking the time to find out what was wrong

Bob Allen camping at the Aransas National Wildlife Refuge, 1946. Courtesy of Alice Allen.

was the last thing Allen wanted to do. Instead, he stocked up on aspirin and went back into the field.

Young Bobby began assisting Allen in the field whenever possible and had learned to identify the whooping crane families. Father and son seined for whatever lived in the marsh, set up camps in various locations on the refuge, conducted waterfowl counts, and took notes of any whooping crane tracks they came across. Most mornings started out with temperatures below freezing, warming to the forties with the mercury occasionally bumping up into the low fifties. The terra firma beneath their feet was anything but; the ground had taken on a fluid quality like the soft, spongy belly of a mythical creature.

On one wet, cold day in the second week of January, while seining near Camp Pond, the territory of the South Family, Allen and Bobby came across a mud flat pocked with numerous crane tracks. The flat was littered with empty shells of blue crab and razor clams, evidence of the

South Family's latest meal. Allen was curious to know what water source fed the pond and brought in the crabs. The only way to find out was to trek across the marsh. They had covered fewer than 100 yards when it began to rain, turning the mud into a glue-like slop. First Bobby lost his boots, then Allen. In his struggle to keep from falling, Allen broke his only thermometer. They returned to camp, donned dry clothes, and were trekking toward Mullet Bay by noon, taking a different path through a narrow inlet. Suddenly, the channel opened up like a fan, spilling water across the flats. Allen could see it now: the cranes' seafood stew was washed in during high tide.

Since the cranes were active, Allen decided to spend at least another night in the field despite the foul weather. That evening found father and son wet and dirty, eating beans in their tent, and saving their last change of dry clothes for another day's work. When dawn broke the next morning, they packed up their equipment and returned to Camp Pond only to find it deserted. Allen knew from his experience with the spoonbills that all good things come to those who wait. Allen and Bobby hid themselves in a brush of live oaks and settled in. After several hours, their effort paid off, but Allen almost missed the event. He had returned to camp to refill the stove with gasoline. Bobby stayed behind, scanning the salt flats for any sign of the big white birds. All of a sudden, the South Family flew in and began plucking crabs from the water. Then the Middle Family glided in low just a few feet above Bobby, who did not have to be told to flatten himself to the ground and stay hidden. The cranes landed in the same area a few yards away. Bobby couldn't believe what he was seeing. Up until now, the families remained in their own territories, miles away from each other. Allen returned just as the two dominant males challenged one another in a territorial dispute that lasted forty-five minutes. The Middle Family male charged, running toward the South Family, his neck outstretched and his spear-shaped beak pointed straight ahead. Although he remained on the ground, he flapped his wings and let out a high-pitched bugle call. The female and chick watched as the male pulled up short in front of the South Family male. Then the Middle Family female joined her mate in sending out staccato alarm notes that resonated through the air and echoed across the marsh.

Allen would witness many territorial disputes in weeks to come, but watching this lengthy display was like having a front-row seat on the past,

Jan. 10, 1947 – Middle + South family groups —
"Mixed Quartette" Performance – 2:05 P.M. – 2:55 P.M. –
(Aransas Refuge, Texas)   GRUS AMERICANA
R.P.A.

Sketch of the Middle Pond and South Family groups entitled *Mixed Quartette*, by Bob Allen. Published in *Audubon Magazine*, May-June 1947, and reprinted in Allen's 1952 monograph. Courtesy of *Audubon Magazine*, New York.

looking back in time to when the whooping crane reigned as an abundant and viable tertiary consumer in their vast habitat. Allen wrote in his journal that evening, "We returned to camp, stiff and wet, but pleased at our good fortune in watching the unusual two-family dance."[12]

Finding the cranes was no longer a problem. Family territories had been discovered and documented. Now Allen had to get close enough to observe their interactions. Since the whoopers seemed unbothered by cattle grazing in the area, he constructed a blind resembling a ruddy-colored Santa Gertrudis bull. He stitched together a swatch of red canvas and stretched it over a rudimentary bovine-shaped wire frame. For the final touches on his hideout, he cut openings in the head where the nostrils would be to use as peep holes. The structure was large enough for Allen to stand upright.

On the first day in the field, the only thing he gained was cold, wet feet. The next day, the cranes failed to show themselves. Not true for another local resident: a bull trotted up, agitated over the presence of the odd-looking challenger. Thinking of Ernest Hemingway's story about bullfights in Spain, Allen composed in his mind his own tale, which he entitled "Death in the Morning," and then a more likely publication, a newspaper headline, "Bird Watcher Gored by Bull."[13] Unable to escape the blind without giving himself away, Allen sat stock still while the bull locked eyes with his intruder. Either Allen won the stare-down or the bull lost interest, for after several minutes, it turned and walked away. After this incident, Allen thought the blind a failure; weeks later, however, he put it to good use.

By year's end, Allen knew the intimate details of whooping crane life on the refuge in Texas. He was certain that their numbers were closer to twenty-five. He knew what they ate and where, which of the fourteen groups claimed which territories; he could recognize the difference between alarm and mating calls, understood the intricacies of the food web and the role the cranes played as a prey and predator, and understood changes in water levels and flows and salinity concentrations. With the crane count completed, Allen shifted his focus. He now watched for changes in their behavior, a signal that the breeding cycle and subsequent migration was on the horizon. On December 17, Allen observed the Middle Pond Pair. One of the birds, probably the male, leapt several feet straight into the air and flapped its wings. Allen looked around expecting to see another family coming in to challenge the Middle Pond Pair. When Allen saw that the pair was alone, he suspected the male's actions might have been the beginning of a mating dance. The female watched and quickly lost interest, possibly sending a subtle message to her mate that the time was not right.

The next display didn't occur until January 10. It was the male again who took the lead, this time adding a few fancy steps to his quadrille. He pumped his bill up and down, rose in the air and took flight. His mate followed, and both returned within a few minutes. Then, on January 26, a warm and mild day, Allen watched the Middle Pond Pair again in what he believed was their complete dance. The almost-erotic display ended with the cranes rushing toward one another "bouncing as if on pogo sticks."[14] The dance lasted four minutes.

In the weeks that followed, other crane families engaged in similar behavior. At first the displays were infrequent and sporadic. As the weather warmed and the days grew longer, the migratory dances increased and became more elaborate, almost like a ballet unfolding in the marsh, acting out the ancient ceremonial courtship. During Allen's second year at the refuge, he eloquently described the Middle Pond female and her youngster enjoying the water just days prior their migration: "They were standing in water about 15 inches deep. The female would crouch hesitantly, like a bather cautiously feeling the water with an exploratory toe. Then she would dip all the way under, except for her head and neck, splashing up and down, shaking her partly open wings, wiggling her tail and throwing her head about so that her crown stroked the feathers of her back. The immature Whooper imitated all this awkwardly."[15] When the male joined them, the female turned on the chick and chased it into the reeds.

With the media interest in the cranes' survival escalating, *Life* magazine contacted John Baker. The magazine wanted to send a photographer to spend time with Allen at the refuge in the hope of bringing back an exclusive photo of what was becoming America's favorite bird. In 1934, when Baker took charge of Audubon, he turned his attention to the birds along the Texas coast. This became his pet project, and he planned to see that every aspect of it was attended to properly. Concerned that the magazine publish the "right kind of publicity," Baker planned to drive the photographer all the way to Texas "to educate him."[16]

Opting for a quicker means of transportation, John Baker and photographer Andreas Feininger, who specialized in landscapes and urban scenes of Manhattan, flew to Corpus Christi and arrived on the refuge on the morning of January 26. Allen had his doubts as to *any* photographer's ability to capture the cranes on film given the inclement weather on the refuge and the difficulty of getting close to the birds—something Allen had accomplished only occasionally. But being the gracious host, Allen agreed to assist Feininger in whatever needed to be done.

The day Feininger arrived, the blustery weather had cleared, and the sky offered a perfect blue backdrop. Feeling optimistic, Allen set up the bull blind near camp. After performing a simple surgery on the bull's side to position Feininger's 20-inch camera lens, Allen situated the photographer inside. The South Family, who usually fed nearby, stayed away the entire day.

When Allen and Feininger arrived at camp the next morning, a thick fog had settled in, reducing visibility to a few yards. Suddenly, the South Family, parents and chick, strolled by, coming within touching distance of the bull blind. Feininger rushed to the truck and grabbed his camera. Then, as if knowing they were being watched, the cranes quietly strolled into the fog and disappeared. On the third day, Allen, Bobby, and Feininger rose at six o'clock. Feininger was set up inside the blind well before dawn. Allen left the photographer a couple of sandwiches, a jug of water, and a stool. Feininger arranged his equipment and waited. Not long after dawn the South Family called from Bloodworth Island a half mile away. The sun rose and a fog drifted in again. Feininger watched and listened, hoping the birds would move in closer.

Allen, Bobby, and Charles "Olaf" Wallmo, Allen's assistant, went in search of more cranes around Mustang Lake; they planned to return to check on Feininger around noon. Early that afternoon, their truck slid off the road, the axle buried deep in mud. The only way to pull it out was to use the tractor, which was parked at headquarters 10 miles away. And the only way to get to headquarters was to walk. When Allen returned for Feininger nine hours later, the photographer had the look of a man given in to defeat. During that long, tedious day, not one whooping crane had come into view. That evening brought with it more rain and wind. Feininger was scheduled to stay for only one more day.

The next morning, Allen and Bobby moved the blind to what they hoped would be a more favorable location. In the faint light of dawn, the South Family flew in and landed, marched around their territory, and sent out alarm calls. Feininger rushed inside the blind and readied his camera. Allen and Bobby flopped down in the marsh grass and crawled a safe distance away. Apparently more curious than alarmed over the activity in their territory, the crane family trooped over in single file, coming to within a few yards of the photographer's lens. In his excitement, Feininger, tried to move the blind and follow the birds for a better shot. Alarm calls went out again, and the cranes began moving away. With the blind tilted on its side and resembling an inebriated cow, Feininger managed a few shots. Despite the poor lighting conditions, he came away with three decent photos. On March 3, 1947, the South Family—father, mother, and chick, whose rust-colored head showed just above the grass—made their debut in *Life* magazine. It was just what the public wanted to see. This one shot heightened the public's emotional interest in the cranes' fate, giving Allen new hope for the species' future.

Later that winter, the use of the blind resulted in more spectacular photos, this time of the dominant Middle Pond Family, who had displaced the South Family from their territory. The photographers inside the blind were Allen's old friends, artist Roger Tory Peterson and ornithologist Allan Cruickshank.

In that first winter's study, Allen learned how tenuous the cranes' existence really was. The open salt flats provided the cranes with an abundant supply of blue crab and killifish as long as the rivers and inlets fed the bay. Although the winter of 1946–47 had its share of rain, one season of drought could have proven disastrous for the dwindling population. When water tables were low, the birds were forced to move inland to forge for food in taller grass, putting them at greater risk of predation by bobcats and coyotes. Allan was especially concerned over a lone crane living in the marsh. The first time Allen spotted him, something didn't ring true. He pulled out his binoculars and watched the bird's movement. The bird seemed strong and healthy. Then Allen noticed that one wing hung low. It was obvious that this whooping crane would not migrate when spring rolled around. Allen hoped his solitary crane could somehow, against all odds, manage to avoid predators alone in the vast marshland.

With all the naturally occurring environmental problems, the cranes faced more apparent dangers. Boat traffic in the Intracoastal Waterway, which bisected the refuge, was increasing. Planes from the nearby Naval Air Station in Corpus Christi, flying training exercises over the numerous islands, often frightened the birds. Allen feared the disturbance would cause the cranes to wander off the refuge, as was the case with the cranes on Matagorda Island during World War II, when pilots dropped bombs while on training missions. Also, it was only a matter of time before oil

companies began drilling in the marshes nearby, resulting in further dis-
turbances. One oil spill could wipe out the entire whooping crane habitat. With their nesting site believed to be in Canada and still unknown,
the dangers they faced during their 2,500-mile migration, and the hazards
developing on their fragile coastal habitat in Texas, saving the whooping
cranes suddenly became even more crucial.

That spring, while the adult crane couples engaged in their nuptial
dances, a prelude to their migration, Allen prepared to follow them north.
For now, more than ever, the cranes needed all the help they could get.

II

Somewhere up North, 1947–1950

If I leave here tomorrow
Would you still remember me?
For I must be traveling on, now
'Cause there's too many places
I've got to see.

Lynyrd Skynyrd, *Free Bird*

4

Things of Value

At the turn of the twentieth century, a betting man would have been wise not to wager on the whooping crane's odds of avoiding extinction. Fossil records showed the species' numbers peaked during the Pleistocene epoch, when environmental conditions were optimal; a shallow sea and bordering marshland, the whooping crane's only habitat, covered much of North America. As global conditions changed and the sea receded, the whooping cranes, for reasons unknown, did not adapt as did their cousins the sandhills, who had moved inland and claimed a wider, more varied niche. Whooping cranes cannot reside above a 3-foot contour line beyond sea level, choosing instead a brackish marsh ecosystem, which unfortunately has a tenuous food supply. The original migratory flyway, the swath down the middle of North America that at one time extended from central Canada south into western and central Mexico and eastward to Florida, has shrunk to a mere sliver. In the 1500s, the whooping crane population was believed to be around 10,000. As the Great Plains became settled, the species had reached the critical stage, shrinking by 90 percent to between 700 and 1,400 in 1870. Their original breeding ground in the United States, which extended from North Dakota southwest to central Illinois, a distance of more than 1,000 miles, was deserted by 1894. The wetlands necessary for migratory stopovers and nesting had been drained for agricultural use. By 1922, the only known nesting site in southern Saskatchewan was also abandoned.

As the species began to disappear, natural history museums became desperate for whooping crane skins and eggs to add to their collection before it was too late. Egg hunters raided the few existing nesting areas in North Dakota, Minnesota, and Iowa.

At this point, all the conservation efforts in the world would not stop the species from declining. The life cycle of the whooping crane is a slow and fragile one. Raising the young from hatchling to adulthood is much harder than it sounds. Biology's rule of thumb is that the fewer the off-spring, the greater the chance of survival. What is also true is that the larger the animal, the more time and energy are required to raise it.

Whooping cranes mate for life. During their thirty-year lifespan, one crane pair, if lucky, might raise roughly a dozen young cranes to adult-hood. So many factors work against them. And the crane parents seem to know this. Unlike smaller avian species like sparrows and warblers, which frequently renest and lay clutches of numerous eggs, whooping cranes breed once a year, producing two eggs, but usually raise only one to ma-turity. Despite the vigilance of both parents, the chicks often fall victim to predators or succumb to disease. If the chick survives the first six months, it must make its first long migratory trip down to Texas. Eighty percent of crane fatalities occur during the six-week migration periods in spring and fall; especially vulnerable are the young, inexperienced whoopers, who sometimes collide with power lines.

In early February 1947, various heads of the USFWS and the National Audubon Society convened at Aransas to discuss the third Canadian search. Studying the reports of the two previous attempts, a general plan was drawn up. John Baker pulled out all the stops and contacted every connection possible. Requests for more volunteers were sent to Dr. Gus-tav Swanson, director of research with the USFWS. Since Fred Bard was unable to return to the project, Baker requested that the Provincial Mu-seum in Regina donate equipment instead. When Allen asked for two pilots to assist in conducting the extensive aerial search, Baker sent out a call for them as well.

In preparation for the trip north, Allen spent the next several weeks catching up on paperwork, part of which included reviewing the proofs of *The Flame Birds*. Eleanor King urged Allen to return the proofs as quickly as possible so that the manuscript could be ready for its spring publica-tion date. Allen's writing extended beyond his book on the spoonbills; part of his assignment with Audubon involved providing articles for *Audubon Magazine* and other publications. Writing had become as much a part of Allen's life as studying birds. Years earlier, he began a routine that eventually developed into a daily ritual. He rose well before dawn and wrote at least 1,500 words before breakfast. Given his preference for writing longhand, Evelyn would later take his notes and type them after her husband left for the field. When an extra typist was needed, "K" Wilkinson assisted.

Since Pettingill did not have enough time to document the cranes' arrival to their major stopover site en route to Canada the year before, Allen planned to spend a few weeks in North Platte, Nebraska, for this sole purpose before heading to Saskatchewan. Annual record keeping of the number of cranes migrating over the Platte River began as far back as 1912. With only eight whooping cranes reported migrating through between 1941 and 1943, Bob Allen described later in his Audubon research report that the situation was "a four-alarm fire" compared to the smoldering conditions of the previous eighty years.[1]

The timing for Allen to begin his trip north was perfect. Andreas Feininger's whooping crane photographs in *Life* magazine had just been published. The general public's excitement grew as news of the expedition hit the newsstands. Communities near the cranes' stopping places were put on alert. Seth Low, refuge manager at the Salt Plains National Wildlife Refuge in Oklahoma, spread the word to the nearby towns of Jet and Cherokee. U.S. Game Management Agent Melvin Ramsey and State Game Protector Arthur Jones were doing the same around one of the country's largest wetland ecosystems, Cheyenne Bottoms Wildlife Area and Quivira Wildlife Refuge near Grant Bend, Kansas.

Occasionally, the publicity generated by the media backfired, and Allen and Audubon had to rebut what had been reported. On March 1, 1947, the *Saturday Evening Post* printed a story advising anyone seeing a large white bird to "rush to the nearest phone and report your experience to any Federal, state, or local conservation official, who will be delighted to get the news."[2] What the article failed to mention was that the whooping cranes migrated along a narrow gauntlet, running from the Texas Gulf coast in a slightly northwesterly direction toward North Dakota. Reports came in from almost every state in the Union and several Canadian provinces. Although most of the reports were discarded, Allen was encouraged by the public's willingness to assist. In the wake of the *Post*'s proclamation came the article in *Life* magazine that accompanied Feininger's crane photos informing its readers that Allen had planned to "trail them [whooping cranes] by plane to their hidden nesting grounds."[3] The public took this literally, and Allen was left to explain on numerous occasions that following slow-flying cranes was not possible and that the noise of the aircraft would scare the heck out of the birds, disrupting their flight. At one point, someone spread a rumor that the scientists planned to place a radar band on the leg of each whooping crane, thus allowing pilots to track the birds with a radar-equipped aircraft. Audubon did not take the rumor seriously. The United States Air Force did. Audubon received a letter from the government stating in no certain terms that the scheme would not be allowed.

~

As Allen made his way to Nebraska, folks spotted his car with its government license plates and approached him with questions, eager to hear reports of his progress. When he arrived at the Hotel Pawnee in North Platte, the designated headquarters for this leg of the journey, dozens of eager members of the Lincoln County Sportsmen's Association and the North Platte Bird Club greeted him, ready to lend a hand. The eager delegation of birders would prove invaluable during Allen's five-week stay in North Platte. He needed to verify and document every whooping crane sighting that came in.

Among the crowd of people at the Hotel Pawnee was Wilson Tout, owner and publisher of the *Lincoln County Tribune*, author of *Lincoln County Birds*, and president of the Nebraska Ornithologists' Union. Tout put Allen in touch with local pilots, who were delighted to fly the ornithologist over the river. On March 24, Jimmy Kirkman, the *Telegraph-Bulletin*'s sports editor who eventually became mayor of North Platte, published an article outlining Allen's endeavor and providing the public with a detailed description of whooping cranes. The headline of Kirkman's article read, "Allen Here, Awaits Flight of Crane."[4] Kirkman urged anyone who saw a bird resembling a whooping crane to rush to the nearest phone and call the Hotel Pawnee to report their sighting to Robert Allen. "Allen doesn't care whether you are certain or not," Kirkman wrote. "He wants to investigate all possibilities. As quickly as he can, he will follow up the report by airplane and you will have helped out in an important work, for, you see, there are only 29 whooping cranes left in the world."[5]

The first call came in the next day. Between March 25 and April 21, Allen investigated 144 sightings. The messages left at the Hotel Pawnee came from schoolchildren, teachers, businessmen, farmers, ranchers, a truck driver, an airplane pilot, an automobile mechanic, and other citizens who lived in or traveled through the area. Many of the reports were false alarms; none went unchecked. Getting up early every morning and driving west to Ogallala and then east toward Grand Island, Allen investigated every single one regardless of the weather.

The calendar said springtime, but winter had not yet let go of its hold on Nebraska. It snowed on April 4. A week later, another several inches blanketed the prairie. Allen's car did not have a heater. Every few miles he was forced to stop and place his bare hands on the windshield to melt the ice that had formed.

After the mid-April snowfall, the weather warmed quickly, bringing in thousands of migratory birds. Along with the birds came more reports. Bob Allen's popularity in the central Nebraska community grew. He had become a much-sought-after figure. When he wasn't running down crane reports, he gave talks to the Lions Club, the North Platte Bird Club, and classes of eager children at the local schools. KODY radio-station newscaster Joe DiNatali included the crane hunt as part of his daily noontime news broadcast.

On April 9, a call came to the hotel headquarters. An excited KODY radio listener told of a whooping crane feeding among a flock of sandhills near Hershey about 15 miles west of North Platte. Allen spent the entire day tracking it only to discover that the large white bird with black wing tips was a snow goose.

While Allen bounced along the rough country roads of Nebraska, Olaf Wallmo kept watch on the whooping cranes in Texas, hoping to pinpoint the exact day the birds left on their migration. He started out each morning at the refuge headquarters and drove to Dunham Point, the farthest location, covering the perimeter and all the arteries leading to the marshes. The 45-mile trip was conducted three times a week until the end of March. Suddenly, the cranes' behavior changed. What had been a predictable, uneventful routine became a harum-scarum of activity. Territories that had been fiercely adhered to shifted. Wallmo first noticed that the Slough Pair, who occupied Mustang Slough, Redfish Slough, and Mustang Lake, had left their territory. His report to Allen stated: "The

North Family deserted Long Pond and used the shore of Mullet Bay. The Dike Pair had usually been found on the southwest end of Long Pond and the adjacent land-locked ponds south of there. After the movement of the North Family, the Dike Pair expanded their territory, using all of Long Pond and ranging to the shore of Mullet Bay. The Refuge Single, whose earlier preference was near the Middle Pond with the Middle Pair, shifted to Mullet Bay. The Middle Pair, however, still were found mostly in Middle Pond, occasionally ranging to Mullet Bay."[6] To keep up with the cranes' recent movements, Wallmo now conducted his drives daily.

Even though these excursions were tedious, Wallmo's efforts proved beneficial. He discovered a whooping crane living in the southern section of the refuge that had not been seen before. The lone crane was catalogued as the South Single. Wallmo also located the unknown territories of the Dunham Bay Pair and the South Pair.

Learning the exact day of departure was vital to the project, and Wallmo telegraphed Allen whenever a family or single crane left the Aransas Refuge. The Dike Pair took flight on April 7; the Middle Pair on April 9; and the Middle Family, the Bay Pair, and the South Single were gone by April 11. For Allen, the cranes' arrival was like waiting for his old friends to come to town.

Late in the day on April 14, pilot Eddy Brown and his wife reported seeing what they thought were three white cranes flying near Overton. Fortunately, Mrs. Brown filmed the event on her 16mm camera. Allen rushed over and viewed the film. After following up dozens of false alarms, Allen felt like celebrating. The gregarious Middle Family had arrived—in only four days.

On April 12, a storm blew in, spilling 4 inches of rain across the refuge in Texas, preventing Wallmo from attending to his daily scouting. On April 14, he searched on foot and found only three cranes feeding along the shore of Mullet Bay. An aerial search over the refuge was arranged on April 19; no cranes were found. Wallmo telegraphed Allen that the entire flock was under way. He concluded that the storm had been the precipitating factor in their departure.

Within a few days, all the cranes except five had been accounted for. The North Family of three and the Slough Pair had not yet appeared. Chances were these five were traveling together since they lived on neighboring territories at Aransas. For two days, Allen had run down numerous reports; all turned out to be false alarms. Could the cranes still be on the refuge and Wallmo had simply missed them? Allen knew that was not the case. He trusted Wallmo's assessment. Allen began to suspect the worst. For years, whooping cranes had been shot during their spring and fall migrations. The greatest number met their demise when the birds landed to rest and feed along the confluence of the north and south forks of the Platte River. Had he been overzealous with his plea to the locals to watch for and protect the cranes? Had he provoked a hunter who felt the whooping crane cause was frivolous? Allen had given it his best. All he could do was wait.

At 7:35 a.m. on April 19, Earl Mathers, attending to his farm chores, noticed five large white birds in his pasture. He hopped into his truck and drove a mile to the nearest phone. Fifteen minutes later, Lee Jensen, the state conservation officer at North Platte, called Allen with an urgent message: "Get out to Earl Mather's [*sic*] farm near the diversion dam. Earl just called in to report 5 whooping cranes on his place. Looks like the real thing!"[7]

Allen sped down Route 30 and reached the Mathers' farm in minutes. Mrs. Mathers was waiting on the porch. She directed Allen to the stubble field behind the barn where her husband waited. Allen found Mathers pacing in his field; the farmer did not look happy, having lost sight of the birds. The two men walked to the river and stood on a high berm overlooking the river bottom. Allen's hopes were dashed when he noticed a flock of at least a hundred white pelicans. Somewhat impatient, Allen told the farmer that the birds he saw were most likely pelicans. Mathers puffed up with indignation and responded: "Mr. Allen, they were *not* these pelicans here. I've told you what they looked like and I'm sure they were the birds you're after."[8]

Giving Mathers his due, Allen rushed to the airport, located a pilot, and was soon flying transects over the South Platte. Within ten minutes, he saw five white specs in the distance along the river bottom. The pilot dropped down to an altitude of 100 feet to give Allen a closer look. In his excitement, Allen almost dropped his camera. That evening he returned to the Mathers place and apologized to Earl. The North Family and the Slough Pair were safely feeding in a corn stubble field. Later that spring, two of Allen's photographs showing the five cranes on the Mathers' farm were published in *Audubon Magazine*.

Wallmo's timely departure reports provided Allen with valuable information about the crane migration. The birds covered the 920 miles between the Texas coast to North Platte, arriving four to seven days later, averaging between 130 and 230 miles per day. Using this information, Allen could predict when the cranes would cross over into Canada. The bad news was that once they flew into the wilds of Saskatchewan, their route was anybody's guess.

Years later, Allen reflected on his experiences along the migration route across America's heartland. Over all, he was pleased with the response and assistance of the folks who came out to help spot the whooping cranes. The whooper fan club seemed to grow every year. Now and then, however, Allen would run up against someone who strongly expressed his or her opposition to saving the whooping cranes. Once, he received a letter from an angry farmer in Saskatchewan who wrote that the effort to save the whooping crane was a waste of taxpayers' money, and that they [his neighbors] intended to ameliorate the problem by shooting whooping cranes whenever the opportunity arose. In a letter to the editor of a leading newspaper, another disgruntled reader wrote:

I myself do not give a whoop for the whooping crane. From what I have observed and read he is a dim-witted gawk of a bird whose pate has become more or less addled in the course of time until now he is not quite sharp enough mentally to be up to the fundamentals of procreation. This in a world where stupidity is nothing unusual is nevertheless pretty dumb and to my thinking deserved everyone's acquiescence to the idea that as far as extinction is concerned the sooner the better. . . . Don't you think in all honesty that our children's children's children will respect our memory more if we forego the expenditure of whatever monies are being spent to preserve these birds and leave them—these kids unborn—just ever so little of a bank balance with which to face the exigencies of that world of tomorrow?[9]

The above excerpt of the man's eloquently written postulation found its way into Allen's book *On the Trail of Vanishing Birds*. He responded that part of the reader's concern made sense, and then, with uncharacteristic sarcasm, he agreed with the guy by adding, "stupidity is not unusual in this world of ours," and suggested that there were other more important things to leave children than a bank balance.[10] It became evident a few years later that those opposed to the cause were not bluffing. Twenty-two whooping cranes were lost during the three-year migration period between 1950 and 1952. This represented a loss of 43 percent of the population since 1938.

Despite the hostile attitude shared by a few, the majority of Saskatchewan citizens were enthusiastic about having the cranes fly over their province. Fred Bard continued to educate the public, resulting in many locals embracing the large white birds as their own personal icon. Once, when a family of whoopers rested on Rice Lake near Saskatoon, a reporter rushed out and snapped their photos. The next day, the two birds appeared on the front page of the *Star-Phoenix* with the headline: "Star-Phoenix Photographs Rarest Bird in World, Whooping Crane."[11] A few days later, hundreds of Saskatchewanians visited the lake to see the birds. The publicity resulted in folks from across the county seeking more information about the cranes.

Allen continued to stress the importance of educational programs for hunters who lived along the Central Flyway. A leaflet, published by Audubon that year, was distributed to hunting clubs, showing the difference between whooping cranes and similar-looking birds. The leaflet also explained the ramifications of the loss of one single bird.

Allen saw to it that articles about the whooping crane were published in hunting magazines, farm journals, and conservation newsletters, and that educational materials were distributed to Junior Audubon Clubs, 4-H Clubs, Future Farmers of America, and the Boy and Girl Scouts. In his whooping crane monograph, Allen stressed the importance of education. The only drawback was the time it took for the public to understand the severity of the situation. And time was something the whooping crane did not have.

5

Unforgettable Days

In keeping with his promise to Evelyn, Allen wrote in his acceptance letter to John Baker that the family would accompany him while in Canada, adding that he would do a better job if he were "leading a normal life with my family around me and my favorite cook dishing out hot meals on order."[1] The companionship of his family notwithstanding, their assistance in camp would come in handy. "The children are big and husky and can even help me with my job now and then."[2] He sent Baker a list of equipment needed for a six-week camping trip in the primitive area of Saskatchewan.

Although Audubon was generous with outdoor equipment, tents, camp stoves, food lockers, cook pots, tarps, and batteries, Evelyn made her own list to prepare the family for an adventure unlike anything they'd ever experienced. She packed the station wagon with clothes for inclement weather, extra blankets and raingear, first aid kits for minor emergencies, and games and books for entertainment. Then, having gathered enough Calvert lessons for the duration of their stay in Canada, Evelyn and the kids joined Allen in North Platte on April 26, and the family set out in two cars for the Canadian wilderness the next day. Allen had since learned to drive, but because of his dubious driving skills, Bobby and Alice chose to travel most of the trip with their mother. Riding with Evelyn also meant that Alice could sing her favorite tune as many times as she liked. Jack McVea's song "Open the Door, Richard" had just hit number one on *Billboard*'s "Honor Roll of Hits." When Alice rode with her father, he limited the number of times she could sing the song to five and only if she hung her head out the window.

The Allen caravan arrived in Regina on May 1. Eager to get started with the next phase of his project, Allen met Fred Bard in his office at the museum to finalize the details for the search. Pilot Bob Smith, the USFWS flyway biologist who worked with Bard and Pettingill in the previous searches, would join Allen around the second week in May, and the two would begin aerial surveys over Allen's two prime targets: the Slave River and Lake Claire in northeastern Alberta and Great Slave Lake in the southern district of Mackenzie. According to reports, the cranes' path seemed to fan out after flying over southern Saskatchewan before disappearing northwest of Meadow Lake. Pettingill agreed with Allen's assessment. There were two others areas of interest based on previous crane sightings and migration patterns: one extended from Beaver River in east central Alberta north to Clearwater River, a glacier-fed river in southern Alberta; the other was the area around Nipawin on the Saskatchewan River north to Prince Albert National Park east to Montreal Lake and into The Pas, Manitoba. Pettingill's team had searched the Nipawin area in 1946, but a meeting of the minds agreed that it deserved another look. Then Allen received a letter from Charles Broley, who had led the Save-the-Whooping-Cranes campaign in 1946. Based on sighting reports he'd collected, he urged Allen to focus within 100 miles of Prince Albert. He believed that Pettingill's search had failed because he worked too far north. Broley also cautioned Allen that whooping cranes usually nest by June 1, and if spring arrived late, the birds might not nest at all. Allen filed away this piece of information with all his other data.

While Allen and Bard were finalizing their plans, John Baker contacted Larry Walkinshaw, requesting he assist Allen in the hunt. Walkinshaw, who was very eager to lend a hand, could do so only during his vacation time in May. He solicited the help of friend and fellow naturalist Walter Tholen. The two men agreed to foot the bill until funds could be found to cover their expenses. In a letter to Bard dated May 15, Walkinshaw was more than willing to "beg rides with anyone who will be doing bird work over the areas which I have to cover."[3] Baker agreed to help find money to hire a pilot for Walkinshaw and Tholen. It was decided that Allen would search the Beaver River area and Walkinshaw and Tholen the Nipawin area.

While waiting for Smith's arrival, Allen searched for a suitable place to set up a base camp. Since Meadow Lake was the last known area over which the whoopers had been seen flying, Allen decided to start there.

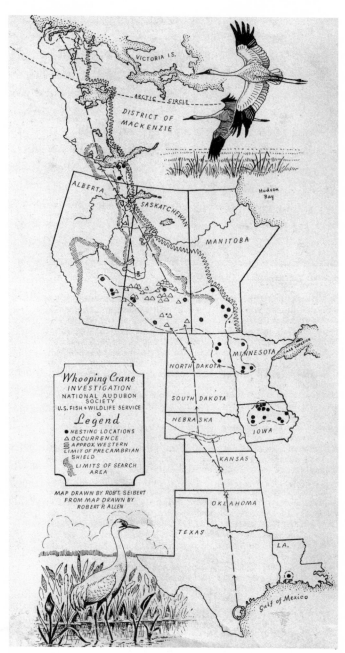

Map showing the whooping cranes' migratory route from Texas to Canada, along with potential nesting locations. Published in *Audubon Magazine*, January-February 1948. Original map drawn by Bob Allen. Courtesy of *Audubon Magazine*, New York.

He and his family arrived in Meadow Lake on May 11. If Allen thought the reception he received in North Platte was encouraging, the greetings in every town and settlement on the way to Meadow Lake were akin to movie-star fame. The media blitz had everyone on the lookout for migrating cranes. Allen's Audubon entourage couldn't be missed: a station wagon with Texas plates pulling a trailer of camping gear, followed by a U.S. government sedan, had the locals out on the muddy roads within minutes of Allen's arrival.

For the next two days, Allen met with Jim Barnett, the district game superintendent. With Barnett's field staff assisting, they studied the migration reports and maps of the area. Finally, Bob and Evelyn loaded up on staples, left the frontier town with their two children in tow, and headed deeper into the bush. Forty-five miles later, the road dead-ended at Flotten Lake. At 1,600 feet elevation, the small aspen lake is hemmed in between steep hills. White birch and spruce provide a canopy over trailing wild strawberry, bearberry, and lowbush cranberry bushes; the air is redolent with the fragrance of wild roses. Thick mosses cushion the hard ground. The shoreline offers ample space for pitching tents and the lake a bounty of trout. From the south, a floatplane had easy access to landing.

A light rain fell as the Allens set up camp on the south shore of Flotten Lake on May 13. Ice still covered much of its surface. That first night, a cold front blew in. The wind kicked up, the rain intensified as the temperature dropped to just above freezing. Hail fell. Between downpours, Allen and Bobby gathered firewood, and in an attempt to keep the wood dry, they filled every inch of spare space in both tents. The weather scarcely improved over the next week.

Inclement weather notwithstanding, Flotten Lake was an avian paradise. On the few occasions when the clouds burned off, the 3:00 a.m. sunrise brought with it a splash of color that commanded an audience, and the Allen family began to look forward to the early-morning show. Rays of light penetrating the misty haze spotlighted the avian menagerie that had settled on the lake. A cacophony of trills, hoots, warbles, grunts, whistles, and squawks sounded like an orchestra warming up for a symphony. Flocks of western and red-necked grebes floated regally across the surface. Loons claimed a nesting site on the north side of the lake, the wind carrying their eerie bird howls over the water and into the woods. Canada geese, their long necks arched, giving them the appearance of floating teapots, glided alongside hooded mergansers with their fan-shaped crests and pinpoint golden eyes. Mallards dabbled at underwater vegetation, upending their backsides and creating an illusion of small tee-pees floating on the water's surface. Sooty gray American coots gathered in clusters too numerous to count. Ruby-crowned kinglets, no larger than a pocketknife, arrived to begin nesting in the high, spindly branches of the spruce trees. Deer could be seen blowing frost as they foraged for nuts and the ever-scarce green leaves. Allen wrote: "Those first days at Flotten had been unforgettable. In its own way, the spell of stormy weather had made our camp life interesting and exciting, so that we cherished the most ordinary things. To be able to sit quietly for a moment instead of chopping firewood, to put on a pair of dry woolen socks, nicely warm from hanging in front of the fire, to lean back at sundown, after a hot supper, watching the embers in the open hearth and listening to the many voices on the lake—these were simple pleasures that we enjoyed to the utmost. There were moments when I almost wished we might stay right here, undisturbed and forgotten."[4]

Perhaps the whooping cranes felt the same, returning every spring to their northern home. The cranes have an inborn urge to leave their paradise in Texas and return to the place where they were hatched, to build a new nest, lay their eggs, raise the hatchlings, and take their new offspring back to Texas before the winter weather sets in.

Despite his family's enjoyment of the outdoors, after that first week, Allen prayed he'd made the right decision to bring them along into the Canadian wilderness. For nine-year-old Alice, life on Flotten Lake was like living in a natural amusement park. Bobby had his moments of fun, but for an adolescent who enjoyed the outdoors as much as his father, Bobby at times seemed lethargic, and Evelyn became concerned over her son's uncharacteristic behavior.

A week passed, and Allen still had not heard from pilot Bob Smith. The groceries were near depletion, and their gasoline lantern and camp stove had broken down. Allen and Bobby made a foray back to Meadow Lake to restock and to check at headquarters for word from the pilot. While there, Allen visited the office of Imperial Oil and was pleased when the company agreed to set up and fill a 1,000-gallon gasoline tank on Flotten

Lake. Once Smith arrived and they began their search over Great Slave Lake, they could refuel whenever necessary. The news from headquarters was a letdown: there were no messages from Smith.

That afternoon, Allen talked at length with a man named E. B. Erickson, who had lived in the area most of his life. Erickson described, in detail, observations he'd made years ago when the whooping cranes were more plentiful. Just 3 miles from Meadow Lake, he'd watched, mesmerized, as a pair of cranes danced. That encounter had occurred forty years ago, but the image was as vivid to Erickson as if it had happened yesterday. Allen took notes, confident the old man's story was genuine for his description of the whoopers' dance matched what Allen had witnessed in Texas.

Living in the backwoods of Saskatchewan required the understanding of certain social graces. Since travel in the area was difficult, it was customary for locals to grant favors, such as the delivery of information and supplies to the outlying areas. With no word from Smith, Allen and Bobby prepared to return to camp. One of Allen's new acquaintances, hearing of his departure, asked the ornithologist if he'd deliver a box of strawberry plants to a man named Dave Lachausseur, a French-Canadian trader who lived in a settlement on Waterhen Lake. Allen had run across Lachausseur while in Meadow Lake earlier that month. Lachausseur was articulate and jovial, and Allen admired the man's gumption in his endeavor to eke out a living in the desolate wilds of Canada. Bobby was eager to see the goings on at the native village, and Allen agreed to make the delivery. With sketchy directions and a promise that the road was clearly marked, they started out. Finding the Waterhen River was easy. Crossing the waterway was another matter entirely. The current, too swift and deep to drive across, had Allen standing on the riverbank scratching his head over the situation. A crowd from the settlement had gathered on the other side. Realizing that the driver of the car and his son wished to cross the river, they began the construction of a temporary bridge by laying down wood planks. Their work completed, they motioned for Allen to cross. He managed to keep the car on the makeshift bridge and made it safely to the other side. He and Bobby thanked the men and continued on.

Within moments, the road metamorphosed into a narrow trail better suited for foot travel. Drooping limbs hung from above. Tree stumps rose from the ground as if they had no intention of having their lives cut short.

As Allen swerved to avoid a stump, another snagged the car's rear end, causing it to stall. Not having planned on a backwoods adventure, Allen had left his axes, saws, and various tools back at camp. Just when he and Bobby considered walking the rest of the way, Lachausseur's booming voice brought them to attention. Delighted that his strawberry plants had arrived, and since favors were always repaid, the trader grabbed the rear bumper and lifted the car over the stump. That day's adventure provided story fodder for the Allens' evening meal.

—

As word spread of the American family camping on Flotten Lake, locals began dropping in to visit. Their nearest neighbor, Pete, a mink farmer, often joined Allen on his treks through the woodlands around Flotten Lake. One morning they came across black bear tracks, and another time they stumbled upon an abandoned sweat lodge used by the Cree Indians. Allen befriended two bush pilots, Lefty McLeod and Cliff Lebey, who, after discovering Evelyn's pan-baked cornbread and syrup, made regular appearances. Local ranger Elmer Johnson often came by to go over maps of the area with Allen. Jim Barnett brought mail, and Mr. Erickson found his way to camp a few times just to check on their progress. On those days when the weather was too cold and miserable to venture outside for any length of time, Evelyn taught her children and kept them busy with assignments from the Calvert lessons. Those were also the days when Allen pulled out his bottle of aspirin to quell the recurring pain in his arm and shoulder.

—

While Allen cooled his heels on Flotten Lake, Walkinshaw and Tholen prepared to leave Winnipeg on the morning of May 22. Before taking off, Walkinshaw fired off a letter to Baker noting that, having discussed the topic with Allen, he "suggested that $400 could be spent by the National Audubon Society for plane travel for me."[5] Walkinshaw went on to mention that he and Tholen had each thrown in two hundred dollars of their own money. Baker did not respond to Walkinshaw's request. Despite the lack of any reimbursement from Audubon, Walkinshaw and Tholen moved forward with their search.

Initially, Walkinshaw and Tholen had intended to base their search in

The Pas, Manitoba, but after visiting Bert Cartwright, a naturalist with Ducks Unlimited who had a good database of crane sightings, they started out in Yorkton, Saskatchewan, instead. Austin Ingham, an air instructor pilot who had served during the war, agreed to fly them around for fifteen dollars per hour for the first ten hours and ten dollars per hour thereafter.[6] Walkinshaw sent Baker the name of the bank in Nipawin where reimbursement money could be sent.

Ingham would not arrive until May 27. To fill their time, Walkinshaw and Tholen borrowed a car and explored the Rokeby Marsh area near Saltcoats to check out a crane sighting from the previous May. A man named Walter Doman had reported, "The lone white bird, with legs trailing behind and neck out straight in front was calling loudly as it flew over their farm five miles from Saltcoats."[7] After interviewing Doman, Walkinshaw was certain the bird Doman had seen was a whooping crane. Walkinshaw added the sighting to his records.

Once airborne, Walkinshaw directed Ingham to fly his Piper Cub over the marshes around Yorkton. Having found no cranes, they flew over Campbell Lake, then westward over Last Mountain Lake. After waiting out a snowstorm, they combed the lake area again. No whoopers were found.

About 125 miles northeast of Nipawin sat the Little Quill and Big Quill Lakes, whose shores sprouted marshes perfect for whooping crane nests. No whoopers resided there. Walkinshaw then set his sights on an area north of Nipawin, where he had once found sandhill cranes nesting in boggy muskegs. In early May, a farmer had reported seeing four large white birds feeding in a wheat field near the Saskatchewan River. Another farmer flushed several birds from a field near the highway on May 15. He watched them fly over and felt certain they were whooping cranes. The birds were stark white except for the black wing tips. Things in that area of Saskatchewan were looking up.

~

On May 25, still waiting for word from Smith, Allen watched a flock of sandhill cranes fly over Flotten Lake on their northerly migration. The scene was encouraging, although Allen wished them to be their larger, white, more elusive cousins. He then turned his attention to an event he could control. He went back into his tent and uncovered an auto-

graphed book given to him by its author, a biologist who'd visited camp
a few days earlier. Allen added his own ditty on the inside cover, "Alice,
Bombalice, Tywiggily Alice—A nine-year-old girl in a tent for a palace!"
It was a day for celebration—Alice's birthday—the book was what she
had asked for.[8]

Finally, on May 30, Fred Bard forwarded a letter to Allen from Bob
Smith written a week earlier. Smith and a fellow pilot, Dave Spencer, had
flown over the areas of interest in Manitoba and Saskatchewan and had
spotted several white pelicans and swans, but no cranes. Once Smith arrived, he'd be at Allen's disposal. "Wherever you want to search is O.K.
with me as this is your show."[9] He stressed the need of having fuel readily
available at base camp to save time. Allen responded that day, writing that
the fuel arrangements had been made, and he was all set to go.

In late May, Walkinshaw and Tholen met with Len Nelson, a trapper who
had reported seeing as many as twenty whooping cranes in the marsh at
the headwaters of Caribou Creek north of the Missipuskiow River. The
report was more than thirteen years old, but it was worth investigating.
Nelson went on to state that he was sure the cranes used the area to nest;
however, he said that local Indians hunted the birds whenever possible.
He described how one group of hunters set up at the end of the marsh
while another group flushed out their quarry. The cranes were shot as
they flew overhead. He had not seen any whoopers in several years. Another reliable sighting came from Dr. Carlson, a retired veterinarian from
Snowden. Two pairs of whooping cranes had settled in the wilderness
area in the back of his house the previous summer. One pair left, the other
remained the entire summer. One day he watched as they flew to a small
marsh: "They drank like chickens and flew just over the tree tops to the
west."[10] When Walkinshaw investigated, the marsh had since dried up.

Ingham continued to fly Walkinshaw and Tholen over the Nipawin
area, often at altitudes as low as 300 feet. The Walkinshaw/Tholen team
left no acre unexplored but failed to find any signs of the migrating cranes.
With their personal funds almost gone, Walkinshaw and Tholen returned
to Yorktown on June 1, picked up camping equipment, and covered the
marsh area near Pas Trail on foot once again. After an unsuccessful week,
they gave up and headed to the lake area north of Nipawin.

Summer arrived on June 3, coming in like a dilatory force making up for its tardiness. That afternoon, the temperature shot up into the seventies. In his book *Trail*, Allen described the sudden change on Flotten Lake: "The birds at Flotten were in full voice: chipping sparrows, white-throats, juncos, all trilling for dear life. And the big loons were now at the peak of their vocal efforts."[11] With the bright sun warming the earth, butterflies emerged from their cocoons. Other insects, not so welcoming, arrived too. Gnats hovered in anticipation of sweat breaking out on a brow, mosquitoes fought voraciously for a warm-blooded host, and black ants marched from their hiding places in decaying logs. The birds that called Flotten Lake home nested and laid eggs. Bobby found a clutch of duck eggs on nearby Baldy Island. Evelyn did the laundry and aired out their tents. That afternoon McLeod flew in with word that there was still no message from Smith.

After finding pleasure in the warmth of the day before, the morning broke cold. Alice woke up at 3:30. Allen built a fire in the stove and put on a pot of coffee. While the kids enjoyed the coziness of their tent, Evelyn joined her husband for a walk around the lake. By midafternoon, it felt as if summer had arrived, and with it came more gnats, mosquitoes, and flies. A dead spruce stump seemed to come alive as its inhabitants of black ants swarmed from every crack in the bark. Allen discovered a couple of dead jackfish floating in the lake, and for the first time, Evelyn had to boil water. By the end of the day, Allen had built a dock, making it easier to collect and haul water from the middle of the lake. By Thursday, June 5, it was clear from Allen's journal that he was growing impatient waiting for his pilot. "Time is beginning to hang heavy. I should be up there looking for whoopers!"[12]

At 10:00 a.m. on June 6, Lefty McLeod's biplane appeared over the trees, and Evelyn started mixing the cornbread. He carried with him two letters, one from Walkinshaw and one from Smith. Smith wrote, "hung up here [Edmonton] since Thursday with motor trouble and weather."[13] He hoped to be at Flotten Lake on June 7. Walkinshaw's letter of May 31 reported that in the precious four days, he and Tholen had scouted the Nipawin area east of Candle Lake, north to Big Springs, and east to Deschambault Lake. Flying at 800 feet, they had been able to get a good look at what appeared to be ideal crane habitat. No cranes were found. They had also checked out several sightings of cranes feeding in stubble fields, but none were found there, either.

At 4:30 p.m., Allen heard the whine of another plane. He climbed the hill near camp and spotted Smith's Widgeon circling overhead. With the lake too rough to land, Smith lowered the wheels, set the plane down on Flotten Lake's sandy shore, then maneuvered it into the water and tied it down. Allen and Smith had met during the crane conference in Aransas in January, and Allen was eager to have his family meet the affable wildlife biologist from Mississippi. Smith climbed from his plane, bearing a huge smile and exuding a languid southern charm that was not lost on the Allen family. He staked his pup tent, barely large enough to cover him, near the fire pit. He made himself at home and turned his attention to the kids. Much to Allen's delight, Alice and Bobby took to Smith immediately.

After months of planning, Allen was finally able do the job he was sent to Canada to do, but only with the help of Lefty McLeod. Imperial Oil had not yet made good on their offer to deliver the gasoline. McLeod lent them enough fuel to make a quick flight back to Meadow Lake, where they met with officials at the petroleum company's office. Embarrassed by the delays, they promised to have a truck out to Flotten Lake the next day.

Over an evening meal of trout and cornbread, Allen spread out his maps on a folding table, and he and Smith charted the area that was to be the focus of the hunt. Toward the east, the Canadian Shield abruptly morphed into rocky terrain dotted with deep lakes. Coniferous forest dominated most of the western area. North of the Mackenzie River, mountains spiked upward—certainly not whooping crane habitat. What remained was a swath of land from east of Candle Lake in central Saskatchewan northwest to Primrose Lake near the border of Alberta, tapering northwest up to Lake Claire, which then widened out again, taking in the vast area of Wood Buffalo National Park, the Slave River parklands, and the Great Slave Lake in the District of Mackenzie. Although Allen's map showed a narrow hourglass-shaped region, its size was immense. The Great Slave Lake alone covers 11,030 square kilometers, making it the world's ninth-largest lake, the fifth-largest in North America, and the second-largest in Canada.

After weeks of menial tasks on Flotten Lake, things started happening.

At 5:30 a.m. the next morning, under an overcast sky, Allen and Smith packed their gear. The Imperial Oil truck arrived with the 1,000-gallon tank, situated it on the beach as close to the water as possible, and filled it. Smith, Allen, and Bobby canoed out to Smith's plane and loaded the gear. As a light rain fell, Allen and Smith took to the sky.

At 2:39 p.m. on Sunday, June 8, Allen's hunt for the whooping crane nesting site had finally begun.

They flew nonstop during the daylight hours, covering the Lost Lake region in west central Saskatchewan from Candle Lake in the east to Primrose Lake in the west, taking in Muskeg and Martineau Rivers and Primrose Lake, where two "old-timers,"[14] as Allen referred to them, swore they had seen whooping cranes less than a month before. Most of the area was thickly forested, and the few muskegs were overgrown with bulrushes and tamaracks, not the best habitat for cranes. Primrose Lake, the only area with a suitable marsh, was home to a large colony of nesting western grebes. Colonies of white pelicans had claimed two islands in the middle of the lake. Cormorants perched on any available branches, faces to the sun, drying their stubby, misshapen wings. Feeding on the shore were great blue herons and sandhill cranes. Bonaparte gulls nested in the spruce trees. Smith spotted a pigeon hawk flying low over the water. A few canvasback ducks floated lazily in the middle of the lake, and in the tall grasses nearby, several moose were momentarily interrupted from their grazing by the sound of Smith's plane. A few miles away, Canada geese had settled on Peter Pond, and more white pelicans populated Barney Lake. Still no whooping cranes.

The evenings were spent back at camp on Flotten Lake with Allen writing his daily reports. Smith tinkered with his plane and entertained Bobby and Alice, often taking them fishing. On one such trip, Alice reeled in a 2-foot-long jackfish, providing supper that evening. When bad weather kept them on the ground, Allen and Smith scrutinized the maps, cut firewood, and satiated themselves on Evelyn's cooking. She'd become quite adept at frying up batches of bannock, a Native American bread similar to baking-powder biscuits.

Meanwhile, Walkinshaw and Tholen were winding things down. They had spent their last dollar on plane travel. Walkinshaw wrote his second report to Allen on June 12. The letter was fraught with hope and frustration. "We have spent about a week in the country north of here [Nipawin] but have seen no cranes. Reports come in regularly of cranes being seen but most of them turn out [to be] something else and many are indefinite with little information—not enough to be helpful. If we had a plane [we] could do a lot more but am unable to swing any more flying financially."[15] He went on to write that John Baker had not come through with financial assistance and, what's more, had not answered any of Walkinshaw's letters. "I am rather disgusted after offering him my time and spending several hundred dollars myself in the search," Walkinshaw wrote.[16] Despite his frustration, Walkinshaw continued to search, spending three days on Alfred Johnson's farm near Snowden, walking almost every square foot of marshland.

~

After eight days of flying over the most promising sites in Saskatchewan, covering more than 2,000 miles and not spotting a single crane, Allen scratched the area off his list and decided it was time to head north. Making sure Evelyn and the kids were well stocked in groceries and firewood, Allen and Smith left camp, flew to Meadow Lake, collected mail, and then continued on to Prince Albert, where they met with Walkinshaw and Tholen at the airport. The four men compared notes and exchanged information. For Walkinshaw and Tholen, it was an end to a few exasperating but exciting weeks. Walkinshaw's vacation time was over; he was regretfully returning to Michigan. In his final report, Walkinshaw wrote that he was impressed with the "fine work" Allen was doing and felt certain the cranes' nests would be found soon as a result of his arduous efforts.[17]

For Allen and Smith, the second leg of the search was about to begin. The plan was to tackle the immense area in the northeast corner of Alberta and the Great Slave Lake in the Northwest Territories, flying over each and every lake, marsh, and any acreage that looked promising. After two days of bad weather, the sun rose in a cloudless sky. Smith turned over the engine for a final check and did not like the rattling sound coming from within. The repairs were minor but would take most of an entire day to complete. Allen and Smith checked into the Marlboro Hotel. While Smith worked on his Widgeon, Allen visited with Gordon Lund, a naturalist who lived in the area and occasionally worked for the USFWS.

Just before noon on June 18, Smith and Allen were in the air again and on their way to check a few remaining lakes near Prince Albert. Flying over Birchbark, Candle Lakes, and Egg Lake, they spotted ideal marsh habitat and pristine shorelines, but no birds. Over Swan Lake, they noted a Franklin gull colony, a few white pelicans, and one bald eagle. Their puzzlement over the lack of any substantial bird life was understood when logging colonies and numerous populated Indian villages came into view. During the winter, these settlements were void of human inhabitants, but in the summer, the population swelled with natives arriving to reap the resources nature provided.

On the morning of June 20, Allen and Smith flew over Garson, Gipsy, Gordon, Graham, and Campbell Lakes, covering all the territory south of Waterways, Alberta. When Smith's fuel gauge dipped toward empty, they put down at the Waterways airstrip outside of Fort McMurray and hitched a ride into town with the airport manager. Once there, they headed straight for the Canadian Pacific Airways (CPA) office to procure fuel. The attending agent would not sell them gasoline without a letter of authority. Smith wired Edmonton, and arrangements were made to fill the Widgeon's tank the next morning at eight o'clock. The agent, now satisfied that he would receive payment for the fuel, agreed to find transportation for Allen and Smith back to the airstrip whenever they were ready to leave.

Since Fort McMurray was strategically located and had an airstrip, Allen and Smith operated out of the river town for a few days. They checked into the New Franklin Hotel, the local gathering place. That evening a crowd of locals Allen described as a "motley crew"[18] poured into the bar and commenced carousing. Their party lasted throughout the night. Tired from lack of sleep, Allen and Smith arrived at the CPA office early the next morning to find that the surly agent had reneged on his offer. Allen and Smith had to take a six-dollar taxi ride to the airstrip. They finally got under way around eleven o'clock.

For the next two days, Smith flew while Allen snapped and documented photos of deltas, marshes, meadows, prairies, woodlands, rivers; few of these areas looked like promising whooping crane habitat until they flew over Lake Claire and Chipewyan Lake, an area that resembled the marshes on the Aransas Refuge in Texas. Bulrushes, blue joint, and plugamites (reed grasses) grew thick. The common Franklin gull nested in the grasses, along with pintail, canvasback, red head, mallard, coot, baldpate, scaup, and teal. Encouraged, the two men zigzagged for 330 miles, expecting to see the large white birds at each turn. Again, no luck.

After studying the charts and maps again, Allen was more certain that this area had probably been void of whooping cranes for decades since their migratory stopovers in Illinois, Minnesota, Iowa, and North Dakota had been turned into farmland. But the area had a certain feel about it— nothing Allen could put his finger on—just a hunch, but at this point, even a hunch could not be discarded.

On June 23, Allen and Smith moved north toward the Slave River near Fort Smith in the District of Mackenzie and the Alberta border. Fort Smith had a small airstrip, making the area another good base from which to operate. A community log cabin was home for the next few days, not the best accommodations, but the place was warm and dry. Cots in the cabin's loft went for fifty cents, hot meals for a dollar, and sandwiches were a bargain at twenty-five cents for two. Unlike the other men staying in the cabin, whose mood was lighthearted and jovial, the nest hunters, with only two days left, were more anxious than ever.

Their eagerness grew the next morning as Allen and Smith flew over the Slave River Delta. The broad, flat river delta, resplendent with every shorebird imaginable, appeared to be ideal habitat for nesting cranes. Shallow marshes, fed by several rivers and tributaries, meant abundant food. The most encouraging factor was the lack of human settlements.

Could they have saved the best for last?

But when they flew over the shores of the Slave and Buffalo Rivers, across the plains of the Grand Detour, and on to the Tethul and Taltson Rivers to the east, again, no cranes. Still hopeful, Allen advised Smith to turn his Widgeon west toward the delta along the Slave and then to Fort Resolution, to the south shore of Great Slave Lake, and on to Hay River. The day's search ended in disappointment.

Later, Allen learned that the lake's northeast shores had been heavily prospected since the early 1930s, when Gilbert LaBine had discovered pitchblende, the ore that yields uranium, near Great Bear Lake north of Great Slave Lake. Then in 1935, gold was discovered, and another wave of adventurers poured in to claim a piece of the action. With all the human activity and increased development, it was no surprise to Allen that the whooping cranes were absent from this area and no doubt had been for some time.

On June 25, Allen and Smith took to the sky for what was to be the last day of the 1947 hunt. By eleven o'clock, they were over the headwaters of the Mackenzie River and found the overgrown, wooded shoreline "unsuitable for whoopers."[19] Then, farther north to Big Island and Deep Bay, just three hours away from the Arctic Circle, they found a landscape covered with tundra grass, what Allen referred to as a "marshy slough,"[20] which pocketed the area near Slave Point. The northern extension of Great Slave Lake had remained untouched by the warm weather, as made evident by the huge ice sheets still covering the surface. When the terrain turned from muskegs to coniferous forest, Smith turned the plane south. Once more they scouted the lake's southern shore, then crossed into the northern section of Wood Buffalo National Park for one final flyover.

As Allen and Smith approached Buffalo Lake, clouds darkened the sky. Smith turned the plane eastward in an attempt to avoid the worst of the storm, but when they crossed over the Sass River, they ran head-on into what appeared to be a solid wall. Smith's attempt to outmaneuver the thunderstorm had failed. Fierce wind tore at the small plane, and within seconds, all visibility was gone, as if they'd flown into the mouth of a cave. Smith fought the storm in total darkness until, miraculously, the clouds parted, offering a few rays of sunlight. Back on course and lucky to be alive, Smith landed the plane in Fort Smith. They had logged fifty-five hours and fifteen minutes of flight time and had crisscrossed 5,750 miles over western Canada. Allen crossed the last search site from his list. No whooping cranes were found around the Mackenzie River. No sign of them along the shores of Great Slave Lake. Not a single whooping crane spotted in the Lake Claire area of Alberta or around Nipawin in Central Saskatchewan. At 2:25 p.m., the 1947 nest hunt came to an end.

6

Small Families

Bob Smith flew Allen back to camp on Flotten Lake, where Evelyn and the kids had been awaiting his return. By no means had they felt abandoned in his absence. During the ten days Allen was away, Bobby and Alice entertained themselves by dressing up as Indians and jumping out from the woods to scare Evelyn whenever the opportunity presented itself. A string of visitors wandered into camp and kept the Allen family company, many drawn by Evelyn's cooking, others by curiosity, and some out of concern. All left, however, knowing that this reserved, dignified pianist who'd graduated from Juilliard in New York City was one powerful woman, one who could hold her own in the Canadian wilderness. After six weeks, leaving camp was bittersweet. They were eager to return to civilization, but the time spent as a family, gathering wood, cooking over an open fire, enjoying the bird serenades, and listening to the sounds of the forest as it settled in for the night were moments they would probably not experience again. On the morning of June 28, the Allens broke camp and left for home.

As far as the whoopers were concerned, Bob Allen had two pressing goals to accomplish within the next few months: return to the Aransas National Wildlife Refuge and delve deeper into whooping crane behavior and prepare for next summer's hunt. But first, he and Evelyn planned to find out the reason for Bobby's continued sluggishness. They headed for St. Louis and the comfort of Evelyn's parents' home, where she took Bobby to see the Sedgwick family doctor. Allen began preparing his report. There were letters to answer as well, many from colleagues who'd participated in the search in previous years. They offered Allen encouragement and advice for the next time he headed north in search of the cranes.

Allen also corresponded with friends, keeping them abreast of his activities. While in Canada, he'd purchased a wooden carving of an owl and sent it to Roger Tory Peterson. Peterson responded with a heartfelt thank-you note. "Just the thing for my paint brushes," he wrote; "and every time I take out a red sable brush, I will be reminded of you."[1]

The failure of the 1947 hunt did not squelch the public's enthusiasm for the Whooping Crane Project. If anything, the interest only intensified with the anticipation of another chapter in an intriguing mystery, a mystery anyone could help solve simply by keeping abreast of the latest developments. Newspapers, magazines, and newsletters continued to report on the latest progress. As for the misleading articles, they, too, continued to surface. A Canadian publication, *Maclean's Magazine*, in an effort to gain additional support for the project, wrote in their November 1, 1947, issue that the cost of the failed searches amounted to seventy-five thousand dollars. Where the magazine came up with that figure was a mystery. This misinformation spurred another rumor that the taxpayers were footing the bill. Those who felt saving the whooping crane was a waste of government dollars had a heyday with that one. Audubon had to go on the defensive and explain that the actual amount was nowhere near the exorbitant costs reported by the magazine, that many governmental services volunteered personnel, that the nest hunters often hitched rides on prearranged flights, and that the expenses were paid entirely by Audubon. Allen responded to these erroneous accusations in his second whooping crane report: "The total amount of each taxpayer's direct contribution to our search, including the waterfowl surveys that took up much of our time, wouldn't cover the cost of a penny post card to their congressmen."[2]

A month later, *Time* magazine, clearly sympathetic to the whooping crane cause, wrote that excessive hunting had forced the big white birds, a species not adapted to cold climates, farther north toward the Arctic. Allen had to explain that there was no evidence that the cranes had been pushed that far north.

⁓

In the wake of the failed hunt, Allen and Audubon were presented with a reason to celebrate. *The Flame Birds* was on the shelf and had received some promising reviews. Fellow ornithologists who'd read the book thought it exceptional. Olin Pettingill wrote, in a letter to Allen: "The

Flame Birds is excellent! I hope that the publisher is promoting it properly so that it will bring home some bacon."[3] Roger Tory Peterson and his wife, Barbara (who was Allen's secretary in New York during his early years with Audubon), sent along their congratulations to Bob and Evelyn: "Bob has the gift of story telling which is so rare amongst scientific men."[4] Baker was supportive as well. In August, he sent out Audubon circulars promoting the book and, later that year, featured it in the Audubon Christmas circular. After sending out an extensive mailing, announcing the book's release, Dodd, Mead's secretary R. T. Bond predicted "the literary sky ought to be filled with spoonbills."[5] Numerous ornithological journals gave it glowing reviews. However, sales were not what everyone had hoped.

The Allens were back in Tavernier in August, and waiting for them was a letter from Bob Smith saying: "I miss the ogema bunch [his affectionate name for the Allen family] every day. My stay at Flotten Lake was the high point of the entire trip and I am looking forward to the time when I can sit around a fire complete with coffee pot with the entire Allen family once again."[6] He signed off, giving his best regards to, "Evelyn, omiskisheesh and ogema jr,"[7] his wilderness nicknames for Alice and Bobby, respectively. Evelyn attended to the correspondence from friends, and Allen caught up on Audubon business. Less than two weeks later, they had the car and trailer packed again.

By the first week in September, a full six weeks before the whooping cranes were due to arrive from their mystery site in Canada, the Allens were in Hopper's Landing, Texas. They unhooked their trailer and rented cottages number three and four. The two cottages, one for Bob and Evelyn and one for Bobby and Alice, were connected by a carport. A small, screened porch overlooked the bay. Both places were little more than efficiencies, a rectangular room with a kitchenette on one wall, beds on the opposite wall, and a bathroom built into one corner. They moved in what little furniture they had brought with them. Once the radio was plugged in and the station tuned to *The Jack Benny Program*, the Allens felt quite at home. On one of their first mornings, Alice's misgiving over the separate living quarters from her parents vanished upon discovering that the tooth fairy had still managed to locate her pillow the night before.

A few days later, Evelyn enrolled Bobby and Alice in school. The Labor Day weekend gave Bobby a chance to introduce his little sister to life in Hopperville before their first day in class. The year prior, Bobby had made friends with Hopper's teenage son, Carlton. The boy was a master oyster shucker and owned his own boat. He had taught Bobby how to shrimp, and soon the two boys had resumed shrimping together. Alice befriended Carlton, too, and was delighted when he introduced her to his horse, Tony. Before long, Alice had learned to shuck oysters and head shrimp. To earn pocket money for the jukebox at Hopper's store, she took a part-time job on Hopper's seafood assembly line.

The focus of Allen's second winter investigation would be on the crane's main food source, blue crab. He needed to learn more about the crustacean itself, the niche it occupied, its life cycle, and reproductive patterns. To do that, Allen needed a healthy supply of crabs to observe. He and Bobby baited crab traps with jackrabbit meat and set up several stations at Rattlesnake Pond.

Once Allen had his study under way, he traveled to New York City to attend the National Audubon Convention, where he presented the results of the 1947 hunt. Although this was the third failed search, the organization was enthusiastic over Allen's methodical scouring of the Canadian wilderness, and expressed certainty that next year's expedition would prove fruitful. Once his report was delivered, Allen hightailed it back to Texas to document the arrival of his beloved cranes.

In mid-October, the first whooping cranes began arriving. Allen had learned to recognize the different families, and this year he planned to observe them as closely as they would allow. Creeping up to them in their territory was out of the question. He needed them to come to him. Bobby helped Allen build a portable blind and set it up outside an enclosure where corn was spread out daily to entice the whooping cranes to feed. What Allen hoped to observe were juveniles interacting with their parents. A single crane flew in on October 21, followed by the Mustang Slough Pair, who appeared sluggish and inactive, having probably arrived the night before. By October 26, eight whooping cranes were back on their winter turf. Still no youngsters. By the end of the month, three more were spotted, all adults. Then, as November rolled around, the families flew in: three on the first, one on the third, another on the eighth, and sometime during the first week of December, a female came in with her chick. Allen reasoned that the whooping cranes arrived in three waves: the singles, followed by the pairs without young, and finally the families, who took the longest time, having to accommodate their young with more frequent resting and feeding stops.

With the arrival of the youngsters came other signs of fall. One morning Allen looked up and saw a cloud of black and orange. Swirling like a delicate autumn scarf blown by the wind, the image folded on itself and fluttered to rest over the bushes along the bay shore: tens of thousands of monarch butterflies, the only known migrating insect, passing through Texas on their way to Mexico. That same day, as Allen had his scope on a crane family and a pair feeding in a ditch near Redfish Slough, a barge entered the refuge and motored alarmingly close to the spillway. A man standing on the deck raised his shotgun and blasted a flock of geese and widgeons. The whooping cranes, about 600 yards away, raised their heads, but remained in the marsh. Allen couldn't make out the lettering on the barge, but was delighted when Carl Hopper's boat, the *Flora Hopper*, came in on the trespasser's wake. Even before Allen's arrival in Hopper's Landing, the Hopper family had proclaimed themselves stewards to the whooping crane flock. The next day, Allen had the identity of the barge and was able to report their poaching. Also coming to the refuge in search of food were red wolves. As long as the cranes stayed below the 3-foot water zone where they had a clear view of the landscape, they were safe from the canine predators. All the same, Allen noted their location and documented their movements as well as he could. With the opening of deer season, more hunters came to the refuge, although the deer population was scarce. After the incident with the barge, Allen suspected many of them were there to poach ducks.

Once the entire flock had arrived, the next few weeks were taken up in territorial disputes. Families and pairs tend to return to the same territories each year, but challenges to these locations still arise, especially from single males who attempt to establish their own territory and find a mate. Allen witnessed the well-established Middle Pond Family drive out the Summer Pair, the two injured, nonmigratory cranes that had intruded when the Middle Pond Family was away feeding. The Middle Pond Family male charged the Summer Pair, extending his neck and long beak and flapping his wings. Unable to fly, the Summer Pair strutted away, looking over their shoulders as if unimpressed by their rival's display. This casual retreat seemed to agitate the Middle Pond male even more, and he raised his head and called loudly, "Ker-lee-oo."[8] His mate joined in the vocal warnings and continued until the Summer Pair had moved an acceptable distance away.

The challenges for this male seemed endless, perhaps due to his coveted territory or his aggressive nature. Allen's normal course of action was to move his portable blind to different areas on the refuge, observing several families for short periods of time. However, he wanted to watch this family for several consecutive hours. Unforeseen circumstances and bad weather prevented him from immediately doing so.

Allen spent most of Thanksgiving morning with Bobby at the refuge headquarters, working together on the outboard motor, then driving across the refuge and checking water levels after the heavy rains from the week before. They stopped at camp for a quick lunch. Allen had planned to station himself at the southern end of the refuge. That plan was forestalled when he became ill and returned home. Thinking it was something he had eaten, Allen spent the next two days in bed. When his condition worsened, Evelyn drove him to the hospital in Corpus Christi, where he was diagnosed with tularemia, otherwise known as rabbit fever, a disease caused by the bacterium *Francisella tularensis*, and contracted from infected rabbits. He most likely became exposed while baiting crab traps. Luckily, Bobby had not.

Today the disease is fatal in about 5 percent of people who go untreated. In 1947, streptomycin had just been approved for use. With its approval came the warning of side effects, the most serious of which was deafness. Just three months earlier, Doctor Glover in Tivoli had given Allen a thorough medical examination and found Allen "vigorous and robust and in great health."[9] Doc Glover recommended the treatment but left the decision to Allen. He took the injection, stayed in the hospital for two days, and was back to work the next morning at 8:30 for a prearranged meeting with a family friend and distinguished visitor. Connie Hagar had requested that Allen show her his now-famous whooping cranes. He had no intention of disappointing her.

For Allen, the streptomycin worked, but the illness had weakened him. His arm and shoulder pains were still bothering him, and the effects of tularemia did not help matters. After spending a day on the refuge with Connie Hagar, Allen was out in the field the very next morning, conducting a crane count.

Keeping her husband from working, even when physical difficulties arose, was something Evelyn knew was futile. Five days after Allen left the hospital, he returned. This time it was to admit Evelyn for a minor medical complication. Although not happy with her misfortune, the incident gave her husband the rest he needed, for he refused to leave her side until she was back on her feet four days later. He might have even joked with Evelyn about her going to extreme measures to keep him at home.

Day after day, Allen checked on his birds, worked on his reports, and escorted more visitors around the refuge. On December 19, he was finally back with the Middle Pond Family. He set up his blind, baited the area with a bag of corn, and waited. The Middle Pond Family, the New Family, and the Summer Pair were all within sight. As expected, the Middle Pond male rushed the Summer Pair and spent the morning fussing over their presence near the pond. With the territorial dispute occupying these two families, the New Family was free to gorge themselves on the corn near the blind. Allen watched their cautious approach: 400 yards, 150 yards—Allen readied his camera—at 75 yards, the family, no longer leery of the blind, picked away at the corn as Allen snapped off a roll of film. After feeding for three hours, the family stayed in the area preening. With the birds content, Allen decided to have lunch until he realized he'd left it in the Jeep. Unwilling to leave the blind and risk missing another display, Allen stayed put. He was happy he did. Within a few minutes, the New Family male invited his mate to engage in a mating dance. He bowed to her, raised his wings, and leaped into the air. The female mimicked his movements, stopping to bump her offspring out of the way. The young bird, uninterested in his parents' amorous activity, moved to the side and continued foraging in the marsh. After a while, the female seemed to grow bored with the affections of her partner and joined her chick. The male settled down as well only to be annoyed a few moments later by the challenges of the neighboring Dike Pair as they invaded the Middle Pond's turf. Suddenly, the entire Middle Pond Family flew toward the Dike Pair's territory and landed within a short distance. The Dike Pair seemed to get the point, and the afternoon's territorial challenges were over. Allen had spent more than four hours crouched in the blind, sketching the display and taking notes.

Ten days later, he was back for another marathon observation. This time his subject was the Extra Family, a female and her chick, named for their attempt to claim a buffer zone between the dominant Middle Pond

Family and the Dike Pair. Allen speculated that the Extra female's mate had died along the migration route, which explained her delayed arrival on the refuge. By the time she reached Aransas with her chick, all the territories had been claimed except for some unoccupied areas near Mustang Lake and Dunham Point.

Allen set up his blind around eleven that morning, spread out the corn, and watched as a herd of cows wandered in, chasing the whoopers away and eating the bait. When the last cow walked away around one thirty, the crane family waiting nearby, moved in to feed on what remained. Within three minutes, an alarm call went out. It was the Dike Pair sending warnings to the Extra Family, which was now in the pair's territory. As the Dike male rushed at the Extra female, the Middle Pond Family flew in and joined the skirmish. The immature Extra ran toward the northeast with his mother following close behind. The Dike male and then the Middle Pond Family rushed the immature Extra. Each time the youngster's mother came to its defense. Finally, the Dike Pair stalked off toward the bay while the Middle Pond Family patrolled the perimeter of their territory, calling out warnings. This confrontation lasted almost forty-five minutes. While watching this aggressive display, Allen concluded that without a male in the family, it was difficult for a female and her young to establish their own territory.

The Extra mother and her juvenile took to wandering along the swampy areas of oak brush far away from the others. When all had settled down, the whoopers spent the afternoon feeding and preening. With crane groups now surrounding him, Allen wrote in his journal: "I'm stuck! Can't escape."[10] By three o'clock, he had once more spent four hours crouched in his blind. Not wanting his presence known for fear of causing another territorial dispute or having the birds become used to seeing him around, he was determined to wait them out. An hour later, the cranes were still preening. When they started moving again, Allen thought he had his chance to leave the blind; then the Middle Pond Family came back to feed again. The Middle Pond youngster initiated a game of chase with the grackles and ducks. At dusk, the mosquitoes began to swarm. The cranes would not leave, and neither would Allen. Then it became evident that the family had decided to stay for the night. Once it was dark enough, Allen slipped away, delighted with the day's encounter, but wondering if his corn-bait idea had worked too well.

In December, Allen received a letter from Roger Tory Peterson, who would be in Texas on January 2 and wanted two days of birding with his old friend and Connie Hagar. He also asked about Allen's health. "What's this I hear about your playing with rabbits?"[11] Allen chuckled, but mentioned to Evelyn that he felt his general health was still "off its stride."[12] Evelyn made him an appointment with Doc Glover. The good doctor gave Allen a dose of penicillin and told him to take it easy. Taking it easy to Allen meant not working in the field for a day or so. That afternoon when he and Evelyn returned from Tivoli, Allen pulled out his journal and drew a design for a whooping crane decoy, which included a string attached to the neck so it could be raised and lowered from his blind. It was made of real cow skin and actually moved. Two days later, Allen was back in the field with the decoy finished and set up in the marsh. Then he set about designing another bull blind similar to the one he'd built the previous winter, except this one would fit two people inside. It was Alice who helped him build this one.

On Saturday, January 3, Allen spent the entire day with Roger Tory Peterson and Connie Hagar exploring Goose Island, Little Bay, and Moore's Pool, where they noted the arrival of tiny yellow-headed verdins, pine warblers, pyrrhuloxias, vermilion flycatchers, and ruby-crowned kinglets. The following day was spent on the refuge with the focus turned to the whoopers. Allen was proud to introduce his two friends to all six families with their gangly youngsters.

While Allen worked on his report, John Baker was fast into arranging the 1948 hunt. He'd written to Gustav Swanson with the USFWS, giving him bits and pieces of Allen's progress. Baker asked Swanson to keep Olaf Wallmo on board as Allen's assistant at the Aransas Refuge. And in true Baker fashion, he reminded Swanson of the agreement to continue allowing Allen the use of a four-wheel-drive vehicle while in Texas, as well as providing him with a plethora of supplies and equipment: "strands of wire, signs [sic], provisions for patrol, corn and other grains for experimental feeding, oats and fertilizer for planting, making available necessary tractor and farm machinery, plus help, installation for recording wind direction and velocity."[13] Most important to the project's success in Canada (and most costly) was an additional allocation for a pilot and plane during June and July. That pilot would most likely be Bob Smith, whose enthusiasm for the Whooping Crane Project had not waned one bit.

Alice Allen, age eight, at Hopper's Landing, Texas, standing by the frame of the bird blind Bob Allen eventually used to view the whooping cranes at the Aransas National Wildlife Refuge, 1947. Photo by Bob Allen. Courtesy of Alice Allen.

That winter, when not in the field, Allen pored over the mounds of migratory bird data. One factor became clear—migratory waterfowl: ducks, geese, and swans consistently followed the northward flow of the Athabasca, Slave, and Mackenzie Rivers through Saskatchewan. It stood to reason that the whooping cranes would take the same route.

Allen decided to focus the next hunt near the three rivers since this was the only area that had not been thoroughly explored. Although the search target had narrowed considerably, the region encompasses more than 500,000 square miles. The District of Mackenzie covers much of the Northwest Territories, extending all the way to the Arctic Ocean and including habitat that was suitable for waterfowl. The various reports coming in from Canada were not ignored. Three in particular caused Allen to widen the northernmost area of his search location.

A pilot with the Royal Canadian Air Force (RCAF) had read the November 1947 article in *Maclean's Magazine* and sent a letter to the Canadian Wildlife Service. He was certain he'd seen whooping cranes living around tundra lakes near Kugmallit Bay in the Mackenzie Delta region. His description was accurate, not only of their physical features, "of tremendous size,"[14] but also their behavior. Sandhill cranes, snow geese, and white pelicans all gather in flocks, unlike the whooping cranes, which are territorial and stay together in small families. "They [whooping cranes] live on the lakes in pairs and occasionally one bird by itself."[15] The birds the pilot saw were most assuredly whooping cranes. He documented the coordinates of the location: 69° 10' north, 133° 40' west.

In a direct line south of Kugmallit Bay, Lac La Martre sticks out like a right thumb between the narrow piece of land connecting Great Bear and Great Slave Lakes. Edward A. Preble, an acclaimed naturalist who had spent much of his time along the Mackenzie River studying birds and mammals, contacted Allen. Preble had accompanied Allen's boyhood idol, Edward Thompson Seton, on his journey near Great Slave Lake in 1907. Seton and Preble had witnessed the flight of four whooping cranes over Athabasca Delta. He encouraged Allen to continue his search of the Great Slave Lake. He even went as far as sending along a map he and Seton had used, and told Allen that the details of the sighting were described in Seton's book *Arctic Prairies*. Another report came in from Ian McTaggart Cowan, a zoology professor at the University of British Columbia. He knew of a Hudson's Bay employee who had seen whooping cranes near Padlei east of Fort Rae as recently as 1942. All these reports concurred with several documents Allen had in his file that dated back to the late 1800s when whoopers were seen in this area on numerous occasions. Allen was more certain than ever that he was on the right track to finding his birds.

7

Vanished

With much regret, Allen made plans for the 1948 hunt that did not include taking the family along. After several examinations, Bobby had been diagnosed with diabetes. Evelyn did not want her son living in the wilderness hours from the nearest doctor. Years later, when she reflected on their life on Flotten Lake in the summer of 1947, she shuddered to think of Bobby trudging into the woods for firewood with an ax almost as big as he was tall resting on his shoulder, and the realization that medical help, if needed, was hours away. Since the family had been on-site the previous summer, they knew firsthand the importance of Allen's mission, and they insisted he continue. Besides, it was time for them to go home. While Allen prepared to head north, Evelyn drove Bobby and Alice back to Tavernier. Two additional passengers made the trip—Alice's pet horned toad and her new Dalmatian, Texie.

Upon their return to Florida, Evelyn and the kids attempted to pick up where life had left off six years earlier. They moved back into the rental house on Lowe Street where they had stored their belongings before leaving. Modern conveniences were beginning to make their way to the Upper Keys. Most dwellings and commercial businesses had electricity, albeit unreliable. Constant interruptions in service occurred when large birds perched on the utility wires or a high wind blew in across the water, damaging the lines. Indoor plumbing reached the homes through a central water pipe coming from Homestead. This service, too, was unreliable. The pipe lay above ground and ran along U.S. 1. Occasionally, a tipsy driver ran off the road and over a pipe, leaving the residents without water for long periods of time. Regardless, Evelyn and the kids were happy to be back among their close friends in Tavernier.

Jack and "K" Wilkinson had purchased a home near the Allens. Evelyn worked at reestablishing her music studio, while "K" devoted her time to improving the intermittent school system in the Upper Keys. She attended school board meetings and worked on establishing an effective PTA. As more children enrolled and attendance became steady, "K" suggested Evelyn put up notices and offer piano lessons. Within a few weeks, Evelyn had a steady stream of music students, some of the families paying tuition in the form of fish caught that day.

⁓

With his family settled back in Tavernier, Allen finalized matters in Texas before heading back north to Canada. John Baker doubled-checked to make sure the CWS and USFWS were ready with the helicopter and fuel to prevent any delays in getting started once Allen arrived.

Beginning in April, newspaper stories and editorials appeared almost daily announcing Allen and Bob Smith's second search and reminding the public of the whooping cranes' dire status. On May 1, the *Saskatoon Star-Phoenix* published a lengthy editorial by Pat Stockton describing the whooping crane mating dance: "As well as being one of nature's greatest lovers the whooper was the first jitterbug."[1] Along with the story was a photo from the University of Saskatchewan museum showing a whooper towering over the much smaller blue heron. An uplifting editorial appeared in the *Toronto Globe and Mail* on April 30 from a supporter who wrote, "But the very fact that in these troubled times people should actually be devoting their energies to something quite removed from politics, atomic bombs, and making money and other such mundane activities, is refreshing."[2] A couple of weeks prior, the *Milwaukee Journal* had reported that Allen planned to follow the cranes north in a plane, although this was not true. To give the newspaper credit, the story went on to clarify that the plane would not follow so closely as to frighten the birds. Overall, Audubon was pleased with the media coverage.

Again, the press had the public stoked. This was to be the big year; fingers were crossed and hopes were high that Allen and Smith would get the job done.

⁓

Allen's preparation that spring involved more than monitoring the cranes' activities; he also needed to stay abreast of what was happening around the refuge. Whooping crane survival depended upon locating and preserving their nesting site and protecting them during migration, but also paramount was saving the integrity of their winter home. As part of the agreement to establish the Aransas National Wildlife Refuge back in 1937, the USFWS had to agree not to terminate a mineral lease on the property held by Continental Oil Company while the company continued to operate. Not long after the first of the year 1948, Allen learned that Continental Oil had subleased its rights to the Western Natural Gas Company of Houston, which planned to begin drilling in Mullet Bay and Camp Pond, prime whooping crane habitat. Upon hearing the news, John Baker was outraged. He set up a meeting with L. F. McCollum of Continental in their New York office, and arranged for Allen to meet in Houston with Continental's vice president, Charles A. Perlitz; Dr. J. A. Culbertson of its geological department; and H. O. Weaver, Western Natural Gas Company's secretary-treasurer. Exercising his negotiating skills, Allen succeeded in persuading the oil company to cease its drilling between October and April, lay conduits under roads, allowing for the continued natural flow of water between ponds and marshes, and discontinue using gas flares. Continental Oil also promised to consult the USFWS and Audubon before deciding on any future drilling locations. Allen described these meeting as "friendly."[3]

This wasn't the first time Allen sat across the table from oil company executives. Back in 1941, Baker had sent Allen to issue a warning to an oil company that was drilling in San Antonio Bay near the Second Chain of Islands. Oil had leaked from barges, producing an oil slick that flowed dangerously close to crane habitat. Allen came away with a sincere apology from the company.

On several occasions toward the end of March, while on patrol of the refuge, Allen caught sight of cranes flying higher than normal, at times disappearing from view. To him, it seemed as if they were flexing their flight muscles in preparation for the long migration ahead. During the first week of April, three families departed the refuge; the other families took to the sky between April 10 and April 18. Allen remained on the refuge until mid-May, completing his reports and gathering equipment to take to Canada.

Olaf Wallmo and the rest of the refuge staff wished Allen good luck.

He picked up the used car he'd bought in San Antonio and drove north via a detour through Jamestown, North Dakota, to investigate an abandoned whooping crane breeding site. He left Minot, North Dakota, at 8:30 a.m. on May 30 and didn't arrive in Regina until 4:00 p.m., a distance of a little more than 200 miles. The car, in dire need of an engine overhaul, had him stopping every few miles to add oil (19 quarts) and gas (168 gallons).[4] Customs delayed him for another hour. Halfway to Regina, just outside of Macoun, Saskatchewan, he threw a fan belt. Fortunately, he found a repair shop on the side of the highway. Then on the outskirts of Regina, bad roads slowed him to a crawl, turning a four-hour trip into an all-day ordeal. By the time he pulled into site No. 9 at the auto camp near the museum, it was too late to do anything but unpack a few things and count the number of oil quarts left. His spirits were high, however. Allen's journal notes mentioned putting on a pot of Mello Joy Cajun coffee, his favorite brand he'd brought with him from Texas.

Bob Smith joined him the next day. Before they got down to bird talk, Smith wanted updates on the Allen family, and Allen was more than willing to oblige.

Unlike last year's hunt, this one began right on schedule. In preparation for the trip, Smith had his Widgeon undergo its 100-hour check at the Regina airport, then had the cabin stripped bare to accommodate their 1,300-pound payload.

At noon on June 3, the fourth nest hunt was under way.

The flight out of Saskatchewan's capital had Allen and Smith over the headwaters of Last Mountain Lake within minutes and then over acres of barren ground. Their first stop was Prince Albert, where they spent the night with Gordon Lund and his family, and became acclimated to life in the bush with their first meal of caribou tongue. Early the next morning, they interviewed the locals, gleaning any information that would help them locate their quarry. An eighty-eight-year-old prospector, also named Bob Smith, bent their ears with stories of his experiences along the lower Mackenzie more than fifty years prior. As entertaining as he was, his information was of more historical than scientific value.

The flight to Alberta over Watchusk and Gordon Lakes, an area known for nesting and breeding for several waterfowl species, especially the white pelican, proved disappointing. As Allen and Smith approached the area, it became evident that seeing anything, much less a white bird with black wing tips, was impossible. The sun, dimmed by a thick, gray cloud of lingering smoke from recent forest fires, obscured visibility. Smith was forced to land in Fort McMurray a few miles to the northwest. With the plane tied down on the airstrip, Allen and Smith made their way into town. A train derailment just outside of Fort McMurray had the locals gathered around in an uproar. Avoiding the commotion, the nest hunters checked into the McMurray Hotel and made for the dining room for a much-needed meal and brew, only to discover that the restaurant had eighty-sixed most of the menu items. One of the derailed train cars had been carrying food staples and the beer supply. Allen reported their stay as "a quiet evening in McM, eating ice cream and drinking water."[5]

Despite the still hazy sky, they took off the next morning toward Lake Claire and Athabasca Delta, in the southeastern section of Wood Buffalo National Park, an area Allen was eager to search. Smith flew transects over every acre while Allen snapped photos and took notes. The park was established in 1922 to protect the remaining wild herd of wood bison in North America. By the time Allen and Smith reached the area, the skies were clear and the park's namesake could be seen thundering across the plains. Allen reported: "It was a magnificent sight, these huge animals roaming at large and under primitive conditions. We saw two big buffalo wolves trotting along on the rear flank of one herd, the nearest group of cows and calves apparently paying no attention to them. After all, in a completely wild state the wolves have always been there, and so are simply an accepted and integral part of the scenery."[6]

While flying over the Athabasca Delta, they conducted a duck count of the 500 square miles of marshland. In abundance were mallard, pintail, northern shoveler, widgeon, scaup, blue-winged teal, redhead, white-winged scoter, gadwall, green-winged teal, bufflehead, ruddy duck, and goldeneye, but no whoopers. That night, they bunked at the Mackenzie Hotel in Fort Smith and hoped for an early getaway to Great Slave Lake the next morning.

June 6 greeted them with a heavy drizzle and a report of a stationary 4,000-foot overcast covering Fort Resolution, their targeted search area.

By noon, it was evident that the weather was not going to clear. Instead of losing the entire day, they altered their plans and flew toward Fort Simpson, where the Liard River spills into the Mackenzie River. Their light breakfast and scant meal from the night before had them on the ground near Hay River at 1:00 p.m., looking for food. Max Krap's café had recently opened, and the proprietor offered a limited menu. The noon special that day was cold meat, bread, tea, and pie for a dollar. While waiting for their meals, Allen mingled with the locals, took out his notebook, and sketched a native family of six who were enjoying hot tea and pie. These humorous drawings, along with sketches of birds, found their way into his field journals.

By 3:30, Allen and Smith were back in the air and flying over new territory. Ahead loomed the Mackenzie Mountain Range, its ominous peaks rising more than 9,000 feet and silhouetting sharply against the blue sky. Smith dipped low over the muskegs, allowing Allen to document the duck species nesting along the lake. If they continued on the same route toward the north, they'd be well over the Arctic. At 5:30, feeling cramped and bleary-eyed from being in the cockpit for so many hours, the two nest hunters called it a day. The settlement where they planned to spend the night was 6 miles from the airstrip. They hitched a ride on a freight canoe headed down the Liard River and arrived at the camp of local game warden Vic Shattuck before dark. Shattuck had other visitors that evening, and the party stayed up late, talking about the intricacies of life in the sub-Arctic. Around midnight, Shattuck passed out eiderdowns (the camp was not outfitted with heat), and each man grabbed a few feet of floor space and called it a night.

Allen and Smith woke early to the aroma of a hot breakfast. During the meal, Allen expressed his concern over the canoe trip back up the Liard, against the river's flow. As they packed their gear, Shattuck graciously rigged their canoe with an outboard motor and Allen and Smith were off on the river and in the air before noon. Their next stop was the town of Norman Wells, located on the north bank of the Mackenzie River. A rich oil deposit had been discovered in the area in 1911 and a refinery built in 1937. It was operated by Imperial Oil, the town's largest employer. As they flew between the white-toothed peaks of the Franklin and Mackenzie Mountains, rain began to fall without mercy. Through the heavy squalls, Smith spotted the airstrip in Norman Wells. They were on the ground at

2:48 and in a cottage owned by Imperial Oil shortly thereafter. Unlike their previous stop, this camp was outfitted with plumbing, hot water, and real beds. Allen wrote letters and turned in early.

Cold temperatures, high wind, and a low-cloud ceiling kept Allen and Smith on the ground the following morning. Finally, by two that afternoon, the weather report from Aklavik came in; the ceiling had lifted, and Allen and Smith took off. Within an hour, the fog returned and with it sleeting rain, dropping the temperature in the cockpit to freezing. Luckily, they'd purchased heavy underwear before leaving Norman Wells.

The fog cleared just as the headwaters of the Mackenzie River came into view. This massive waterway originates from Great Slave Lake and flows north, eventually spreading out over more than 150 miles of shallow ground, before emptying into the Beaufort Sea. The Dene legend has it that one summer, the rains failed to fall and the people began to starve. The Great Master sent a giant ball of meat rolling down the land, gouging a deep crevasse and throwing off bits of food. The crevasse filled with water and the Deh Cho, the Mackenzie, Canada's longest river, was formed.[7] From the cockpit, the wide river glistened below, majestic in its twisted form, giving credence to its legend.

Soon, they were skimming over the vast Mackenzie Delta in the far northern reaches of Allen's search area. The delta begins at Point Separation and is bordered by the Richardson Mountains on the west and the Caribou Mountains on the east. In the spring, the snowmelt fills the river, which in turn empties into three channels—the East Channel, the Middle Channel, and the Peel or West Channel—and creates a maze of streams, lakes, ponds, alluvial islands, and shallow, meandering channels, making the delta navigable only between May and October. The delta has the largest concentration of pingos (conical-shaped islands formed by ice-age uplifts) in the world. Approximately twenty-five thousand small, ever-changing lakes dot the landscape.

Scanning the lakes below, Allen and Smith saw that most were still frozen, and the bird life was slim. That afternoon, a thick fog bank formed over the Arctic Red River, a tributary of the Mackenzie, blocking out visibility below. Suddenly, Smith caught sight of a narrow slit in the fog and decreased altitude. "Bob brought the little amphib down close to the main stream," he wrote, "where we skimmed along over great islands of rotting ice that were moving swiftly for the open sea farther north."[8]

Smith landed on a mud bank on the West Channel just a few miles from Aklavik. A group of four men gathered to watch as he maneuvered the plane as close to the shore as possible. Allen remembered advice he'd received from a friend who had visited here years before. Because the folks who lived in this remote region of Canada saw so few visitors, they were often leery of unannounced arrivals. Allen planned to make a good first impression. Determined to win over the four men who had gathered, Allen smiled broadly, grabbed the towline, stepped out onto the nose of the Widgeon, and tossed the rope. Two men caught it, but made no attempt to tie down the plane. Allen decided he'd make the first move. He would step ashore and greet them with a firm handshake. "I stood up on the nose and, grinning cheerfully at our new friends, leaped for the bank. I made it all right, smack into that black, silty mud, hip-deep."[9] The four men, Hudson's Bay manager, Bill Carson, a man named Roberts who was an agent with Imperial Oil, a local game warden Bud Boyce, and Ward Stevens, a biologist with the CWS, who was engaged in a muskrat study, laughed at their visitor's graceful display and then, using planks and logs, hauled Allen from the mud.

Allen learned that his old friend's advice was not necessary; the men were eager to assist in any way possible. Boyce invited Allen and Smith to stay the night at his new, well-heated home. They took him up on his offer, promising to be gone after they refueled in the morning. Boyce chuckled, put on some music, pulled out his bottle of libation, and told them to get comfortable. Imperial Oil's entire cache of fuel was swept down the river in a recent flood. Hundreds of drums of gasoline were lazily floating somewhere downstream on the Mackenzie River. Royal Canadian Mounted Police had organized a search, and a fresh supply was en route from Norman Wells.

What was to be a one-night stay turned into a week. Always the optimist, Allen completed his June 8 journal entry with, "We're settled in Bud's house with record player, oil furnace and Demerara [rum]. Wotta life!"[10]

Aklavik is located on the western shore of the Peel Channel, where the river forms a "U" as it meanders across the delta. There was not much to do in the town of four hundred at that time of year. The gathering place, the North Star Inn, was deserted, since the locals were away hunting muskrat on the delta. The hunting season was scheduled to end on June

15, at which time the small settlement would swell to more than 1,000 rab-
ble-rousers eager to sell their goods and begin celebrating before heading
out into the icy water to fish. Wondering how to fill the hours, perhaps
days, in the sleepy settlement, Allen and Smith jumped at the chance to
accompany two Canadian Mounties on an excursion to a Loucheux trapper's camp up the river. This was in the same area where the Mounties,
after organizing what became known as the biggest manhunt in Canadian
history, had killed the infamous Albert Johnson, a.k.a. the Mad Trapper,
in a shoot-out sixteen years earlier.

Seeing the delta at eye level from a canoe gave Allen and Smith an entirely different perspective. It was easy to understand how a fugitive like
Johnson could elude the police for weeks before capture. The seemingly
flat, soggy ground, fraught with meandering channels and vast muddy
bayous, looked as if it could swallow an entire fleet of canoes. At the first
camp, hundreds of muskrat pelts hung drying on frames, awaiting transport, some destined for Aklavik and others for Edmonton. It was evident
that the Loucheux population who inhabited the area had prospered
from their bounty. The settlement had many of the modern conveniences
seen in more developed areas: washing machines, battery-operated ra-
dios, movie theaters, and ice cream shops. Smith had learned of a local
girl who was known for her skills as a seamstress. Word was sent out that
an American wanted a muskrat parka. She seemed to materialize on the
spot and took Smith's measurements. In a couple of days, he was proudly
decked out in his new garment. What made this coat special was that the
young woman had shot and skinned the animals herself.

A few days passed, and Allen began noticing the birds along the pe-
rimeters of the settlement: flocks of the common short-billed gull; the
large, aggressive pomarine jaeger, which feeds on small gulls and lem-
mings; long-tailed jaegers, the smallest jaeger, which nests in the Arctic
tundra and migrates along the Washington coastline; and the Wilson's
snipe, whose flexible bill is almost as long as its body. Several of the natives noticed Allen's interest and began educating him on the birds' common names. When Allen asked about the whooping crane's native name,
he was sad to learn there wasn't one.

Allen and Smith cleaned out the plane, rearranged their gear, listened
to the local radio station incessantly play the latest hit recording by a local Eskimo band, and waited. On June 10, Smith volunteered to fly over

N.W.T. 1947

Sketch of Cree Indian from the Northwest Territories. by Bob Allen, 1947.
Published in *Audubon Magazine,* January-February 1948. Courtesy of *Audubon Magazine,* New York.

the area and assist the Mounties in a search for a lost man and boy who had failed to return from their canoe trip the day before. A few gallons of fuel were found, and while Smith flew the Mounties over the area, Allen filled pages in his journal with sketches of the townspeople. His favorite subjects were the Northwest Territories Cree Indians, two priests, an Anglican and Catholic, who tried to outpreach one another on their Sunday radio broadcasts, and a shy woman named Elizabeth who spoke very little, but giggled while Allen sketched her washing clothes with her two young children.

Saturday morning, June 12, a new crisp sheet of snow hid the muck that had refused to dry for the past few weeks. Allen decided that Aklavik, despite the unscheduled grounding, would make a suitable base for exploring the surrounding area once they resumed their flights. The gas barge had not been retrieved, and the supply from Norman Wells, which was shipped on Wednesday, had still not arrived. The only good news was that the two missing men had found their own way back into town.

To alleviate the tedium of having to wait until they could resume their search, Mountie Ed Phalen invited Allen and Smith to the weekly movie at the Hotel Aklavik. "Afterwards, with Ward Stevens, we sat in North Star Inn and drank coffee while Bing Crosby sang *Deep Purple* on the jukebox. The sun was brilliant at midnight when we walked back to the house."[11] The next day, Allen spent a quiet Sunday with Ward Stevens on a lake near town, documenting thirty-two different bird species.

When Monday rolled around, the solitude of the previous week was lost in a flurry of activity. The locals arrived with their muskrat catch. Men, women, children, and dogs crowded the docks. Shortly before noon on June 14, the gas barge pulled up from Norman Wells. Allen and Smith watched as the unloading began. They hoped to be in the air by late afternoon. But in all the chaos, it was evident that the task would take hours. Allen walked back to the lake, where he spotted a hoary redpoll, a finch sporting a red-capped head, which had not yet migrated to the Arctic Circle, and added it to his journal list of delta birds. Seeing the unusual tiny bird turned out to be the high point of the past two days.

In the intervening time, the snow had melted, but the weather remained cold and rainy. Once back in the air, the nest hunters flew toward the Eskimo Lakes and were surprised to find every one frozen over. The Beaufort Sea was a solid slab of ice from the shoreline to as far as the eye could see. Ducks, geese, and whistling swans picked their way along the perimeter. Allen became hopeful when he spotted a flock of sandhill cranes. But the big white bird was nowhere around.

During down time in Aklavik, Allen enjoyed mingling with the locals. A teacher at the Anglican School asked if he would talk to the schoolchildren about the whooping crane hunt. He was surprised and pleased to learn that the class was well informed about the plight of his subject. Pictures and drawings of birds, including whooping crane, covered the classroom walls. The students were eager for updated information, and Allen won them over immediately. "In the plump and handsome faces before me there was an almost electric attention. When I asked for questions at the end of the talk half the hands were in the air at once."[12] Allen also told them about life in Texas where the cranes enjoyed winters free of snow and ice. Giggling erupted over that bit of information. Living in a frozen climate eight months out of the year with winter snows reaching to rooftops made mild, warm winters unimaginable for the local children.

After his school visit, Allen had gained a fan club. Several boys waited at the riverbank each day for the plane to appear over the horizon. As soon as he stepped from the plane, the boys pumped Allen with questions, hoping to be the first to hear news of his success in finding the nesting site. As time went on with no encouraging news to report, the number of boys dwindled daily until finally the welcoming committee disappeared completely. Allen could deal with frustration of not finding the birds, but seeing the disappointed look on the faces of the children in Aklavik was another thing altogether: "The silent treatment we received from those native children was the bitterest pill we had to swallow. We would slink back from the landing as if we had just been caught kicking a dog. Both of us had moments at that time when we felt that we were complete failures and might as well give up the whole thing. It was a very humbling experience."[13]

The summer finally wrested away winter's hold on the Northwest Territories. With the ice breaking up, Allen and Smith were back in the air on June 16. They flew transects over the Caribou Hills, Cape Dalhousie Peninsula, Parsons Lake, McKinley Bay, and all the deltas in between. Allen documented populations of scaup, scoter, pintail, mallards, and whistling swans. The next day, they flew low over the thawing tundra, and they watched a grizzly bear charge a couple of nesting whistling swans. Smith banked the plane and flew back around. The grizzly stood on stump-like hind legs, raised his head, and shot the pilot a threatening glare. Smith dipped lower, playing chicken, until the bear took off running. Smith yelled some obscenities as he flew past. "I always wanted to cuss out a grizzly bear. Notice how surprised he looked? No one ever talked to him like that before."[14] Allen laughed, and the tediousness of that afternoon's search was broken.

Allen spent Sunday, June 20 at the North Star Inn, reading and answering mail while Smith gassed and oiled the Widgeon. Monday morning, they were off again. During that week, they flew over Richards Island, Liverpool Bay to the Anderson River, and over the Kugaluk River Delta. They got word that the ice over the Eskimo Lakes had broken up enough for them to land the plane and search the shores of the lake region. Ward Stevens joined them on June 25, and the three men set out for a camping trip along the southwest shores. At 2:20 p.m., Smith had them on the water just a few feet from land where delicate violet crocuses and clusters of the white sticky flowers of Labrador tea grew in abundance. Catkins, the long cylindrical flowers of ground birch, heavy with pollen, drooped from the trees' branches.

After camp was set up, Smith grabbed his fishing tackle and walked to a nearby stream. In less than an hour, he was back with a huge smile on his face and several good-size trout dangling from his stringer. As he pan-fried their evening meal, he bragged about his fishing prowess. Allen joked that Smith's catch was due more to the trout's curiosity about the chrome spoon he had used as a lure than to his fishing skills. Smith responded with raised eyebrows and hushed Allen by offering him a second helping of fish.

The next morning they woke to a choir of songbirds: the robin's *cheerily, cheer-up, cheerily, cheer-up* melded with the *sweet-sweet-sweet* of the yellow warbler. Tree sparrows and fox sparrows chimed in. Hudsonian curlews probed their long bills in the wet sand. White-fronted geese, whistling swans, long-tailed ducks, pomarine, and long-tailed jaegers flew in and covered the lake's surface. A trek through the marshes and reeds sent a few great blue herons squawking overhead, but no whooping cranes were found.

By the end of June, Allen had a thorough population estimate of the waterfowl that inhabited the entire Mackenzie Delta. Ducks, as a collective family, were the most numerous at 369,000. Three species of geese numbered 21,000, whistling swans numbered 16,000, black brant, 2,300, and 3,200 sandhill cranes. With the entire 4,700 square miles of delta explored, it was time to move on. Allen had his sights on the Anderson River Delta east of the Mackenzie, where in the 1860s, fur trader and writer Roderick Ross MacFarlane had reported seeing whooping cranes migrating in from the south.

Sunday, June 27, Allen noted in his journal that he and Smith observed the Sabbath by sleeping in. Smith had caught cold during their stay at Eskimo Lakes and needed to recuperate. While relaxing, they kicked around the idea of making a side trip over the Yukon before leaving the area. July 2 dawned clear and calm. Smith suggested they take advantage of the beautiful day and make an unscheduled trip to Old Crow since they were flying over the Yukon. On his way to the plane, Allen stopped mid-step. "You mean, Old Crow, on the other side of those mountains?" he asked. "Yep," Smith responded, "Old Crow."[15] Allen expressed his doubts over the weather on the other side of the Richardson Mountains, but his pilot merely smiled and shrugged. At 11:45 a.m., Smith had his Grumman Widgeon heading in that direction.

The Richardson Mountain Range, the northernmost vestiges of the Rocky Mountains, rise to more than 4,000 feet and run northwest to southeast, making up a portion of the Yukon/Northwest Territories border. The village of Old Crow is the only settlement in the Yukon that, even today, does not have road access. It is also the only village north of the Arctic Circle. Today the population hovers around three hundred Vuntut Gwitchin First Nations. There is archaeological evidence that supports the possibility that the Old Crow area might have been one of the earliest-known sites of human occupation in North America.[16] Back in 1948, it was little more than a cluster of log huts on a ridge overlooking the Porcupine River. Most who gathered here did so to hunt caribou, as it is located on the Porcupine caribou-migration route.

As the mountain range came into view, so did the violent Rat River, tumbling over rocky slopes and spilling into the steep canyon below. Up ahead, the Bell River joined the Rat, and the two forces collided, sending a deafening bellow that bounced off the canyon walls. Smith kept the plane low to avoid the strong unpredictable air currents swirling near the mountain summit. Alpine meadows covered the slopes where mountain sheep had purchase. As Smith maneuvered the plane between the narrow mountainous gap, Allen took note of their surroundings. "On one of these a light-colored mountain sheep stared at us without moving, as staunch as the rocks about him. Then the pass narrowed and the sides grew steep until we were flying through a winding canyon, with the river a thin torrent 1,000 feet beneath us. The canyons of the Bell twist and turn every which way, so that we were constantly banking around great steep walls of rock and slipping this way and that to keep as near the middle of the cut as possible."[17]

Smith, probably a bit cocky over his skill at flying them safely out of the canyon, decreased altitude over the basin so Allen could conduct another bird count. Here, they found the largest concentration of waterfowl since they had begun the 1948 expedition. The shallow ponds and lakes were home to scoter, baldpate, scaup, pintail, golden-eye, oldsquaw, canvasback, Canada geese, and sandhill cranes—all told, an avian population of more than 150,000 birds. Allen estimated 56.2 ducks per square mile. No whooping cranes were seen.

That afternoon, they reached Old Crow. As Smith scanned the river below for suitable water landing, the Loucheux gathered on the riverbank, intently watching the plane's approach. Smith brought the Widgeon down, bounced a couple of times, and fought the strong current to the shore. Corporal Kirk, an officer with the Mounties and the only white man living in the settlement, and the local shaman instructed two villagers to pull the plane in and tie it down. Kirk shook his head as the two scientists hopped ashore. Seems that Smith had chosen a precarious section of the river for landing. Just below the surface were dozens of wooden stakes the locals used for securing their fishing nets. Had the river level not been unusually high, the plane would have no doubt been impaled by a stake and flipped over. Smith smiled upon hearing what he had just done and shrugged again, acting like the daredevil he was.

Allen, Smith, Kirk, and the shaman talked birds for a couple of hours. When it was time for Allen and Smith to fly back over the mountain, Kirk enlisted them on an important mission—a delivery to Aklavik. He handed Allen an envelope. Inside was a love letter from a Loucheux girl to her beau. Allen may not have found any whooping cranes that day, but he had a chance to make a young couple happy.

As Allen and Smith walked back to the shore and boarded the plane, thunder cracked just beyond the mountains and storm clouds boiled overhead. Smith was certain he could outfly the rain. Ten minutes after being airborne, droplets splattered the windshield. Allen glanced above and the gray cloud he had seen earlier had turned black. The Bell River below was now an angry torrent from the runoff spilling in upriver. Moments later, a gale-force wind struck the plane as the black cloud descended. Smith nosed the plane down toward the river and caught sight of the rising foam 100 feet below. He leveled off just above the river and fought to keep the Widgeon from being sucked into the growing vortex. "Never did the little craft seem to have such speed!" Allen wrote. "In close quarters like that her 110 miles per hour gave us the sensation of riding an unguided missile up a blind alley. It was a nightmare!"[18] Up ahead everything went black.

Smith craned his neck to keep the Bell River in sight as it cut left and right and back again through the sheer rock before spilling into the Rat River. They picked up the Rat and followed its course until the faint light came into view. As if an annoying fly had flown into its mouth, the mountain gorge spit the Widgeon out over the flat land of the Mackenzie Delta. In the delta's vastness, the storm lost its fury. Allen glanced over and was relieved to see the human side of his partner—sweat ran down Smith's face.

That evening, they sat at the now-crowded North Star Inn in Aklavik enjoying a hot meal prepared by the establishment's cook, the benevolent Mrs. McNeice. The return trip from Old Crow had both men shaken and questioning their decision to fly over the mountain. But they took solace in knowing that elsewhere in town a happy young man was reading his girlfriend's letter.

During the remainder of July, Allen and Smith concentrated their search over the rest of the Anderson River Delta. The Anderson River originates from Great Bear Lake and flows north to the Beaufort Sea between the Mackenzie and Coppermine Rivers. The RCMP, when learning of Allen and Smith's intention of camping in this remote region along the Arctic coast and conducting a ground search, loaned the two nest hunters a Winchester rifle. The grizzlies in that area were a factor to be reckoned with. Besides, if Allen and Smith were killed by a bear, the Mounties, having too much work on their hands, were not keen on filing death reports. Smith perhaps regretted cursing out *Ursus arctos horribilis* on that sunny afternoon near Eskimo Lakes.

As the Anderson River flows into Wood Bay, it forms several channels around mounds of high ground. Smith landed the plane near the largest of these islands, and he and Allen waded ashore in icy waist-deep water, carrying their equipment and supplies above their heads. Proclaiming the ground suitable, they set up base camp. A few hours later, the tide had risen to within a few feet of the tent, providing their camp with a natural moat. The moat, they joked, would keep predators away. As if in punishment for mocking the tundra gods, fresh tundra wolf tracks, as large as a human hand, pocked the mud surrounding their tent every morning.

Even though the daytime temperature on the Anderson Delta bumped up into the high eighties, the evenings heralded in the cold. The terrain was void of firewood; a single-burner gas stove provided them with warmth and a means to cook. When the tide was low, every nesting colony of black brant, glaucous gull, jaeger, king eider, and scoter was explored and documented. Since the black brant, also called real neglek by the Eskimos, outnumbered all the other species, Allen and Smith named their island Real Neglek.

During one of the nest-counting forays, Allen was determined to photograph a nest of black-brant eggs, but the geese spooked too easily. Using two canoe oars and burlap sacks, he constructed a blind and set up his camera equipment. Smith retreated a safe distance to watch. The nesting goose appeared mesmerized by the presence of the blind. Finally, she waddled over, poked her head around the burlap, and stared Allen directly in the eye. She ran back to her nest, then returned to the blind for another look. This behavior continued, back and forth between the nest and the blind, with the goose peering at Allen from one side and then the other. The comical display had Smith doubled over with laughter.

Allen never got his photo. Concerned with the goose being off her eggs for too long, he gave up and left. "If you had ever gazed into the eyes of a real neglek you would understand my emotions. There was no further choice in the matter. I pulled down the screen, rolled it around the paddles, and hightailed it out of there."[19]

Allen and Smith were back in Aklavik in mid-July, preparing to finish up their search before the weather turned cold. Allen wanted to have one more look at the marshes between Great Bear and Great Slave Lakes. As they were making plans to leave on July 20, an unexpected front blew in from the northwest. Within minutes, the wind had increased to gale force, and Allen and Smith rushed to tie down the plane. Then the clouds split open, dumping buckets of rain that didn't let up for three days. Finally, on the afternoon of July 23, the storm clouds dissipated. The sky turned a brilliant blue, then just as quickly, faded to gray. The two men hurriedly packed their equipment, said good-bye to their friends, and with high hopes, headed toward the one remaining region left to explore. They got as far as Norman Wells when another wave of bad weather swept in, grounding them for two more days. Good flying weather presented itself on July 25. For the next three days, they covered the area from Norman Wells all the way across the Coppermine Mountains. Over the Coronation Gulf, they flew transects, covering each square mile. The gulf is open to the Arctic Ocean via the Dease Strait and Queen Maud Gulf Straits on the east and the Dolphin and Union Straits on the west. Compared to the Mackenzie and Anderson Deltas with their abundance of waterfowl, the area around the gulf was almost barren. A few glaucous gulls and oldsquaw ducks were scattered about the coastline; it was clearly not whooping crane territory.

By July 28, all of Allen's search sites had been covered, but the area between Great Bear and Great Slave Lakes continued to occupy his thoughts. He wanted to have one more look; Smith agreed and left a flight plan with Canon Webster at the RCMP headquarters. At three that afternoon, they headed for Eldorado and Yellowknife. At four, as they approached MacTavish Arm of Great Bear Lake, a storm hit like a surprise slap in the face. The rain reduced visibility to zero, and the wind tossed the plane like a dry leaf in a tornado. Just as Smith began muttering his prayers out loud, a clear patch in the clouds opened below, and a body of water came into view. The surface of Hunter Bay on Great Bear Lake rippled with white caps. Smith took his chance, dove toward the water, located a protected cove, and landed safely. The rain finally turned to a steady drizzle, and fog rolled in. Using every rope aboard, they secured the Widgeon to the trees that grew along the water's edge and settled in to wait out the bad weather. Smith pulled out his chrome spoon and caught a couple of trout. After a satisfying meal, they unrolled their duffle bags and bedded down for the night inside the plane.

At midnight, Allen and Smith were startled awake. Something had grabbed onto the plane and shook it like a toy. It bounced and slammed onto the rocks. They scrambled out and realized the wind had shifted, and their safe haven had disappeared. Flying the plane to another location was not an option. A few more minutes of battering, and the Widgeon would be in no shape to fly. Allen and Smith lowered themselves into the frigid water, grabbed the wing tips, and prayed the storm would end soon. Rain flew in torrents, chunks of ice bobbed around them, occasionally knocking them off their feet. By the time the wind shifted again, and the storm blew out, the nest hunters had been in the icy water for more than sixteen hours. The air temperature, remaining in the sixties, saved them from hypothermia.

Too tired to assess the damage, they crawled back into the plane, ate what was left of their rations, and slept for the next fourteen hours. When they inspected the plane the next morning, they found the paint scraped off the bottom and sides, but the Widgeon was intact. However, another beating like the night before could leave them stranded on Hunter Bay. Using branches from a tree Smith chopped down, they pushed and guided the plane to a safe distance from the rocky shore. At first, it appeared that the only damage was a flat tire on the starboard side. Upon closer inspection, Smith feared that the hydraulic retracting gear might be damaged. If the wheels could not retract, they would not get off the water.

It wasn't until nine that night that the wind subsided enough for them to attempt a takeoff. Smith worried that the battery might be dead, as it had not been charged since leaving Coppermine. The men held their breaths, the engine turned over, the wheels lifted. In less than an hour, they were safely taxiing to the shore of the Canadian Air Force base in Eldorado. Upon arrival, Allen and Smith discovered that their flight plan had not been received.

One of the Air Force commanders, hearing of their plight, offered Allen and Smith beds in the officers' quarters. The next day, Smith gave his plane a thorough check. It was flyable, but the carburetor and generator needed repair. Much to Allen's consternation, finishing up a second search around Great Slave Lake would have to wait. Instead, they limped into Prince Albert, Saskatchewan, on August 4, ending the 1948 search. The two nest hunters had given it their best shot and hadn't found a single whooping crane. Allen concluded his report with, "It was as if they [the whooping cranes] flew North each spring and vanished from the face of the earth."[20]

8 ～

The Story of Rusty

Allen left Regina the second week in August 1948 and returned to Tavernier. Using the mounds of data he'd collected while studying the cranes
at Aransas, investigating their stopover in Nebraska, and discovering
potential habitats in Canada, he began working on his whooping crane
monograph. Audubon was uncertain about any future organized whooping crane hunts. John Baker had not given up, however, nor had Allen.
But there were other bird species in immediate trouble. During the next
three years, the USFWS biologists kept an eye out for the cranes while
conducting their annual waterfowl surveys. Bob Smith, who also never
gave up hope of finding the nesting site, conducted most of those surveys.

Allen spent the next six years shuttling between Florida, Texas, and
various locations in the Caribbean. Audubon and the USFWS still had
the responsibility of saving the whooping crane, but the project would
take a different course of action, one that caused a division among Audubon members. Everyone agreed that finding the site was vital; time was
running out. The whooping cranes were hanging on, but just barely. If a
different plan were going to be used, it needed to be put into effect immediately.

Audubon had considered experimenting with the breeding of captive whooping cranes during the initial planning of the Whooping Crane
Project in 1945. At such time, Allen clearly stated his opinion on the direction the project should take. Breeding cranes in captivity would eventually result in the loss of certain behaviors; the most significant was the
one that held the key to the mystery. Since migration is a learned crane
behavior, whooping cranes raised in captivity would not migrate. If the
wild flock disappeared, the elusive site would never be found. Refusing

to budge on an issue was not how Allen operated. "No matter how attractive and interesting they [captive whooping cranes] can be under such circumstances," he wrote, "they are not whooping cranes in the fullest sense. Their wild spirit and fierce nature tamed, their majestic flight denied, the thrilling drama and mystery of their annual migrations abruptly stemmed—these things cannot be permitted. Of course, the two injured birds already in our hands were another matter altogether."[1] Allen, strong-willed and outspoken, was also a team player. Debating the issue only wasted precious time. As long as his friend Bob Smith was flying over the Canadian wilderness, Allen felt the new plan had merit. Ever the diplomat, he drew both sides together, and the next phase of work began in the fall of 1948. Just to be sure of his position, he reiterated, "It should be understood at once that the primary object of our investigation was to provide for the future survival of the whooping crane in the wild state."[2]

~

It was a nice summer day in Brady, Nebraska. Henry George's two young daughters were riding their bicycles down a dirt road near their home when they came across a tall, white bird fluttering in a field. Amazed at the bird's size, almost as tall as they were, the girls stopped to watch and noticed its huge wing drooping almost to the ground. They rushed home and told their father. George drove along the field until he cornered the bird along a fence line. Despite its mangled wing and injured eye, the crane put up a fight, jabbing with its beak and thrusting about with its one good wing, before George captured it. He brought it to a private bird sanctuary owned by the Gothenburg Gun Club near North Platte, where it was positively identified as a whooping crane, its injuries apparently caused by a gunshot wound. The bird was placed in a pen with nonreleasable sandhill cranes, Canada geese, and various duck species. The next day, Thursday, June 11, 1936, the Lincoln County Tribune ran the story reporting that a "large white Heron" had been found and taken to the sanctuary.[3]

Twelve years later, Allen stood looking at the whooping crane as it peered back, extending its large neck over the top of the fence. He wondered how anyone could have mistaken this 5-foot-tall bird for a heron. He was also curious as to why a whooping crane had been found in the Midwest during the summer, weeks after the time of migration.

Allen contacted Jack Kennedy, whom he'd met and interviewed while in North Platte in 1947. The elderly Kennedy was the director of the gun club and a wealth of information. He told Allen stories about seeing flocks of whooping cranes numbering as many as fifty roosting on the river bars and feeding on frog eggs in buffalo wallows near where the George girls found the injured bird. This had occurred decades ago, but he still remembered them combing through fields of buffalo grass, pecking at insects. He even watched as they turned over and broke up cow chips to get at beetles. He witnessed migration takeoffs and watched as the birds rose higher and disappeared into the northwestern sky. So moved was he by seeing dozens of whooping cranes flying in V-formations that he painted a picture to immortalize the scene. Kennedy had also taken a photograph in 1905 that showed a proud hunter holding a dead whooping crane by its beak. The bird, its wings extended to show its 7-foot wingspan, was almost as tall as the man who had killed it. Kennedy had shown Allen the photograph and the painting. Allen later included both in his whooping crane monograph. When Allen asked Kennedy if the Gothenburg Gun Club would lend Audubon their bird for the captive-breeding experiment, he was delighted to do so.

The average lifespan for a whooping crane is thirty years. The Gothenburg crane had to have been at least fourteen years old when Allen found it. Despite its captive life, the crane was anything but tame. Allen watched as it chased the captive sandhills cranes, reclaiming a small portion of the sanctuary as its territory. The bird's aggressiveness was encouraging. Maybe it wasn't that old, after all. The caretakers at the sanctuary reported that the crane's behavior was ornery from day one, and the bird had never taken kindly to humans or any of its cage mates. They had given it the name Old Devil. A truck was sent for, and the bird was transferred to the Audubon Zoo in New Orleans, where it would join what all hoped would be its future mate.

—

In 1940, the rains in southern Louisiana flooded much of the area in Vermilion Parish. Thirteen remaining whooping cranes of the nonmigratory colony, which were living nearby, sought higher ground on the White Lake wetlands near Gueydan. When the water receded, only six cranes returned. A short time later, an injured whooping crane was brought to the Audubon Zoo in New Orleans. It had apparently been shot and was believed to have been one of the missing cranes. At the time Old Devil arrived, the Louisiana crane had been living in the zoo for eight years.

To get an idea of what he would be up against in the breeding of two captive whooping cranes, Allen began looking for stories of whooping cranes held in captivity and was surprised to find several. Most of the cranes were flightless due to injury. One such bird, turned pet, was owned by a Dr. Cook of Cottonplant, Missouri, and was purported to have lived for more than thirty years. On Jose Maria Negrete's estate in Mexico, the Mexican Hacienda El Molino, several whooping cranes had been kept as its main attraction. In England in the early 1900s, the Duchess of Bedford owned eleven different crane species, including whooping cranes. Allen also discovered that a female whooping crane had lived on Lord Lilford's English estate for almost forty years beginning in 1892. What perplexed Allen was how the North American bird had ended up in England in the first place. Lord Lilford's whooper had befriended another female crane, a Manchurian. The two nested together, with the female laying infertile eggs for many years.

More recently, in December 1946, when Allen was looking for whooping cranes among the salt domes along the Louisiana Gulf coast, he ran across an interesting character named McIlhenny, whom the locals called Mr. Ned. Mr. Ned's family had lived on one of the salt dome islands since the early 1800s. He told Allen that he had hunted whooping cranes as a child in the 1880s, when the species was abundant on the tallgrass prairies near the Calcasieu, Bayou Cannes, Mermentau, and Vermilion River bottoms. Mr. Ned had also captured several whoopers and raised them in captivity, reporting that they made excellent pets until they began eating his mother's chicks. By 1890, the Plume War had taken its toll on the bird population in the area. Thousands of egrets had disappeared almost overnight, and Mr. Ned had stopped hunting and established a bird sanctuary. He captured eight snowy egrets and raised them in captivity, and then released them during the fall migration. They returned the next spring, bringing with them several other migratory species. On that same salt dome now sits the manufacturing facility of the McIlhenny family business, the Tabasco Sauce Company, maker of the world-famous hot sauce. Today the sanctuary, Bird City, is still a migratory stopover for birds and one of the largest egret rookeries in the country.

In all the stories Allen had collected, including McIlhenny's, not one told of whooping cranes breeding in captivity. Notwithstanding, a concerted effort would be made.

The two whooping cranes were sent to the San Antonio Zoo to be "rested and conditioned" by aviculturist Fred Stark, who had had notable success in breeding and raising cranes.[4] After a thorough examination and pronouncement of good health by Stark, they were driven to their new home on the Aransas Refuge in Texas, where 150 acres of rich marshland had been selected. The habitat was ideal: narrow-leaf cattails for nest building, tall cattails in which to hide it from predators, and plenty of the cranes' favorite food (blue crab, mud shrimp, frogs, and snakes). As an added healthful bonus, yellow corn soaked in wheat germ oil would be put out each day.

The whooping cranes arrived in October 1948 and were released into the pen. Early on, before Old Devil's gender had been determined, refuge manager Bud Keefer began calling the bird Petunia. When it was revealed he was a male, Petunia became Pete. When it was discovered that the New Orleans crane was a female, its name was changed from Joe to Jo, short for Josephine. Old Pete and his younger mate Jo hit it off immediately. In December, the scientists were delighted to witness the new couple performing their species' mating dance. As spring approached, the dancing became more frequent. Allen, at home in Tavernier working on his monograph, was kept up to date by Keefer. By the end of April 1949, Keefer noticed a change in the cranes' behavior. Whenever the corn was distributed, both cranes usually rushed to the fence together. On April 27, Jo came alone to feed, and the next day, Pete arrived by himself. They continued to take turns feeding, then Keefer noticed a nest among the cattails. On April 30 he found one fawn-colored egg, and on May 1, another.

During the time of the Plume Wars, when certain bird species were declining, natural history museums and private collectors placed large bounties on bird eggs. When Allen was compiling information for his whooping crane monograph, he contacted many of these museums requesting data on whooping crane eggs. Most were happy to comply. As a result, Allen analyzed the size, shape, and color of more than sixty-two whooping crane eggs. Very little was known about their nests, and Allen was eager to study the structure and add the information to his monograph.

On May 4, Keefer entered the enclosure and set up his camera equipment at what he thought was a safe distance away. Pete was on the nest. Jo took on the role of defender, rushing at Keefer and jabbing his thumb hard enough to draw blood. She then grabbed his sleeve and pecked Keefer on the top of his head. Pete merely watched as his mate defended their nest. Keefer got the photos he wanted and retreated before Jo could inflict serious injury. Later, Keefer and Allen reflected on Pete's behavior. Was his nonaggression typical of a crane on a nest, or the behavior of a "senile" bird?[5]

As the anticipated date neared, like an eager grandfather, Allen packed his bags and headed for Texas. He arrived on May 12. By the time he got there, Keefer and his assistant had built an observation tower near the nest so a constant vigil could be kept. The nest was well hidden among tall cattails, its location evident only when Pete and Jo stood over it. While seated, the cranes and their nest were well camouflaged. Allen installed a 19.5× spotting scope, allowing him to see the cranes even through the vegetation. From the tower, Allen was careful to document the nuances of the expectant couple's activities, since this was most likely the first time a human had witnessed whooping crane nesting behavior. He began his observations at 5:00 a.m., not leaving his station until 7:30 each evening. His detailed drawings were published in 1952 in his monograph *The Whooping Crane: Research Report No. 3 of the National Audubon Society.*

One afternoon, Allen watched as Jo approached the nest for her turn at incubation. She raised her wings and poked aggressively toward something in the cattails. Pete, who had been fussing over the eggs and was eager to be relieved, froze. Jo sounded an alarm call and charged. Suddenly, a deer dashed away from the nesting site with Jo in pursuit. Avian intruders were a different matter. Both cranes became extremely aggressive, calling loudly when large birds flew over. Smaller birds species such as terns, gulls, willets, black skimmers, and plovers were an annoyance, but not worth the time and trouble to chase away. As time went on, Pete became more and more determined to keep out every single wading bird that approached. He flew into fits of rage when egrets, herons, or even the spoonbills came within 100 yards of the nest. He was relentless in his efforts to evict them, often chasing the birds from one end of the enclosure to the other. Allen described Pete as looking "dirty and ruffled" after running through the marsh.[6] As hatching time grew near, Pete's aggressiveness intensified. "Sometimes," Allen wrote, "after a series of exhausting chases, he walked back toward the nest dripping wet and black underneath from the splashing mud. He was a game old warrior and did the best he could."[7]

One day while Jo was sitting on the nest, Allen observed Pete in a panic, jumping to and fro, flapping his wings and lunging at something in the grass. Allen pulled out his binoculars and watched as Pete pranced around a cottonmouth whose head was in striking position. To Allen's amazement, Pete stabbed the snake to death, and then took his time swallowing the entire reptile. The caught snake offered a rare treat. Since blue crabs were not plentiful at the time, most of the cranes' food forays among the cattails turned up crayfish, aquatic insects, mollusks, and on occasion leopard frogs, which according to Allen's observation, "were stalked with wonderful patience."[8]

Overall, Allen was impressed with the crane couple's attentiveness to their future progeny. Despite all the intrusions, the cranes never displayed the slightest inclination to abandon the nest. In collecting whooping crane information, Allen discovered that there was one intruder that would cause a wild whooping crane to flee. George B. Sennett, an egg collector from Erie, Pennsylvania, told of the time he stalked the nest of a pair of whooping cranes. As he approached, the birds flew off and landed nearby. He dropped down and covered himself with grass, lying stock-still, waiting for them to return. The male returned after half an hour, while the female, more cautious, continued to watch the area where Sennett had hidden himself. Fifteen minutes later, she apparently felt safe and returned to the nest to incubate her eggs. Sennett was fewer than 25 yards away. He proudly writes in his report: "I could see her wink her eyes watching me and her mate constantly. Her eyes gleamed like fire. How anxious and how handsome, was ever a sight so grand. . . . The male stood on the ridge watching her closely for a few minutes, when feeling all was safe he calmly commenced to preen himself in grand style and shortly walked off away from me the proudest of birds. . . . I slowly arose, turned and gave her one barrel as she was rising from the nest and the next before she had gone six feet and dropped her in the water."[9] It was stories like this that stuck in Allen's craw and made their way into his publications, making him more determined than ever to keep these birds around.

The story of Jo and Pete had John Baker and USFWS inundated with letters from people requesting to visit the refuge and see the cranes during this time of incubation. The *Corpus Christi Caller-Times* released a story on May 8 announcing the project. Publicity over Jo and Pete was a double-edged sword. Audubon needed the continued support and sympathy for the protection of this disappearing species, but having hundreds of people vying for space on the observation tower while Allen and Keefer documented the event could not be allowed. Despite Jo and Pete's protectiveness of their nest, too much commotion could jeopardize the project. Had there been any possibility of releasing the cranes back into the wild, human contact would have to be avoided entirely. With several governmental agencies involved, a number of individuals claimed authority over the birds. John Baker, Bud Keefer, Albert M. Day, director of USFWS, and Clark Salyer II, refuge chief of the USFWS, often disagreed on who would be allowed to observe and take photographs.

Larry Walkinshaw, who had been part of the 1947 search, arrived on the refuge and was given permission to join Allen on the tower. Allen was pleased to have his fellow nest hunter assisting. Walkinshaw's knowledge of sandhill nesting behavior clued them in on what to expect.

Pete and Jo took turns incubating the eggs, relieving one another six times during the day. When the outside temperature increased, the amount of time they sat on the nests decreased. Pete's time on the nest during the day was longer than that of his mate, 70 percent to her 30. Since Allen was not able to observe them around the clock, he was unsure if Jo picked up the slack at night. Walkinshaw had documented similar behavior with the sandhills—the males spent 63 percent of the daylight hours on the nest. It was theorized that the male's duty at night was to stand guard while the female incubated.

For twenty-three days, the parents faithfully attended to their eggs. Then, on the twenty-fourth morning, Jo and Pete began acting strangely. Instead of the normal turning and rearranging of the eggs, the attending parent poked at the nest, impatiently standing and sitting every few minutes. Suddenly, both parents poked at the nest one last time, turned and walked toward the marsh, and for a brief moment, engaged in the mating dance. When Allen and Walkinshaw investigated, they found the eggs smashed. It was obvious they were infertile.

Disappointed, but not discouraged, Allen returned to Tavernier. With everything in place, they'd try again to breed the birds next year. On July 21, Allen received a call from the new refuge manager, Julian Howard. At 6:15 a.m., Russell Clapper, refuge clerk, had been awakened by an alarm call. When Clapper investigated, he found Jo in an agitated state. He woke Howard, and when both men searched the pen, they found Jo standing alone near a pool of water with Pete lying nearby on his back. The Old Devil had apparently died of natural causes.

To keep Jo in the maternal frame of mind, another male crane was needed, and Allen knew right where to find him, if, that is, the bird was a male. Allen was almost certain it was, judging by its size and demeanor when he first saw it. He was also certain that, although the crane had a bad wing, he was otherwise in great shape. This was the crane Allen and Wallmo had seen in February 1947 when they tried to encircle it and approach it. "We never had a chance! Old Crip calmly hiked up his bad wing and, head high, started off with those steady 23 inch strides that a whooping crane uses when he wants to run down a skittering blue crab or outwalk a couple of boy scouts, which is what we soon felt like."[10]

There was only one way to find out for sure if the bird was a male. That next spring, after consulting with Baker, Allen called Howard and gave him the go-ahead to round up a posse to search for the crane with the crippled wing. The bird was located, captured, and placed in the enclosure with Jo. All uncertainty about the newcomer's gender disappeared when Jo and her new young companion took to one another and almost immediately the prenuptial dancing began. Although his injured wing kept him from flying more than a few yards, he was otherwise a promising specimen.

In March 1950, the two cranes built their nest in their enclosure, and on April 22, Jo laid one egg. Not having exact data on the incubation period, although it was believed to be around thirty-five days, Howard and the rest of the refuge staff conducted a dawn-to-dusk watch.

Around the May 1, Allen had just returned to Tavernier from an investigatory mission in Mexico on behalf of John Baker and Audubon. Waiting for Allen was word from his fellow whooper snoopers, an unofficial club of refuge observers, that the hatching was near. He packed a fresh bag, threw it in the back of the station wagon, and rushed to Texas. This was one event he would not miss. He barely made it.

On the morning of May 23, Jo refused to leave the nest when Crip tried to relieve her around ten o'clock. This was the thirty-second day of incubation. "We scarcely slept that night. Early on the twenty-fifth we climbed the tower and waited impatiently for the light to increase enough so that we could see what had happened. From the behavior of both parents it seemed certain that the miracle we had been hoping for had actually taken place."[11]

Whooping crane fans across the country were waiting for news of the hatching. On May 8, *Life* magazine had published a story entitled "Whooping Crane No. 38?" Along with the article were four photos showing Jo and Crip engaging in the mating dance and one photo showing Jo standing next to the egg.[12]

Allen, Howard, and Clapper took turns watching through the telescope. The cranes were obviously attending to something. The tall grasses around the nest made it impossible to see. At 6:30 the next morning, Allen saw him. He wrote, "He was so tiny I could scarcely believe my eyes, but there he was, a rusty-colored, downy little thing, moving about on the nest on wobbly legs and being dutifully cared for by both parents. The miracle had happened! 'Rusty,' the first whooping crane ever hatched in captivity, had entered the world at an unknown hour during the night of May 24–25."[13]

Allen observed Rusty again on day three. He was out of the nest, running across Crip's feet, and stabbing at his father's bill, eager to be fed. Although the telescope offered them a close look at what was taking place 200 yards away, those watching longed to hear Rusty peeping as Crip fed him. Allen recorded the following scene: "Then Crip bent over with a soft and graceful tenderness, and finding the tiny mouth with the tip of his great bill, fed him. In all my experience with birds, this was the most wonderful, and the most moving scene I have ever witnessed."[14]

Allen's elation was short-lived. That afternoon, Rusty followed his parents through the grass. A short time later, turkey vultures circled overhead. A caracara flew in and landed. Allen was unable to see what was happening, so Howard rushed back to headquarters and returned with his rifle, which was equipped with a powerful telescopic sight; still they were unable to determine why scavengers were gathering. That evening,

Jo and Crip sent out alarm calls. Through the scope, Allen noticed raccoons running near the nest. A storm blew in that night, dropping the
temperature and bringing rain and heavy wind. At dusk the next day, Jo
and Crip were still at the nest. Later that morning, they wandered off.
There was no sign of little Rusty. When the two cranes were a quarter-
mile away, Allen, using a battery-operated field telephone, called Howard.
When the refuge manager arrived, they entered the enclosure and began
the search. Rusty had disappeared and was never found.

Despite the authorities' attempt to control who was and who wasn't
allowed on the observation tower the previous year, the event of 1950
brought 1,694 visitors from across the country and Canada to the refuge
to witness a once-in-a-lifetime occurrence. Reporters arrived, and soon,
photos appeared in national publications. When Rusty disappeared, radio stations across the country announced the loss. The story was picked
up internationally. One concerned citizen from Greenville, South Carolina, wrote a letter to the *News* editor imploring people not to forget the
big picture: "We read and exclaim about the little whooper, forget him
the minute he disappears and all the while the National Audubon Society
is struggling to provide sanctuaries in appropriate places where not only
whooping cranes but other birds, threatened with extinction, may have
some natural privacy and protection to make comebacks."[15]

In the six years after Rusty's disappearance, twenty-three whooping
crane chicks successfully migrated to Texas. Allen still had hopes for the
breeding couple and recommended that the experiment continue, but it
was evident where his focus lay: "It seems clear that we must make these
wild birds our chief concern. In their continuing ability to return each fall
with young lies the whooping crane's only real hope of survival."[16]

III

The Hunt, 1951–1963

Hold fast to dreams,
For if dreams die
Life is a broken-winged bird
That cannot fly.

Langston Hughes, "Dreams"

9

A Sudden Change of Plans

Allen was fully aware that taking the whooping crane species from near-extinction to a thriving population was not going to happen in his life-time, but Rusty's loss was a bitter blow. If the nesting ground could not be located and the captive-breeding program proved unsuccessful, seeing the whoopers disappear was something that Allen might indeed witness. The only thing to do was to keep trying. Back in Tavernier, he continued to work on his whooping crane monograph, compiling years of data, which included the cranes' history, details of the four failed searches, and information on their habitat and behavior he had gathered while in Texas, all the while keeping tabs on the two captive whooping cranes.

In preparation for another breeding season, Jo and Crip were confined to a smaller enclosure equipped with barbed wire and an electric fence to deter raccoons. The smaller habitat was intended to allow the parents to more easily defend their territory and protect their young. That spring Jo laid two eggs. Ensuing floods washed them away. All the same, there was every belief that these two healthy birds could indeed produce young under optimal conditions. What those optimal conditions were apparently led to disagreements.

In December, George Douglass, superintendent of the Audubon Zoo in New Orleans, sent a message to Julian Howard at the Aransas Refuge that he wanted his crane back. The bird he claimed belonged to the zoo was the male Crip and not Jo, since Jo, as he now believed, belonged to the zoo as well. The story of Jo and Crip had been big news, and updates appeared in newspapers across the country. An article in the *Racine Journal Times* on Wednesday, December 12, 1951, reported: "Tuesday, the Audubon zoo's superintendent, George Douglass, said he planned to come to

Texas and claim his bird—he says it's Crip, the male—and return with it to Louisiana Saturday." Julian Howard retorted, "Douglass couldn't get Jo or Crip without a fight."[1]

A lot had happened since 1945, when Douglass had agreed to participate in the captive breeding of whooping cranes in Texas. As it turned out, the tug-of-war that broke out over Jo and Crip might have been the result of a political situation between the States of Texas and Louisiana. The USFWS has jurisdiction over all migratory birds, but state authority is given decision-making rights over their management. Just a few weeks before Douglass sent word that he wanted his crane back, the State of Louisiana had planned to send several of their pelicans (the Louisiana state bird) to St. James's Park near Buckingham Palace in England. Texas acted first and supplied the birds instead. This could have been retaliation for losing the battle to tax Louisiana shrimp boats to keep them from harvesting shrimp off the Texas coast. Regardless, Douglass claimed that any future responsibility of breeding captive cranes should be left to him, having lost faith that the boys in Texas, namely Julian Howard, could get the job done. In turn, Howard claimed he lacked faith that Douglass could do any better. Hard feelings developed between the two. Newspapers reported the story of Jo and Crip's imposed separation. The story of American's favorite bird couple splitting up had citizens outraged. Finally, the USFWS intervened, and when Jo was taken to New Orleans, Crip accompanied her.

Two years passed. When the cranes made no attempt to nest in New Orleans, Baker tried to persuade Douglass to allow Audubon one more shot at breeding Jo and Crip in a natural habitat—the proposed location was the Rainey Wildlife Sanctuary, where whoopers had nested decades ago. After all, the sanctuary was located in Louisiana, which should have pleased Douglass, but before Douglass could respond, the USFWS vetoed that proposal and the birds remained in the zoo.

A year later, the controversy over who possessed jurisdiction over the two cranes lingered. John Baker sent Joe Hickey, with the Department of Wildlife Management at the University of Wisconsin, a letter agreeing with his decision not to engage in an "official discussion of this matter" while attending American Ornithologists' Union's next meeting.[2] Allen attended that meeting and urged the parties involved to quit their squabbling over the birds' ownership; such endeavors were a waste of time. He went on to reiterate that the salvation of the whooping crane would be in the hands of the wild flock instead of the captives.

For now, Jo and Crip lived contentedly in the Audubon Park Zoo in New Orleans, but made no attempt to build a nest until 1955, when Jo laid two eggs. As hatching time grew near, a television cameraman, on the scene to record the event, got too close to the nest and frightened Crip, who accidently crushed the eggs. A year later, Jo laid two more. Four days after hatching, one chick disappeared; it was believed to have been snatched by a rat or predatory bird. The second chick died of a fungus forty-five days later. Not to be defeated, Douglass arranged for a roof to be built on to the pen. For good measure, the rodent population at the zoo was exterminated. The next spring, Jo laid two more eggs. Both hatched without incident.

Jo produced thirteen hatchlings while in captivity: only four grew to adulthood, and none reproduced. She died in 1965, a victim of Hurricane Betsy, which swept through Louisiana that September. In January 1967, Crip was transferred to the San Antonio Zoo and paired with the resident whooping crane, Rosie, who had shunned all previous suitors. On July 9, 1967, they produced a female chick, Tex. Because of the young chick's health problems, Fred Stark was assigned the task of raising it, which he did—by hand in his living room, resulting in her imprinting on humans. She was eventually sent to Patuxent Wildlife Research Center near Baltimore. Once Tex reached maturity, she was paired with a male named Canus, but Tex did not recognize herself as a whooping crane. In 1975, George Archibald, an ornithologist and founder of the International Crane Foundation, brought Tex to Wisconsin, where he taught her the whooping crane mating dance, hoping to induce her into laying eggs, which he would then artificially inseminate. After several failed attempts, Tex produced her first chick, Gee Whiz, on June 1, 1981. A few weeks after Gee Whiz hatched, a raccoon killed Tex. Gee Whiz went on to produce seven offspring. His grandfather Crip, whom Allen first noticed on the Aransas refuge in 1946, lived to an estimated age of thirty-three. He died of natural causes on March 27, 1979.

—

In October 1950, while attending the American Ornithologists' Union Conference in Minneapolis, Allen had to cancel the remainder of his sessions and fly home. The shoulder and arm pain that had bothered him while on the Texas refuge spread to his neck and back, and this time the pain was unbearable. Once back in Tavernier, he made several inquiries and located a specialist in New York. The doctor diagnosed a slipped disk. Allen left the office wearing a plaster neck cast and returned to his project in Texas. On his first boat trip to count the cranes, the cast limited his mobility. Allen stripped it off and threw it overboard. A second opinion revealed that he was suffering from a rare condition called Strumpell-Marie disease; a rheumatoid spondylitis, which results in calcium deposits forming over the spine ligaments. This doctor painted a grim picture: For the next three to four years, Allen's pain would worsen until the entire spine had calcified, at which point the pain would lessen. He would be left with a misshapen back, placing pressure on the ribs, making breathing difficult. Working as a field researcher would be impossible. Allen's life as an ornithologist would be over.

His only option was to try an experimental treatment, which involved heavy doses of cortisone. His doctor warned him about potential serious side effects. After talking it over with Evelyn, they agreed that taking the cortisone was worth a shot. What choice did he have? Less than a month later, he was stalking ivory-billed woodpeckers with Jim Tanner in the Apalachicola swamps. Bob Allen had dodged another bullet.

—

With Audubon having no definite plans to organize another search for the whooping crane nesting site in Canada, Allen was getting antsy. He had always gleaned a certain satisfaction from writing. Compiling the whooping crane monograph was not only cathartic, it fired his determination. But he was a field researcher, and in the field is where he longed to be. He didn't have to wait long.

The American flamingo had all but disappeared from the United States. The remaining populations in the Bahamas and Cuba were now in trouble. At the first Audubon Board of Directors meeting in New York on January 30, 1905, Frank Chapman was instrumental in establishing the Wild Bird Protection Act in the Bahamas and creating the Andros Island Refuge. In 1933, Audubon's president, Dr. T. Gilbert Pearson, established the National Flamingo Refuge in Cuba. Word spread, and the last two flamingo nesting sites drew ornithologists and bird-watchers from around the globe. After World War II, the nests were deserted. It was evident by the condition of the habitat that the flamingos would not return. Their numbers in the Caribbean were plummeting. Allen's mission to Mexico the previous spring alerted Baker to the seriousness of the situation. Baker launched a full-scale investigation, assigning Bob Allen to the task, not in lieu of, but in addition to the Whooping Crane Project.

The first week of May 1951, Allen was in Mangrove Cay in the Bahamas, standing on the deck of a sturdy 21-foot sloop named the *Alert*. Alongside him was the boat's builder, owner, and skipper, Captain McPhee. A native of Andros, McPhee came highly recommended as a guide and boatman. Scurrying along the deck and preparing the boat to set sail was McPhee's wiry first mate and cook, Herby. Allen's destination was the flamingo refuge on the western side of South Andros. McPhee sailed them to Grassy Creek and acted as Allen's guide over the next several days. The trip was a disappointment. In the island's interior marshes, where fifty years before, Frank Chapman had seen flamingo flocks so large it appeared as if a scarlet blanket had been thrown over the marshes, Allen found a few deserted nests and fewer than a dozen "sad-looking" flamingos.[3] When they arrived back at Mangrove Cay around midnight, Allen asked McPhee if he was willing to sail out immediately for a quick trip to Nassau to check a site of interest. The captain didn't hesitate.

The pleasant sail back from Grassy Creek the day before found its way into Allen's notebook. Light, cheery notes told of sailing home and telling stories of his adventures once he returned. "It isn't that you are glad to see the trip over and done with, or anything like that," Allen wrote, "it is simply that you have another job under your belt, and you can look forward to relating all the fantastic things that happened to you, and to getting cleared away for the next one."[4] And the next one was soon to follow.

The day was May 13.

Allen was an experienced boatman, having navigated a freighter around the world with the Merchant Marine and, later, earning his Third Mate License during World War II. His exuberance might have led to a false sense of security, but in the back of his mind, he was well aware of how fickle the sea could be. You took every day on the water as it came. They were to sail to Nassau and return the next day.

By midmorning, Captain McPhee had maneuvered the *Alert* over the Mangrove Cay shallows and through the barrier reef. As they crossed over the Tongue of the Ocean, the water changed from a glistening aqua to a deep indigo, with the ocean floor instantly dropping more than a mile. The first crack of thunder brought their attention to the few gray puffs forming above the western horizon. Then, like a giant amoeba, the clouds grew and spread in all directions. The storm, miles away, was no real concern. They were sailing east, leaving the bad weather behind them.

Around four that afternoon, their joviality gave away to concern as the wind changed, shifting direction rapidly. Within minutes, a drenching squall spattered the deck and slapped bare skin like steel spikes. With the rain came a deep chill. Then, as suddenly as it appeared, the heavy cloud traveled on. The respite was short. For the next four hours, one squall followed another. By this time, the sloop was racing across the water's surface like a contender in a regatta. Seabirds dove from the sky and flew across the surface. McPhee kept his eyes on the horizon and seemed to navigate by instinct.

By nightfall, the storm worsened. Herby became agitated, and McPhee sent him below to make tea. "Ah'll make you tea aw right, but it's strong coffee for Herby, strong an' bittah," he called as he descended to the galley.[5] McPhee told Allen it was time to check their course. Allen was shocked to see a wooden box loosely tied down to the helm with nothing more than string. Inside was the compass. McPhee aligned the instrument and held it in place with his feet, announcing they should be well over the Tongue before morning.

Herby served tea and johnnycakes, then clambered back across the deck, pulling the sheets and trimming the sails as McPhee shouted instructions in a language Allen didn't understand. With McPhee at the tiller and Herby at the sails, the two men settled into an unrelenting routine. The best thing for Allen to do was stay out of the way. He went below and tried to steady himself in his bunk. The rocking threw him hard against the planking. He crawled back to deck and anchored his feet in the hatchway, preparing to wait out the storm.

After what felt like hours, Allen, cold and drenched and with muscles at the point of snapping, felt fatigue overcome him. He stole a glance at his watch; it was only midnight. The storm unleashed another violent gust, and Allen fought to keep from being washed overboard. Waves exploded and hammered the deck with such fury that it felt as if the sloop would rip apart. It wasn't until Allen looked over and saw that McPhee's stern confidence had eroded, uncovering a look of fright, that Allen became concerned for the first time. McPhee continued to shout instructions to Herby. Allen understood only one word, "hurricane." Herby let go of his native tongue and let spill a litany of "Sabe us, oh Lord above! God in Heaben, sabe us, sabe us!"[6] McPhee ordered Allen and the first mate to lash themselves to the boat.

The first waterspout sliced along the starboard side, then came a second, followed by another and another. Each seemed more powerful than the one before. When Herby's prayers failed to dissipate the storm, he turned to singing hymns, which at first had a hypnotic effect on Allen and McPhee. Suddenly, McPhee broke into a maniacal laughter, sounding more like the voice of Davy Jones than the jolly captain who had sailed them out of Mangrove Cay.

Herby's recital continued, his voice joining the horrendous screams of the hurricane. Then he broke into Tennyson's *Crossing the Bar* and sang: "Sunset and evening star, And one clear call for me! And may there be no moaning of the bar, When I put out to sea."[7] With that verse, Allen looked mortality straight in the face and recognized the irony in his predicament: "What a foolish, unprepared way to die, I thought, out here in these strange waters, in a boat with nothing but a torn patched-up sail, in this day of efficient marine engines. With two men I scarcely know, and who probably don't care if I die or not. And, worst of all, in an unpredicted hurricane, at the wrong time of year. Who ever heard of a hurricane in mid-May?"[8]

A few hours later, a faint light shone on the horizon, but the new day brought little hope. The storm had gained momentum. McPhee was forced to drop the sails and leave the *Alert* to fight the battle herself. The halyards slapped against the mast, threatening to snap it in two. The sailboat rolled from side to side as the wave crests lifted her high above the surface and then mercilessly dropped her into the troughs. McPhee's eyes grew with each approaching wave. Waterspouts continued across the sea and alongside the vessel. Herby stopped singing.

By midmorning, the wind had let up a fraction. McPhee shouted at Herby to raise the reefed mainsail and turn the sloop to catch the wind on its starboard side. Suddenly, a wave rose like a fist and struck the old wooden deck, causing the boom to jibe. The mainsail ripped and the boom hung on its topping lift. It took all three men to haul the mainsail back aboard. As McPhee attempted to secure the mainsail, he lost his balance, barely catching himself before slipping overboard. Once the mainsail was righted, McPhee took his best shot at navigation and pointed his sloop toward High Cay, the closest recognizable land. He sent Herby up the mast for a better look. Herby shouted back, "No lan', nuthin', but watah!"[9] McPhee sent him back up every few minutes and around eleven o'clock, Herby shouted, "High Cay, off to starboard!" Allen described the moment as "being born again."[10] McPhee, however, grew more intense. Allen turned and caught sight of churning water breaking in front of the island and knew what lay ahead.

The barrier reef, jagged and sharp, surrounded the island like a cordon of razor wire. Sailing slowly on a calm sea would give the captain a chance to search for the few breaks in the reef; in a hurricane it was like riding a locomotive into the teeth of a meat grinder. If McPhee missed the inlet, the *Alert* would splinter in seconds, and no one would live to tell about it. Herby shimmied up to the top of the mast, telling Allen not to worry, that he knew the location of a narrow channel, "like the pa'm of my han.'"[11] McPhee shook his head and shouted for Herby to save his cockiness for another fool, reminding Herby that his uncle had lost his schooner, his entire crew, and his life while crossing this very reef. Herby fell silent, and Allen's momentary relief went south.

As the sloop raced toward the reef, Allen scanned the water for any sign of a break in the black underwater ridge. Herby hung from the mast, waving his arms and pointing to starboard side and then to port. McPhee, cursing under his breath, watched Herby's every move. He jibed the *Alert* closer to what Allen feared was impending doom. Sea spray doused the deck as the sloop fell and rose with the swells. Suddenly, the vessel sliced through the reef channel like a jittery thread slipping through a needle's eye. The water near the shore was calm, and Herby dropped anchor. The boat swayed gently for the first time in three days, rocking the men to sleep.

The next day, Allen searched the site on Nassau, but found no flamingos. Captain McPhee sailed them back to Mangrove Cay. Allen bid McPhee a fond farewell, graciously thanking the captain for his heroic effects in bringing the sloop into safe harbor. Herby hastily said his good-byes, leapt from the boat, and disappeared into the crowded streets. McPhee cocked his head in Herby's direction and said, "Rum, th' cheapes' an' th' mostes' he can drink."[12] Allen grabbed his bags and went ashore, determined to follow in Herby's wake.

That Allen charged ahead with his plans after almost dying in a hurricane was no surprise. He contacted Elgin Forsyth, Andros's commissioner, who was in charge of flamingo protection in the Bahamas. Forsyth had been documenting the dwindling colony since the early 1920s. There was no better person to assist Allen in exploring the Marls on Great Abaco Island, and Forsyth was delighted to accompany the ornithologist. It was reported that the brunt of the hurricane had struck the island. If flamingos resided there, hopefully they had been spared.

To keep a tight rein on their purse strings, Allen and Forsyth booked passage on a mail boat. The two men loaded up on groceries and boarded the overcrowded vessel. The 50 miles across the New Providence Channel would have put them at their destination sometime the next afternoon. Early the next morning, the captain made an unscheduled stop off the coast of Hopetown. He disembarked from the vessel, leaving the crew and passengers on board. Allen had picked up enough Spanish to realize the village was the captain's hometown, and a visit had been long overdue.

The mail boat did not pull into Marsh Harbour until after sunset on the second day. Once there, Allen chartered another sloop, the *Ramona R*. He gathered a few supplies with the intention of leaving the next morning. When Allen and Forsyth arrived on the dock bright and early, the *Ramona R*'s owner, Rodney Roberts, was nowhere to be found. After asking around, Allen located Roberts's son, Rodney Jr., who said his father was attending to matters at his farm and should be along shortly. He invited the two men to his home to rest in a spare bedroom; this was Wednesday, June 27. Roberts didn't show until Saturday morning. After much fuss over the final preparations, they finally set sail that evening with Rodney Jr. aboard. Their first stop was to fetch the local flamingo expert Cameron "Happy" Montour. He was waiting with a small unseaworthy-looking boat. Montour paddled across to the *Ramona R*, and as he neared the vessel, he began shouting for a rope; his flamingo boat was taking on water and sinking fast. They hauled the guide and boat aboard and continued on. Allen wondered what he'd gotten himself into.

Roberts anchored the sloop at Green Turtle Cay that night. In the morning, they'd set out for the Marls. Heavy seas kept them in dock, and it was four days before Allen and Forsyth finally reached the place where their search was to begin. Montour directed the *Ramona R* through the channels, meandering around the cays to locations where he promised flamingos were nesting. It wasn't long before the sloop grounded on a sandbar during low tide, which is where they sat until the next morning. They finally reached Mastic Point Cay on July 4.

That morning, Montour stood on the deck of the *Ramona R* and made his grand announcement: it was time to launch his famous flamingo boat and sail to the island! Allen and Forsyth considered the pronouncement and chose to use the *Ramona R*'s dinghy to take them ashore instead. Rodney Jr. joined them. Montour paddled his launch in their wake. Deciding they could cover more ground on foot, Allen and crew beached the dinghy and explored the shoreline. Periodically, they caught sight of Montour, struggling in the shallows, stopping to bail every few minutes. At the end of the day, Allen had not located any flamingos, and neither had Montour.

The next day, however, Montour was successful in finding a nesting site. The nineteen mounds were overgrown and abandoned. Five flamingos flew over, heading southwest. Over dinner of fresh-caught snapper, Allen and Forsyth debated with their guide as to where they would search the next morning. Rodney Jr., listening to their exchange, merely shook his head in dismay. When the sun rose, Montour paddled his dinghy alone toward the Cherokee River. Allen and Forsyth went in the opposite direction. It didn't take them long to discover a small flamingo colony of about two dozen nests. Montour found nothing. They returned to Andros, the expedition having been a complete fiasco. Allen thanked Forsyth and the Roberts and left for the Dominican Republic.

10

A Different Kind of Revolution

Allen's search eventually led him to the small town of Monte Cristi. On July 30, Allen ran into two American entomologists who were working for United Fruit Company. The scientists were fairly knowledgeable on the subject of local birds and directed Allen to the town of Puerto Libertador, where it was rumored that the fruit company's dock manager, George Austin, knew where to find flamingos. Allen checked into a guesthouse. The next morning, he was trekking along Estero Balsa, looking for a sand-bar where Austin claimed he had seen flamingos. Finding none, Allen returned to town, taking a path that led along a series of local huts. Sitting next to one was a suspicious-looking dog that seemed riveted by the stranger in his neighborhood. As Allen approached, he addressed the dog with a friendly, "Nice doggy" greeting, which threw the mutt into a rage.[1] Before Allen could retreat, the dog sank his teeth into Allen's right calf, then, just as quickly, turned and disappeared through the brush.

Allen hitchhiked a ride to the company hospital. It was too early in the morning for doctors to be on duty. An attendant who spoke no English examined Allen's wound. Despite shouting the word *perro* and mimicking a vicious bark, Allen wasn't able get his point across. He found the word for "rabies" in his language dictionary. The attendant merely shrugged. He was not a doctor. All he could do was clean and dress the wound.

Allen took a chance the dog was not rabid and hired a skiff to take him to Rio Tapion. At the mouth of the river where it empties into the bay, debris gets caught and forms a natural barrier, trapping fish in the channels—a perfect place to find birds. As the boat's captain and guide, Alejo, puttered along the red mangroves crowding the shore, an array of wading birds showed themselves: a roseate spoonbill flew by, then a yellow-billed egret, a green heron, several blue herons, tricolored herons, white egrets, and a few long-billed white ibises. Alejo had not paid attention to the outgoing tide, and before long had the skiff grounded in the mud. Alejo's assistant handed out poles and they continued on, poling their way through the mangroves. Suddenly, Alejo pointed to an open marsh flat. A few yards away, mixed in an assembly of wading birds, were at least sixty flamingos. The men left the boat and trudged through the mud for a closer look. As Allen counted and made note of his discovery in his journal, he was astonished when Alejo said that these flamingos did not nest in the Rio Tapion. They had most likely come over from Florida. Allen did not correct his guide, for the ornithologist did not have the heart to tell Alejo that there were no more flamingos nesting in Florida.

Allen moved south to Barahona. His ultimate destination was the town of Jimani near Lago de Enriquillo, on the Haiti/Dominican Republic border. No public transportation went to Jimani, and the only ride Allen found was in a mail car. He and two other passengers climbed in for the 60-mile ride. At each mail stop, more passengers joined them. Eight people were now crammed together in the car. The windows, opened for ventilation, brought in the dust. Then the carrier made another stop. Waiting there was a large woman with an armload of groceries and a small dog. Certain the mail carrier would turn her away, Allen was surprised when the woman yanked the door handle and, without asking, took her seat on Allen's lap. She dropped a load of melons on his feet. Unlike the local cur he'd encountered earlier, who by this time Allen was sure was not rabid, this woman's pooch took a liking to the gringo. For the next hour, Allen rode along, arms pinned at his side, unable to defend himself against the face-licking dog.

When Allen arrived at the Haitian border, he met up with Cesar Alberto Meyreles, the provincial governor, and Dr. Santiago Lopez, a local justice. They insisted on accompanying him to Lago de Enriquillo on his hunt. Lago de Enriquillo, the largest lake in the Caribbean, covers more than 102 square miles and lies 129 feet below sea level. Because of fluctuation between heavy rain and high evaporation, the lake's salinity can vary and, at times, can be triple that of the ocean. Thick, tangled brush woven with prickly cactus grew to the shoreline in several areas. The only way through the jungle was to use a machete. Meyreles talked while he hacked, telling Allen that flamingos were frequently seen in the area, but because of the new roads and villages along the shoreline, he was certain the birds no longer nested there. Meyreles explained that wading birds and songbirds were protected by law, but the government had no agency to enforce it.

Allen was both encouraged and disappointed. He counted more than fifty flamingos feeding in several sites along the shore, but sitting back in reeds, like an old neighborhood gone to seed, were dozens of abandoned nests. The next morning, Allen explored the shore of Lago del Limon, finding even more flamingos, but no nests. Once back in Cuidad Trujillo, Allen went directly to the director general in charge of tourism and explained how the country's economy would benefit if the flamingo population were allowed to prosper. The general was sympathetic, but he was unable to offer assistance. Allen then made his plea to the authorities in Haiti, who explained that as long as the people were poor and hungry, nothing could be done to protect the flamingos. Frustrated, Allen left for Cuba.

In August, Allen arrived in Manzanillo, a coastal town in southeastern Cuba. An old friend to whom Allen referred simply as Arturo had arranged for Allen to cruise up the Rio Cauto on a Navy vessel to search the Cauto Delta. The commanding officer was rumored to be a fan of flamingos and was happy to have an American ornithologist as a guest aboard his boat. When Allen walked into *el capitan*'s office, the man surreptitiously shoved a glass into his desk drawer and began pounding away on his typewriter. When he realized who his visitors were, he greeted them with a welcoming smile and withdrew a bottle and three glasses from his drawer; the visit called for a toast. After the appropriate pleasantries were exchanged, Allen got down to business.

El capitan, ecstatic about their upcoming adventure, was also distraught over a horrible accident: his engineer, the one who operated the crank for the engine, had broken his arm. "Very painful! It was unspeakable. In fact, let's not speak of it again. There are other boats, many other boats. In good time we will find another boat, perhaps a fishing boat, and possibly a fisherman who knows the river well."[2] He suggested they celebrate the good prospects that were surely on the horizon with another toast. Allen complied and relaxed, knowing that his American ways were too *rapidio* in this laid-back country. Then *el capitan* grew pensive; he'd just remembered another difficulty that might forestall their departure.

This one was truly unspeakable. He pulled out a message he'd received that morning—top secret! Then he began to rant, waving the paper in the air. He and Arturo broke into rapid Spanish. When their conversation ended, Arturo grabbed Allen's arm and dragged him from the office. "Never fear, we will talk of plans," he whispered.[3] Allen stole a look toward the *el capitan's* office. As the door swung shut, Allen saw that the rum bottle had made another appearance.

Once Arturo was sure he could speak in private, he spilled out the story, vacillating between English and Spanish. The Navy had been alerted to the possibility of rebels trafficking contraband arms onto the shore near Niquero. It was *el capitan's* assignment to apprehend those responsible for they were surely "Communists seeking to start a revolution."[4] Allen was well aware of rumors of Communists infiltrating the country. When Arturo told Allen that they must be very careful from now on, Allen asked what the *contrabanders* had to do with looking for flamingos. Arturo was aghast. "I told him [*el capitan*] we could not go up the river after flamingos without him, and it is obvious that he cannot go with us until these bandits of *contrabanders* are caught, so we must go with him, of course. It is only being polite to do so. It would have been inconsiderate if we did not offer to help him with the *contrabanders*, when he, *el capitan* himself, has offered to help us with flamingos!"[5] Although Allen could poke holes in Arturo's reasoning, he knew it would have been a waste of time. He was eager to get started and the idea of looking for another guide and boat would only postpone the trip. Besides, Arturo, who was a shoe salesman by profession, was eager for an adventure. Reluctantly, Allen agreed to assist in the hunt for gunrunners. Arturo informed the Americano that there was no hurry: "*manana* will be time enough."[6]

Allen checked into the El Gran Hotel Inglaterra. The next morning, he held a council of war in the open-air lobby. Arturo, his brother Carlos, an engineer on a trading vessel, a friend Aurencio, who owned an old American Ford, *el capitan*, and Allen finalized the plans. Aurencio would drive them to Niquero, some 35 miles away, rent a boat and begin the flamingo/contraband hunt. More amused than apprehensive, Allen described the undertaking: "A party of *viajeros* setting out from a small Cuban town and heading off along a dusty road that can lead nowhere but a dead end down the coast, is evidently quite an event."[7]

Aurencio conducted business along the way, stopping at five sugar-mill villages. As they approached each village, Aurencio announced their arrival with blasts on the horn. The operator of the mill would emerge from his office, and Aurencio would joyously introduce his two distinguished travelers, the naval officer and the Americano bird man. Every introduction called for a celebratory toast. Several hours later, Aurencio swerved into the small town of Niquero. Too late to find a boat, they checked into the Hotel Sixto, the town's social center and meeting place. Present at the bar were another sugar-mill operator, the chief of police, a sailor stationed at the coastal town's office, the mayor, and several other important men. *El capitan* began his long story of top-secret assignments to capture *contrabanders*, and, of course, everyone celebrated his good fortune with multiple toasts. Just as Allen was prepared to depart for his room, Arturo's father-in-law arrived and invited the entire group to supper at his plantation. Everyone piled into the Ford and took off down a muddy road. When they arrived, Arturo's mother-in-law greeted her surprise guests (now filthy from pulling the car from a mud hole) with smiles and words of welcome.

Once back at the hotel, Allen set his alarm for 3:30 and fell into bed. A 4:00 a.m. rendezvous with the captain of the fishing vessel, who had been hired to take them into the Golfo de Guacanayabo, was set. After much rousing by Allen, he rounded up his group. Nursing their hangovers with strong black coffee, they reluctantly joined Allen and boarded the boat to set sail. When it was bright enough to see across the water, the sailor pulled out his .45 and grabbed his binoculars. Allen bit back a smile when he noticed the man's binoculars were opera glasses. Then one of the fishermen spotted something in the distance, and everyone began waving their arms and yelling. Allen pulled out his navy-issued binoculars and disappointed his fellow mates by telling them the object of interest was merely a dead tree stuck on the mud bank. Feeling like a killjoy, Allen admitted that the tree's branches did look like the masts on a schooner. He was surprised when no one believed him. The sailor aimed his pistol as the captain threw down the throttle. With water slashing the stern and dousing everyone aboard, the captain directed the boat toward the target, swerving just in time to prevent ramming the tree.

Finding nothing along the shore, *el capitan* ordered the boat to be taken into the open gulf. Rough seas kicked up. The rocking and rolling motion exacerbated the effects of the previous night's drinking. He then ordered the boat back to dock with the declaration, "In weather like this no *contrabander* would dare come near to the coast."[8] That settled, the military maneuvers were over. Allen, suspecting *el capitan* had another drunken night planned, ordered Arturo to find another car to take them back to the fishing village. The next morning, they would hopefully find another vessel and a captain who did not have his own agenda regarding booze.

Once back in Niquero, Allen's plans changed again. There were no boats available for hire. Instead, he and Arturo took a train from Manzanillo to Bayamo and then a car to Puerto Padre on the north side of the island to the National Flamingo Refuge. Arturo put together another crew, which consisted of his Uncle Antonio, a fisherman, and a "shifty-eyed and evil-looking" guide named Nicolas.[9] Allen's target area was Bahia Malajeta near the village of Jeibara. They arrived as the sun was descending over the water and arranged to spend the night in thatch huts outfitted with sleeping hammocks made from gunnysacks. Shortly, a man walked up and offered to be their group's cook. He said he would take no money, just two bottles of *aguardiente* (a brandy-type liquor) a day, one as the sun rose and one as the sun set. Arturo shrugged his shoulders at the offer, and Allen hired the guy. That evening meal of beans, rice, canned meat, fried bananas, and strong coffee was one of the best Allen had eaten since his arrival.

Having slept well after the much-needed meal, Allen rose early the next morning and visited with the locals. They told him of a *salina* where flamingos had nested in years past. Allen and his group drove to the area, set up camp, and launched the motorboat. As they cruised down the waterway, Allen spotted three boys who proclaimed to be charcoal burners, and asked them about flamingos in the area. "*Muchos flamencos*," they responded. Allen looked around.[10] The boys said the flamingos were no more, and went on to tell of an incident that had occurred two months before. Several flamingos flew in and prepared to nest when hunters came and shot the birds. Since then, none had returned. Dejected, Allen directed the boat back to camp. After a while, a group of men claiming to be *caiman* (crocodile) hunters pulled up to shore. In the bow of their vessel was a dead flamingo. Since they had had no luck finding a *caiman*, they shot the flamingo instead. Taking advantage of Allen's campfire, the men skinned the bird, cleaned it, and threw it in a pot of boiling water for their evening meal. A pack of dogs fought over the dead bird's head and feet. Allen witnessed firsthand the government's inability to enforce its law against killing the flamingos.

The following day was also a disappointment: their guide and flamingo expert, Nicolas, had gotten them lost on the way to Laguna de Amarillo. Arturo and Allen took control of their expedition and located the lagoon themselves. There were no flamingos anywhere around. Realizing they could do better on their own, Allen and Arturo left the others behind and motored up to check out another location. The only flamingos they found were the remains of another flamingo feast; a head and skin, mixed with other refuse, scattered on the beach.

Thinking matters could not get any worse, Allen returned to camp and found their driver and cook passed out on the beach; most of their food was gone, along with the *aguardiente*. Since Nicolas was the only one conscious, he became the recipient of Arturo's anger. The best thing to do was to break camp and drive back to Senor Felipe's beach huts to spend the night. Feeling sorry for the men and their foiled mission, Felipe's wife cooked them a comforting meal, and they retired for the night.

Around midnight, harrowing screams jolted Allen awake. Standing next to him, Arturo was fighting to dislodge a knife from Nicolas's upraised hand. Felipe rushed in with a lantern just as Arturo subdued his assailant by the throat. They tied up the flamingo expert and sat him in the corner of one of the huts. The now-sober cook made coffee. As Allen sat around the campfire, the entire adventure of the last couple of days seemed like some tale straight from a Hollywood movie set. "And there we sat, for all the world, as I thought to myself, like a company of good-natured pirates, fighting off the mosquitoes, gulping our coffee, and harking to the cook as he recited patriotic Cuban poetry."[11] The sun rose, the men were moved to tears by the cook's recital, and Allen began a new day of nest hunting.

At the end of the summer of 1951, it was evident that the flamingo population was in more trouble than Audubon realized. If the birds could not find a safe haven in which to nest, it was only a matter of time before they, too, disappeared. Allen returned to Tavernier more determined than ever to reason with the Cuban government. If Frank Chapman could persuade the government to set aside bird sanctuaries more than forty-five years ago, Allen and Audubon could see to it that the birds that lived there would bring in enough revenue to keep them from becoming a food source for the country's hungry.

Allen returned to Cuba in March 1952 to search the Cauto Delta, the location of the previous year's aborted expedition. Arturo met him at the El Gran Hotel Inglaterra. With a new guide, Julio, and a boatman named Rafael, they set out for the Rio Cauto. On the first morning, Julio took them into one of the many-fingered channels where he was certain flamingos had nested at one time. When the waterway became too shallow to pole the boat, they launched a canoe, and paddled farther up into a narrow mangrove-studded creek. When the canoe scraped bottom, Julio and Rafael volunteered to muck around through the mud and scout the area. Julio proclaimed that the flamingos must be just around the next bend. An hour later, the two men returned, looking embarrassed. Allen and Arturo exchanged glances; it was evident that their guide and his captain had gotten lost. Julio threw a few pink feathers in the boat, hoping to mollify the situation and pull the wool over Allen's eyes. No doubt Julio was unaware that the bird man in their company had conducted an extensive study on the roseate spoonbills. Before Julio could proclaim his discovery of flamingo feathers, Allen pointed to the guide's prize and said, "Sevilla!" the local term for spoonbills.[12] Julio shrugged and turned away.

The next day proved more fruitful. Allen and his *compadres* motored up the Cayo Norte, where Allen counted 610 flamingos feeding along the banks.

There were no nesting sites anywhere.

Allen scoured the rest of the delta and finally told Julio it was time to return to town. When they pulled into the harbor, a stranger rushed up to Arturo, carrying on like a madman. When the shocked Arturo finally found his voice, he informed Allen: "There ees a revolution! Batista has seized the government in Habana an' the president has fled! We mus' get to town at once an' see wha's cooking!"[13]

Crowds had gathered in the plaza. Two men, one in support of the government and one sympathetic to the rebels, were standing on each side of a bandstand, postulating their opinions to their prospective listeners. As the men talked, the crowds shouted in response. Pamphlets were distributed, urging citizens to take a stand for their political party. Allen and Arturo watched as the plaza filled with anxious, angry Cubans. Then the clumping sound of horses' hooves silenced the crowd. Everyone turned toward the main street leading into the middle of town. The Army was riding in, soldiers slashing sabers above the heads of Cubans along the street, others with guns drawn and pointed at the crowd. People flew into a panic, dispersing in every direction. Screams and curses turned to a deafening roar as the mob clambered over one another to escape. Arturo grabbed Allen's arm, and they disappeared onto a back street.

Word spread that Batista's men had taken over the Rancho Boyeros Airport in Havana, and all flights out of the country were canceled. Businesses shut down, and except for the Army, the streets were deserted. Only the bars were open, which is where Allen and Arturo had taken shelter until it was safe to return to the hotel. A few hours later when Allen walked into the hotel lobby, the manager informed him that the police had inquired about Allen's presence in the country. In the morning, Arturo urged Allen to leave the hotel and take refuge at Arturo's father-in-law's sugar plantation, for surely the police were suspicious of Allen's motives. Allen had doubted the seriousness of the situation. After spending much of that evening listening to reports of what was happening in the country, he changed his mind and agreed to leave the city with his guide. Allen was unable to contact Evelyn. For several days he waited in the small village near the plantation. The villagers went about their usual business, but there was unspoken concern on everyone's faces. Finally, when Allen got word that the airport had reopened, he persuaded Arturo to drive him back to Havana, where he caught the first flight to Miami. Once again his flamingo mission was cut short. Adding to his disappointment was a growing concern over the fate of his Cuban friends and the country, which he had come to enjoy despite its idiosyncrasies.

—

In the days that followed, Allen stayed attuned to the situation in Canada. Bob Smith and other waterfowl biologists working in Canada continued to fly over Allen's recommended search area. Smith sent Allen a letter on July 1, 1952: "Two of the elusive great white birds found north of Great Slave Lake—just north of Deep Bay."[14] This was same area Allen and Smith had flown over in 1947 and 1948. Encouraged, the USFWS reported to the *New York Herald-Tribune* on August 6. "This is the strongest clue we've had to the nesting ground."[15] A few weeks later, Smith made another flight over Great Slave Lake. The two birds he'd seen in July were not around. All Audubon needed was a definite nest sighting, and another whooping crane hunt would be off and running. Smith advised Audubon to wait before sending out a ground crew to investigate. There was no place to land a plane, and a ground search would be too arduous.

⁓

In February 1953, Baker was preparing a trip to Washington, where the policymakers were gathering for a whooping crane powwow. Allen sent his charts showing Baker the most logical area and cautioning of the difficulty in landing a floatplane. A ground search of the area, even with packhorses, would require days if not weeks. If nothing conclusive came from the meeting, Allen had planned to return to Inagua the first week in March to continue his flamingo investigation.

Allen also stayed in touch with Bob Smith, a character the Allen family delighted in hearing from, having spent so much time with the waterfowl pilot while on Flotten Lake. Family reports often found their way into Allen's letters to Smith. Bobby was faring well and enrolled at the University of Florida, studying architecture. When asked why he hadn't planned to follow in his dad's footsteps, his response was, "Do you think I'm crazy!"[16] Alice had just turned fifteen and was already proclaiming herself a future career woman. The following year, she finished high school ahead of her classmates and joined her brother as a student at University of Florida. Evelyn, as was now customary, had a long waiting list of music students.

That summer when Allen returned from the Bahamas, waiting for him in Tavernier were the maps he'd sent Baker. Nothing had been decided, although Baker was lining up a potential floatplane along with helicopters and pilots in case he got the go-ahead. He hoped to know one way or another by the third week of July. Allen was making plans to return to the Yucatan with a copy of a promotional flamingo film, provided by Audubon, as ammunition to persuade the Mexican government to establish flamingo refuges. Baker, feeling like this summer would prove fruitful for another crane hunt, urged Allen to wait. Bob Smith was scouting the prime area again and would hopefully return with good news.

None came.

Smith had flown over Great Slave Lake again. He saw nothing. However, a Canadian Army helicopter pilot reported what he believed to be a whooping crane flying close to the area. Then in October, Allen received a telegram from W. Winston Mair, chief of the Canadian Wildlife Service: "Eight whoopers reliably reported south bound along Slave River October 6." After nine years, Allen's prime search area looked more promising than ever. That winter the flock arrived in Texas with three new chicks. The whooping cranes were obviously breeding somewhere.

—

Allen had unfinished business in Cuba. With the revolution slipping into a safe lull, he returned the following spring to resume his search near Cayo Romano along the country's north coast. When he arrived, Allen was put in contact with a man named Erasmo, a taxi driver from Havana, who knew of an active flamingo colony near his home off Mojarra Island. Erasmo had seen them himself just a year ago. He was ready and waiting with a boat and had Allen on the water in no time. As they paddled through another all-familiar mangrove swamp, Allen's elation began to ebb. If the colony was as large as Erasmo had claimed, there should have been evidence of the birds' presence along the way. When they entered the clearing, flamingo nest mounds rose high above the water's surface, hundreds of them.

All abandoned: the deserted mounds stood sentinel like tombstones of the departed.

The men were crestfallen; Erasmo, in tears. The last time he was here, the swamp was ablaze in color, thousands of birds, their scarlet feathers shockingly bright against the blue sky. In the humidity and heat, a shiver went up Allen's spine. Stretched across the water were fishing nets attached to stakes. The boys who were on the boat with them knew the story behind the nets. Poachers used the setup to capture the fledglings before they learned to fly. Frightened from their nests, the birds scampered directly into the webbing and became tangled. Some died on the nets as they fought to free themselves; others continued to struggle until they were plucked off and killed. Hundreds were taken each year.

Horrified, Allen asked how they knew. The boys responded, now embarrassed, that they had been part of the harvest. The young birds were sold for food. Seeing Allen's alarm, they proclaimed they never worried about their flamingo harvests, since there were always more the next year. Allen slumped against a nesting mound, heartsick for the birds as well as the people who were forced to rely on their endangered wildlife for food.

"It's too bad that the flamingos can't stage their own revolution,"[17] Allen said. He wondered where the flamingos would go now to lay their eggs, after nesting here for eons.

The situation in the Dominican Republic and Cuba had proven disastrous for the flamingos, but things were much more hopeful on another island in the Bahamas. And it was only fitting that after so many well-meaning but incompetent and opportunistic guides whose concern for the flamingo was questionable, the man who now carried Allen across Lake Rosa on the island of Inagua would become his lifelong friend.

The industrious Sammy Nixon had crafted his skiff from an old boat he'd found washed ashore during World War II. He knew the flamingos, he knew where they had once nested, and he, like Allen, was passionate about bringing the birds home where they belonged. His efforts would not go unnoticed and eventually landed him a place in Audubon history.

Ever since Allen was a teenager, trudging through Schooley's Woods looking for scarlet tanager nests or Gibson's Swamp studying cardinals that visited his feeders, he hoped one day to lay eyes on a thriving flamingo colony. Thirty-five years later in the early-morning hours of March 20, 1953, as Allen and Nixon floated through a dense mangrove tangle toward Cotton Cay, a high-pitched sound, one Allen had never heard before, split the humid air and seemed to carry with it the twilight of a new day. Sammy smiled and called, "The Lord be praised! That's th' fillymingos!"[18]

The channel, now only a few inches deep, would take them no farther. Nixon tied the craft to a mangrove. As they waded closer, the sound of the flamingo harmony grew to a deafening crescendo. The tree canopy thinned. Dozens of flamingos flew overhead. With outstretched necks and long legs trailing, they resembled scarlet arrows shooting through the air. The mangroves gave way to bulrushes, and the two men stopped in their tracks. "Openmouthed, we stood and stared in silence," Allen wrote. "Through the thin screen of brush we could see a solid band of red. It shimmered and undulated in the heat exactly as if it were a long sheet of flame."[19] Crowded in a small saltwater pond, more than 1,000 flamingos had congregated for a prenuptial celebration. At first glance, what appeared to be a raucous display of leaping, shoving, strutting, and vying for attention of the best mate melded into a ballet of choreographed motions that had the entire group swaying as one giant red mass. Then, as if a silent signal had been passed, the entire group, moving as one, rose and flew off.

That year, Allen arranged for Sammy Nixon and his brother, Jimmy, to be appointed as wardens by the National Audubon Society. With both countries working together, the Society for the Protection of the Flamingos in the Bahamas was formed. In order for the brothers to keep a constant vigil during nesting season, Allen built a permanent structure on Long Cay, which he also used as his headquarters on his numerous visits. Seven years later, the Bahamas National Trust was created to oversee the flamingos' protection. The Nixon brothers spent the rest of their lives protecting and studying the flamingos on Great Inagua. Sammy died in 1986 and Jimmy in 2007. Today, Jimmy's nephew, Henry Nixon, is the current chief warden in the Bahamas, where more than 60,000 flamingos nest each year.

Behind the silver lining of his work in the Bahamas loomed another dark cloud. Allen's pleasure over the accomplishments made on Grand Inagua was dampened by government officials on Andros Island, who promised, but never delivered, plans to develop refuges for their dwindling populations of flamingos. Allen knew that with any effort to make long-term, significant changes there would be successes and failures, as with the whooping cranes. Although rare sightings were encouraging, the whooping crane numbers were not.

The year 1953 brought more bad news: the whooping cranes were in trouble again. The crane count from Aransas came in alarmingly low. Only twenty-four whooping cranes arrived in Texas in that winter. With the two permanent residents in New Orleans, Jo and Crip, that brought the total number to twenty-six. With twenty-five cranes lost during the last five years of migration, Audubon began a new publicity campaign targeting the entire migration route from the wilderness in Saskatchewan to the Texas coast. In September, before the migration was to begin, Audubon utilized every form of media, alerting TV and radio stations, newspapers and periodicals; all received press releases and public service announcements. The State of Nebraska printed a photo of a whooping crane along with the title, "Don't Shoot This Bird!" on the back of hunting licenses. Schools, local Audubon chapters, Scout and Campfire clubs, and any organization that connected people with the outdoors received literature informing them of the crane's sudden decrease in population.

With any campaign that draws attention to an issue, a potential backlash has to be considered. Publicity also stimulated the ire of some farmers and hunters who viewed the whooping crane as a menace. And one irate individual could cause irreversible destruction. The campaign, nevertheless, worked. Only one whooping crane disappeared between the spring and fall of 1954. This success, however, was merely a crest in an ever-moving wave of uncertainty.

There were no plans for a search in the summer of 1954 unless Bob Smith or anyone else spotted cranes in the area north of Great Slave Lake. May turned into June, and no such reports came in.

11 ～

Empty Nest

Wednesday, June 30, 1954

5:00 p.m.

Conditions in the Northwest Territories were right for a thunderstorm —not a surprise at that time of year. The forest service was on high alert; fire hazard classified as extreme. One lightning strike could ignite a boreal forest like a match to dry tinder. Helicopter pilot Don Landells was returning from an isolated section of Wood Buffalo National Park after checking on the status of Fire 24, which had been burning for several days. In the cockpit next to him was G. W. Wilson, the superintendent of forestry. As Landells turned to head back to the station, something in the marsh below caught his attention.

Landells nudged Wilson, decreased altitude, and flew back around; there was no doubt in either of their minds that below, feeding in the marsh, were two adult whooping cranes. That in itself was a rare and wondrous site. Spotting the rust-colored chick following behind was like finding the pot of gold at the end of the rainbow.

Landells radioed the dispatcher at District Headquarters in Fort Smith. For the last nine years, virtually everyone living, working, or visiting the area had been on lookout. They'd seen the posters and pamphlets and read the newspaper and magazine articles. When the call came in, the dispatcher alerted biologist William Fuller, who ran to the radio room and spoke to Wilson.

6:00 p.m.

Less than an hour after Landells saw the whooping cranes, Fuller stood on the tarmac, camera bag in hand, scanning the horizon. He heard the chopper well before it appeared over the tree line toward the northwest.

Landells was required to make another flight back to the site of the fire and deliver a fire pump and supplies. There was room for one more passenger, and Fuller was welcome to come aboard. He could hardly contain his excitement. Five minutes later, Landells had refueled, and the three men were flying toward Fire 24.

7:18 p.m.

The serpentine course of the Sass River came into view. Landells flew low over the marsh, and within moments, Fuller spotted the two whooping cranes wading in knee-deep water. He pulled out his camera and snapped an entire roll of film. Placing one foot in front of the other, in slow deliberate strides, the cranes moved through the shallows. If he hadn't known better, Fuller would have sworn the cranes were posing. Then Landells dipped lower, and the hypnotic moment was broken. The cranes took flight. Landells followed. He got close enough to see the birds' distinctive red heads. Fuller wanted to inspect the area on foot. He knew it was not possible to land the helicopter in the marsh. But the fortuitous sighting by Landells and Wilson was the best news since the hunt had begun almost a decade earlier.

—

Like a living, breathing force, the Keewatin Glacier crept across North America almost 3 million years ago, gouging deep crevasses, uplifting mountains, and leaving debris of boulders in its wake. Below the earth's surface, calcium carbonate leached out and slowly hardened, forming a limestone rock layer, which acted as a filter for the water that percolated through its cracks. Tiny vascular plants grew, their roots penetrating the uppermost layer, weakening the hard surface. Bushes and shrubs took root and continued the process of transforming rock into rich soil. Eventually, birch trees dotted the landscape, depriving the smaller plants of sunlight.

As plant life evolved, so did various animal species. Insects burrowed, birds nested, mammals grazed and roamed. Ten thousand years after the glaciers retreated, nature's balance had stabilized, reaching its developmental climax. In 1922, the Canadian government, in an attempt to protect the natural integrity of the area, set aside 17,300 square miles, establishing the country's largest national park. Wood Buffalo National Park straddles the border of the Northwest Territories and Alberta. The northwestern corner is a vast watershed where the Nyarling, Sass, and Klewi Rivers spill into the Little Buffalo River, which flows parallel to the Slave River and eventually into the Great Slave near Fort Resolution. Sitting north of the park, like an enormous aquatic horn of plenty, is Great Slave Lake, the deepest lake in North America and the ninth-largest on the planet. Fort Resolution is located at the mouth of the Slave River, which marks the boundary between the Interior Plains and the Canadian Shield. One side of the river is bedrock. The other side, where the whooping cranes nest, is an isolated boreal wilderness mixed with a maze of quagmire swamps, hundreds of small springs, and marl lakes less than two meters deep.

It was almost as if the whooping crane had scouted the area thousands of years ago, searching for the most hidden, isolated place to nest. The shallow lakes and ponds offered a bountiful cache of food. Bulrush covered the shorelines. Stands of black spruce, willows, and dwarf birch formed a protective border.

—

Landells, Wilson, and Fuller didn't return to Fort Smith until eleven o'clock that evening. The next morning, Fuller sent a short telegram with the news of their discovery to W. Winston Mair in Ottawa. On July 2, while Fuller composed his detailed report, Mair took it upon himself to send out a wire-service dispatch, alerting the media before informing the other two agencies involved in the project. In the next office, naturalist A.W.F. Banfield was writing a letter to John Baker to give him the news.

The day Baker read the letter, the story had been published in dozens of newspapers across the United States and Canada.

Five days later, Baker received another letter, this one from Mair himself, explaining his decision: "But you may be wondering why we made a release to the newspapers at the same time as informing you rather than after. This action was taken because the birds were seen by others than our own officers and, consequently, we anticipated the possibility that a report might leak out to the newspapers, a report that might be either highly inaccurate or otherwise unfortunate in its content."[1]

Baker immediately picked up the phone and placed a long-distance call to Tavernier. Despite Mair's reasoning, Baker was not happy hearing the news after the fact, and he did not want to chance Allen finding out by reading it in the local paper.

Allen was home working on his flamingo report and enjoying time with his family. He and Evelyn wanted their youngest daughter living closer to home and had been able to transfer Eve to a facility in Miami were they could visit more often. Later that summer, they accompanied Alice to Gainesville for her first day at the University of Florida. Upon hearing the news, thousands of thoughts assaulted Allen's mind all at once. Finding a mated pair and their chick was encouraging, but one nest was not enough to proclaim success. He wanted to speak to Fuller, to Mair, to the pilot. He wanted nothing more than to hop a plane to Fort Smith and begin his third hunt. All of which would come in good time, but the one burning question—where in the heck were the damn birds nesting?—might finally be answered.

When Baker gave Allen the location, Allen chuckled. He knew the area well—his prime target—the infamous site he and Smith had flown over on June 25, 1947, when they ran head-on into a blinding storm. Allen had written in his journal, and later in his field report: "1:40 p.m. Rain squall. Rough going. Poor visibility all the way in."[2]

Baker contacted three oil companies in the area, hoping to arrange for immediate use of a helicopter. Hudson's Bay was the only company that had one available, but not until September. They would, however, supply a Beaver floatplane. Baker told Allen that Mair was willing to have Allen organize another hunt immediately. To channel his elation, Allen hung up and composed a letter to Baker. Using his favorite line, Allen responded, "Our telephone conversation of this afternoon concerning the whooping crane reports from Wood Buffalo Park has been, for me, something like the clanging of a bell to an old company fire horse!"[3] The big question now was whether to take Mair up on his offer or wait until next year, when the nest hunters could get an earlier start. Baker left the decision to Allen.

Allen didn't waver. As much as he wanted to fly to Fort Smith and see the site firsthand, as much as he wanted to get back into the wilderness and trek or canoe, or drop from a parachute, Allen knew he would have to cool his heels for another year. He advised postponing the expedition until next summer. The region was difficult to access. Landing a float-plane would be impossible because of the small ponds, shallow swamps, and ridges of spiky vegetation. There were only two ways to get close to the area, by helicopter or on foot. Since a helicopter was not available, a land entry was the only option. Such a trip should begin no later than mid-June. Also, mid-June to mid-July, when the young whoopers were old enough to be out of the nest and active, offered an optimal window in which to observe them. Considering the time it would take to organize a ground team and reach the area, this window of opportunity was well past.

Baker telephoned Mair the next day, thanked him for his willingness to proceed, but informed him that Allen had decided to wait until the following spring. In the interim, there was much for the three agencies to do to get ready. Mair guaranteed that the Canadian Wildlife Service would continue to scout the area for more whooping cranes and to protect the area by limiting other air traffic over the nesting site.

By July 20, it was confirmed that six whooping cranes were living in the area: two adult pairs, one with a juvenile, and a single bird. Baker, however, needed reassurance that the young chick Landells saw on June 30 was a whooping crane and not an adult sandhill crane, since the sandhills were also nesting in the area. Fuller was not able to substantiate Landells' sighting, for when the trio returned from the fire patrol, the chick was not seen. Fuller questioned Landells extensively, urging the pilot to describe the appearance of the young bird in detail. Landells knew exactly what he was looking at. The whooper was the size of a rooster, reddish-brown in color, larger than a brownish-gray sandhill crane chick. Mair assured Baker that the pilot knew his cranes. "All of us who have flown with Mr. Landells have been impressed by his keen eyesight, and I have every confidence in his interpretation of this observation."[4] Baker was satisfied.

With the media pressing for more news, Mair also promised Baker that details of the site's exact location would be withheld to prevent museum or private collectors from finding their way in. Baker, in his attempt to leave no stone unturned, reminded Mair of his promise in a follow-up letter of August 12 and added that this type of protection be ongoing: "Although you doubtless have Wood Buffalo Park under excellent control from the patrol angle, our experience would lead us to recommend to you the exercise of extreme caution in the period from early April through September each year (assuming that the cranes are nesting in Wood Buffalo Park) because there are individuals who will go to almost any lengths to get a specimen of species threatened with extinction, either the adult, the juvenile, the eggs, or the nest, and these people have more than once proved their ability to succeed in getting into the most inaccessible spots. This includes photographers."[5] Copies of his letter were sent to John Farley, director of the U.S. Fish and Wildlife Service, and Bob Allen.

While the powers that be went full force with planning next year's hunt, Don Landells took the opportunity to keep up with the birds he'd spotted and to discover more. In doing so, his interest in the elusive whooping crane grew as the news reports escalated. One day a few weeks later, Landells wrote to Ward Stevens at the Northern Affairs and National Resources office asking him to contact Allen about a favor. Toward the end of August, the pilot was delighted to have received an autographed copy of Allen's monograph *The Whooping Crane: Research Report No. 3 of the National Audubon Society* in the mail.

—

If Allen couldn't be trekking through the soggy marshland of the Northwest Territories looking for his birds, he could still be productive. With all the publicity announcing the nesting site discovery, Allen, on behalf of Audubon, wrote a press release in September 1954, which also appeared in *Audubon Magazine*, informing the public that it was not time to rest on its laurels. The whooping cranes were still in danger of becoming extinct if trouble befell them during migration. Allen began his editorial: "Another dramatic test awaits the world's last remaining flock of whooping cranes when they leave their far northern breeding ground early this fall and head for winter quarters in Texas. How many will return?"[6] The press release went out to newspapers across the Midwest shortly before the first crane headed south. It might as well have fallen on deaf ears.

In the fall of 1954, only twenty-one of the twenty-four whooping cranes returned to Texas. Shockingly, not one single chick survived the summer and fall to reach Aransas. American's favorite bird was in more trouble than ever.

12 ⁓

Cards on the Table

For the nest hunters and all those concerned with the whooping crane saga, 1954 was an emotional roller coaster. Allen wrapped up his flamingo report, then flew to Ottawa on November 19 to meet with a cadre of Canadian Wildlife Service officials: Chief W. Winston Mair; Mair's assistant chief, Dr. Victor E. F. Solman; chief ornithologist David A. Munro; and wildlife management officer Robert D. Harris. It seemed nothing could be done about the loss of so many birds. Though there had been setbacks in the past and there would be more in the future, the preservation of this species would have to hang in the balance for decades to come. The situation had not reached such disastrous levels overnight, and recovery wouldn't happen with just one or two successful breeding seasons.

That very November meeting resulted in a framework for the 1955 search. An aerial survey would begin between May 15 and 25 with the intention of spotting the incoming cranes before they settled at their nesting site. By that time, the ice would be breaking up. The aerial phase would take about ten days, followed by a ground search led by Allen the first week of June. William Fuller would be in charge of the aerial survey and assist Allen later as needed. The USFWS would allow flyway biologists, either Bob Smith or John Lynch, to participate in both the aerial and ground searches. A budget was set, estimating the cost of the preliminary aerial survey at $1,800 and the establishment of a ground camp at $2,250 (with all but $250 going for the cost of floatplane and helicopter expenses).[1] The six oil and gas companies working in the area would be approached about using their helicopters and pilots, thus saving the three organizations a considerable expense.

It had been almost six years since Allen had seen Bob Smith. Allen was eager to work with his old buddy again. Then, in December, Mair received word from Farley that neither Smith nor Lynch would be available during May. Smith was assigned to conduct a waterfowl aerial survey in British Columbia, and Lynch had duties to attend to in Saskatchewan. As time for the hunt drew near, Allen learned that Fuller would not be available to assist in the ground exploration. He had been scheduled to attend the Alaska Science Conference the first week in June and would then fly to the Yukon to take care of business there. In March, Fuller wrote again saying that the chance of finding a helicopter was slim and that finding an entry into the wilderness and to the rivers for canoe launching was equally daunting. Just as Allen's frustration level rose, a breakthrough came in a letter from Bert Harwell of Audubon, who had explored the area in 1950. He wrote Allen about a new road that had been built across the Salt River that led to the mouth of the Buffalo River, where they could quickly canoe to the Sass River. Allen passed the news to Fuller.

Time was drawing near for the search to begin. After months of planning and corresponding back and forth among the three agencies, the CWS had still not received approval for funds. Allen and Baker were under the impression that the search was a done deal until Fuller began referring to their plans as "tentative."[2] Allen grew concerned and began to have doubts, not only about pulling off the expedition, but also about finding the actual nesting site. On April 4, he wrote Baker about his concerns. Although eager to get started, Allen felt that it would not make sense to launch a ground investigation, spending time, money, and effort if the cranes were not nesting in the location where they had been spotted the season before. The only way to remove this doubt was to plan aerial flyovers, take photographs of any nests, and note the exact site. Until that was done, Allen was not comfortable with proceeding. In his annoyance over the situation, he lifted direct quotes from Fuller's letter, listing all the issues that were now very iffy. Allen summed up his concern: "In general, it seems to me that all the parties except ourselves are shying away from full scale participation in this survey. I don't know if they are simply assuming the unspoken attitude that the whooping cranes might just as well be written off, or if they feel that nothing really worthwhile can be gained by stumbling about over that immense bog up there in the summer months. I wish they would lay their cards on the table. Then we could evaluate the entire problem more closely and make more sense on the subject than we can at the moment."[3] The funds, personnel, and aircraft that were to be supplied by the CWS seemed unattainable. Allen told Baker that these problems needed to be solved before Allen left for Canada.

Since the ground search for the whooping cranes was not scheduled until June, toward the end of April, Allen flew to the Bahamas as initially planned. He had not given up on persuading the government to establish a flamingo refuge on Great Inagua. Although a bit uneasy with the unforeseen developments up north, Allen felt confident that Baker could work out the kinks.

That winter of 1954–55, whooping crane fans continued to visit the refuge in Aransas. A new observation tower had been built, and the Mustang Lake Pair had become celebrities in their own right. In April, Julian Howard began watching for signs of migration. On the twelfth, he noticed a pair of whooping cranes picking through the marsh near Jo and Crip's old pen. It was one of those overcast days where the gray sky seemed to meld with the water's surface. A southeast wind picked up. The pair craned their necks, gained a running start, and rose. Howard expected them to circle and land again. They continued to spiral in a counterclockwise direction, allowing the wind to carry them high with each revolution. When they disappeared into the clouds, Howard drove to the Mustang Lake tower, and using the spotting scope, scanned the sky.

The birds were gone.

Howard was eager to conduct an aerial survey to determine if other cranes had left. The strong wind prevented him from taking the flight. Two days later, when he was able to fly over the refuge, he did not find a single crane. He sent word north. All twenty-one birds had survived the winter, and the 1955 whooping crane migration was under way.

Fuller was in the air on April 30, flying across the Sass River. That afternoon he wired Mair in Ottawa. He'd spotted two whooping cranes from an altitude of 700 feet and within a mile of where he and Landells had seen them on June 30 the previous summer. Now the ground team had a starting point. He felt certain that Allen and one more team member could reach the location carrying minimal equipment, have the rest of the supplies dropped by helicopter, set up camp, and complete the survey in a few days. He analyzed the three possible entrances to the site on the Sass River. Since the terrain was not conducive to trekking long distances, his main objective was to get the men as close as possible to the water. One option was to motor down the Slave River into Great Slave Lake and west to the mouth of the Little Buffalo and down to the Sass. In all likelihood, Great Slave Lake was still iced over; breakup did not usually occur until mid-June. A shorter, more direct route looked promising. They could take the road out of Fort Smith, put in at Buffalo River Falls, then motor into the Sass River. This option was abandoned when Fuller discovered that the bridge over the Salt River, the only route to the falls, had been washed out. Fuller studied the map again and realized that the closest he could get the nest hunters to the Sass was to send them down the Slave River, have them put out at Grand Detour, and then portage to the Little Buffalo. The distance—on foot—amounted to 6 miles. Fuller felt confident that with extra help, Allen and his team would be up to the task. He would hire extra packers to help the team with the portage.

Fuller flew over the Sass one more time and took a good look at the river. It was high on the bank and running swiftly, ideal conditions for travel. Fuller made a decision; although it was early May, the ground search was to begin immediately.

On May 5, Allen had just arrived on the island of Inagua. Waiting for him in Matthewtown was a radiogram from Baker: "Your presence in Fort Smith indicated middle of May. Letter to Tavernier."[4] The letter Baker referred to was one he'd written to Allen the same day, outlining the details and assuring Allen that Fuller had seen two whooping cranes in the 1954 location and that Mair had taken care of all of Allen's concerns. Fuller wanted to begin the hunt by May 15 at the latest. Baker also suggested that, from here on, Allen and Fuller correspond directly and send carbon copies to both Baker and Mair to expedite communication.

The only form of transportation from Inagua leaving immediately was a mail boat on its way to Nassau. Allen hopped aboard, caught a flight for Miami, and arrived in Tavernier on the tenth. Eager to get going, he was disappointed to learn that there was no connecting flight out of Edmonton to Fort Smith until the nineteenth. Then he relaxed, fairly confident the boat down the Sass River would not leave without him.

While Allen bided his time in Tavernier, Fuller hitched rides from any aircraft available to continue documenting cranes and their locations along the Sass River. In doing so, Fuller named the small lake where two cranes had been seen on April 30, Lake A. A pilot with the Royal Canadian Mounted Police arrived on May 15 and flew Fuller over for another look. He spotted one crane flying toward Lake A. The next day, a Gateway Aviation pilot, on his way to Edmonton, stopped in Fort Smith to refuel. Fuller begged another ride and managed to complete another survey, which included a positive sighting on another lake a half mile from Lake A. This time, the crane was sitting on a nest, and the lake became known as Lake B. Three days later, flyway biologist Ed Wellein took Fuller up, and the two men found a crane next to its nest on Lake B, another feeding on Lake A, three cranes milling around two nests on the Klewi River, and two more a few miles away. Fuller knew Allen would be thrilled with these results.

⁓

Bobby Allen drove his father to Miami International to catch the 8:00 a.m. flight to Chicago for his connection to Edmonton. Twenty-four hours later, Allen checked into the MacDonald Hotel, found his room, and crawled into bed. Despite his anticipation of the next morning, Allen fell asleep before the noisy crowd in the lounge knocked off for the night.

The cold morning had just shaken off the frost and was warming up nicely when Allen climbed out of the plane in Fort Smith just before noon on Friday the twentieth. His friend and colleague Ward Stevens, who had since been promoted to superintendent of game for the Territories, was there to greet Allen and help with the final preparations. The first order of business was to introduce Allen to the two men who would make up his team: Fuller's assistant, Ray Stewart, a young biologist with the Canadian Wildlife Service who had been conducting research in the area during the past three summers. This was his first big project. Also selected was Bob Stewart (no relation to Ray), an ornithologist and ecologist with the research division of the USFWS, who had conducted most of his work in the libraries and research facilities behind a desk. Bob Stewart's primary interest was in botany.

The night before the expedition was to begin, Allen, Ray Stewart, and Ward Stevens flew over the site. Fuller wanted Allen to see his search area from the air so he could get an accurate lay of the land. As the pilot descended to 1,000 feet, allowing Allen to scan the intricacies of the Sass River, a white speck slowly came into view. At 7:45 on May 22, 1955, the ornithologist/nest hunter gazed down on a wild whooping crane sitting contentedly on her nest. "I could see that it was turning to watch us as we passed, its head up and its yellow eyes doubtless glaring at us with hostility and a total lack of fear."[5] Allen had waited more than nine years for this moment. It was every bit as sweet as he had imagined.

Allen's elation was short-lived when, moments later, he caught sight of the river. He was told the Sass was not a friendly waterway. Seeing it for the first time, he doubted Fuller's assessment of making the trip in a few days. The distance from where they would enter the Sass to the nesting site was only 16 miles as the crow flies. With the twists and turns, Allen estimated the distance by boat to be close to 70 miles. The first mile alone contained at least forty bends. But that was only the last leg of their river journey. First they would have to motor 45 miles up the Little Buffalo, then begin to portage 6 miles to the Sass. That evening, Allen, the Stewarts, Allen's old friend D'arcy Munro of the Hudson's Bay Company, and Ward Stevens gathered at Bill Fuller's house for supper. His wife prepared a hearty meal for the nest hunters' sendoff the next morning. It would be one of their last comfortable evenings for a long time.

—

Breathing frost and rubbing their arms, Allen and the two Stewarts were in high spirits and ready for an early start. Allen teased Bob Stewart about being a novice camper. This was not only the biologist's first time in the Canadian wilderness; it was his first time to camp. To get him in shape, Allen assigned him the duty of "Chief Woodchopper."[6]

By 8:00 a.m., only one of the eight packers hired to assist in loading the 500 pounds of equipment had arrived. With 45 miles of river to travel that day, they couldn't wait around for the rest of the crew to show up. Fuller managed to round up nine more locals. He then made six copies of Allen's food list; he kept one, gave one to Allen, and the other four were given to several responsible citizens in the area. Stevens was to coordinate the aerial supply drops. The first was scheduled for June 3, with subsequent drops every ten days until mid-July. Allen carried with him a portable radio. At the last minute, Fuller suggested a backup plan. If headquarters failed to receive radio contact from the team by May 27, Stevens would fly over the proposed campsite to locate the team.

At 10:15, the scientists and their new crew shoved off in two riverboats, one pulling an 18-foot canoe.

Fuller waved them off and checked his list one final time, feeling certain he'd covered all the bases.

By 2:40, the team made Grand Detour. When the men stepped from the boats, ice cracked underneath their feet. The packers wasted no time in building a fire and, in a large cauldron, boiled a buffalo steak and potatoes for lunch. An hour and a half later, rested and nourished, they readied themselves to portage the equipment to the Sass River. Allen scanned the surrounding acreage. From 1,000 feet above, the area looked considerably different than at eye level. The only previously documented route from Grand Detour into the wilderness on the banks of the Sass, which followed the buffalo trail, was the one made in 1907 by Ernest Thompson Seton and later referred to in his book *Arctic Prairies*.[7] The experienced explorer had been unsuccessful in his attempt to penetrate this area of the park. Just the same, in Allen's pocket was a copy of Seton's book and the map Edward Preble had sent Allen last December.

Besides sharing this trekking adventure with Seton, Allen had another trait in common with the author, one that caused Allen some concern. Seton suffered from arthritis in his legs, making his trip an agonizing experience. Although Allen's spinal arthritis had not given him much trouble since his cortisone treatments, he was apprehensive about carrying a heavy pack for 6 miles. He later reported that his concern was unfounded. However, Allen was never one to include details of his discomforts in his writing; once he began an adventure, physical ailments were pretty much scoffed at.

Soon the spruce trees gave way to a soggy prairie where the water, at times, rose to calf level. Mosquitoes, having hatched in the shallows a few days before, now swarmed en masse. When the men rounded the bend in the trail, a buffalo herd grazing on the other side of the river spooked and thundered off, their pounding hoofs shaking the earth beneath them and sending echoes across the river valley.

By 7:00 p.m., the crew had reached Long Slough. From here on, Allen and his two colleagues were on their own. The packers unloaded the gear and left, mumbling and shaking their heads over the absurd undertaking the three scientists had planned for the next several days.

Too tired to scout the area, Allen and the two Stewarts pitched their tents. Ray Stewart cooked supper, and after the meal, the three men crawled into their sleeping bags. In the cool evening breeze, they fell asleep to the sound of songbirds singing their evening opera. Up at 5:30 the next morning, Allen wrote in his journal, "Stiff, sore, and ready for coffee."[8] After a quick breakfast, they pushed off down the Little Buffalo River. Along the banks, new sprouts of mossy green cattails poked their heads above the water. In a few weeks, they'd grow tall, creating a maze and blocking out all views of the surrounding prairie. As if to celebrate this new growth, waterfowl abounded—sandhill cranes and lesser yellowlegs stalked around the banks. Horned grebes rested on the matted vegetation. For Allen and Ray Stewart, old outdoorsmen in their element, watching the newcomer Bob Stewart, speechless and enthralled over nature's overwhelming presence, provided an added pleasure.

The temperature rose and fell at the whim of the clouds. Then, as if nature had flipped a switch, a cloud dropped its heavy load, drenching the men and their equipment before drifting south. When the three scientists reached the slough's terminus, they portaged to an Indian winter camp for the night. Without the packers, they had to make several trips to get their equipment to camp. A curious black bear watched from across the river and seemed determined to claim its territory with each pass from the strangers. On their last trip through, not wanting their food supply ravaged during the night, the men stood their ground, caused a commotion, and sent the bear fleeing. At 5:00 p.m., except for the canoe and gas cans, all the gear was stowed. Just as they began to organize camp, another storm blew in, this one flinging marble-size hail that covered the ground in minutes. Huddled under a tarpaulin, they waited for it to blow over.

That night after the daylight had dimmed and the campfire had turned to embers, the wilderness erupted into a symphony of nature sounds. A family of Tennessee warblers took center stage, interlacing their melodious chorus with the singing of thrushes and robins. A raucous refrain from sandhills and swans answered back, sounding more like angry spectators at a sporting event. When the avian sound show ended, a staccato of beats slapped the water's surface—the primal sounds of beavers going about their perpetual dam-building.

Two days later, the mouth of the Sass River came into view. Allen did not like what he saw. Its swift current could best be described as sinister and inhospitable. Yet, they loaded the canoe and put in. Around the first oxbow, they hit a logjam, not a bad one by Allen's estimation. In minutes, they'd cut through, only to find the next jam even larger. They pulled ashore and trekked along the riverbank, finding one jam after another. Later in the summer, the Sass would dwindle to a mere trickle. Now, in May, the river was still in its prime. Over a hot evening meal, they decided to tackle the next logjam in the morning and hope for the best.

With an ax, saw, and otherwise empty canoe, Allen and Ray Stewart set out after breakfast, hoping to dislodge the jam and praying the logs would disperse along the riverbank. Within minutes, the rushing debris hit the next logjam, adding several feet to its height. At this rate, they'd never make it to the nesting site before the young cranes hatched, fledged, and flew south for the winter. Portaging the entire distance through the tightly tangled brush was out of the question.

On the third day of their journey, Allen admitted defeat. "In a word, to say that the Sass is not navigable is putting it mildly."[9]

Allen returned to camp to radio Fort Smith for a helicopter to pick them up. Once back in headquarters, he and Fuller would review other options. They couldn't afford to lose any more time. When he picked up the radio, he heard Ward Stevens calling. Allen spoke his message and hit the transmit button. No response. He repeated his action again—nothing.

Bob Allen's ground party on the Slave River, attempting to reach the whooping crane nesting site in Wood Buffalo, Canada, May 23, 1955. Photo by Bob Allen. Courtesy of Alice Allen.

Bob Allen and Bob Stewart on the Grand Detour Portage on the way to locating the nesting site, May 24, 1955. Photo by Robert C. Stewart. Courtesy of Alice Allen.

Stevens continued to transmit, inquiring about the hunters' progress. With each unanswered message, his concern grew; finally, he told the three men to stand by, that a search pilot would fly along the Sass River the next day. Certain the pilot would imagine the worst when he failed to locate their canoe near the designated area, Allen's only choice was to put in on the Little Buffalo, paddle along the shore of Great Slave Lake, and make for the radio station at Fort Resolution as quickly as possible. This time the swiftness of the Little Buffalo was an advantage. They arrived at the mouth in fewer than twelve hours, a 90-mile journey that, under normal conditions, would have taken two days. In the distance, the huge lake glistened under the sun's dim rays. Despite the breeze, not a single wave broke the surface. As they drew closer, Allen knew instantly their water journey had ended. Great Slave Lake was frozen over.

Ray Stewart contemplating the first of many logjams on the Lower Sass River, May 25, 1955. Photo by Bob Allen. Courtesy of Alice Allen.

At a nearby Chipewyan village, Allen got news from the locals that the lake all the way to Fort Resolution was impassible. Allen and the Stewarts considered leaving their gear at the village and continuing on foot, but without a map or trail to follow, they dared not risk the venture. Allen befriended a Chipewyan native, Isadore Edgerican, who was camping on the river with his family, waiting for the ice to break up so they could begin trapping beaver. Upon hearing of their dilemma, Edgerican volunteered to make the 32-mile round-trip journey on foot to Fort Resolution and deliver their message. Allen and the Stewarts returned to camp and waited. While the Stewarts explored the surrounding area, Allen stayed at camp, nursing a cold with doses of aspirin washed down with black coffee. "I am in bad shape, but perhaps this is the worst day for my ailment."[10] Allen's prediction was correct; his cold ran its course, but the trek to the nesting ground became even more of a challenge.

Edgerican was successful in delivering Allen's message, and at three o'clock Sunday afternoon, May 30, a week after they began, a government pilot by the name of Pat Carey landed his floatplane near the campsite. It would take him two trips to ferry the men and their equipment back to Fort Smith, so they loaded the plane and left immediately. Since Allen was sick, he was on the first flight out. The Stewarts arrived the next morning.

When Allen arrived at the Hotel Mackenzie, awaiting him was a letter from Baker. The situation in the Bahamas looked hopeful at last. The government was considering a flamingo reintroduction program and requested Allen's assistance. Baker hoped to honor the request and have Allen back in the Caribbean as close to July 1 as possible. Allen was overjoyed with the news, but advised his boss that under the present circumstances, it would be best to postpone the project until the following summer. In that letter to Baker dated May 31, Allen also outlined his concerns after the first nine days in whooping crane territory. The site the cranes chose as their summer home, near a black spruce forest, could disappear in flames after one lightning strike, wiping out the entire flock. The Chipewyans' encroachment into the forest to trap beaver could alarm the whooping cranes during the most vital time in their reproductive cycle. Without waiting for any official plan of action, Allen proposed a "government-owned helicopter stationed here permanently" for the sole purpose of spotting fires.[11] He also recommended that the government place restrictions on beaver trapping in the park, possibly halting it altogether after April 1. Allen then visited his friend and birder C. E. Anderson, a chief engineer of a gold-mining operation in the Northwest Territories and a member of the N.W.T. Game Association in Yellowknife. Anderson was moved by the story of the almost-extinct whooping cranes and was willing to assist in the ongoing publicity campaign and take the responsibility of reporting on the cranes' status. Anderson requested the use of any Audubon whooping crane films to show to the association. Allen encouraged Baker to follow up on this request: "This is a new group and forerunner of a new trend in this country up here. They ought to be encouraged in the right direction."[12] Finding the nesting site was just the first step; securing and protecting the habitat offered hope for the whooping cranes' future.

Allen predicted June 12 as the estimated time for the hatching of whooping crane eggs. By Monday, June 6, he felt certain he'd be snapping photos and filling his notebook with detailed descriptions of new crane parents taking turns incubating their eggs. Instead, time slipped past with Allen waiting at the Hotel Mackenzie, rethinking his strategy while Fuller tried to locate a helicopter that could drop them closer to the nesting site. Unless they could select a new location and set up within three or four days, witnessing the hatching of the next generation of whooping cranes would not happen. With anxiety mounting and impatience building like an uncontrollable force, Allen nurtured a hope that a helicopter would be found in time.

Hearing of the stalled Whooping Crane Project, Jerry Webster, with the Ozark Drilling Company working near Hay River, sent a telegraph on June 2 to the district administrator in Fort Smith. Webster was happy to offer the company's helicopter and pilot to transfer the men to their new location. It would arrive in a day . . . or two.

Ray and Bob Stewart set out to do some fishing while Allen prepared a new supply list. Much to everyone's relief, Pat Carey arrived the following day in his floatplane. Allen and Bob Stewart packed the gear while Ray had the easier task of buying groceries. The three days of down time put Allen on the mend. Ray now had the cold. Fuller invited the guys to his house for another sendoff meal—trout caught that day. Then he passed out his good cigars.

On Saturday, June 4, Pat Carey ferried them and their equipment as close to their proposed base camp as a floatplane could manage. As they passed over the area, Allen took note of a huge limestone escarpment nearby. This landmark would help them locate the nesting area. They landed on a shallow lake about 10 miles from the campsite. The next afternoon, Ozark's helicopter pilot, a new hire unfamiliar with the area, met them on the lake two hours after the scheduled time. Exasperated over the pilot's tardiness, but grateful for his assistance, Allen unfolded the map and laid it over a supply box. After a cursory scan of Allen's map, the pilot nodded. It would take at least four trips to get all the 1,000 pounds of equipment to the new campsite. The pilot glanced toward the north, showing his impatience. The northern skies, darkening above the horizon, struck a chord of trepidation.

Ray Stewart and Bob Stewart stranded at camp and waiting for rescue, June 1955. Photo by Bob Allen. Courtesy of Alice Allen.

Ray Stewart, knowing the area the best, left on the first trip. The pilot flew low to avoid the heavy winds, making it difficult for Stewart to recognize the destination. It took longer to get to the escarpment than Stewart had expected; he merely chalked it up to difficult flying conditions.

Watching the helicopter pilot fight the storm on his final landing to pick them up, Allen and Bob Stewart had serious doubts about reaching the campsite in one piece. But four hours later, the task was completed. Allen's sense of foreboding, however, grew. The river seemed larger and more turbulent. The pilot, more anxious than ever to get the hell out of there before the storm grounded him, assured the men that they were fewer than 3 miles from the pond where the whooping cranes nested. The nest hunters stood on the bank of an angry river; overhead the storm clouds danced. The only thing to do was to set up their tents, crawl inside,

. and hope that things would look better after a good night's sleep. Allen's journal notes that evening were unusually concise: "Making camp among 6 billion mosquitoes."[13]

In the wake of the storm, the morning broke damp and muggy. With the heat came more mosquitoes. Allen and the Stewarts set out in the canoe and turned back almost immediately. Again, logjams made this portion of the river impassible. No problem, they'd ditch the canoe and trek to the pond instead. Only 2 miles away, even on foot, they'd reach the site in less than an hour. Noon arrived without success. They returned to camp for lunch, then started out in a slightly different direction. The path through the woods never thinned, and the pond did not come into view. Several hours later, they sat on their upturned canoe, soaked to the skin and filthy. The following morning, another trek into the woods, another disappointment. Again, the notes in Allen's journal were short:

"June 7—*Did not find the ponds.*"[14]

That evening a sobering thought took hold of Allen and resulted in a sleepless night. Allen reached for his journal the next morning. His entry was brief and to the point:

"June 8—*We don't know where we are!*"

Allen and the Stewarts drew the only sensible conclusion after three days of wandering; the pilot had dropped them in the wrong place. Allen swallowed his pride and attempted to radio Fort Smith with another message to send an aircraft to locate them and tell them where they were. Wondering if the Northwest Territories possessed a mysterious magnetic force that interfered with the flow of radio waves, Allen tossed the radio to the side when his transmission failed. He turned to his two partners, "We'll sleep on it and try to talk to Smith [Fort Smith] in the morning."

"June 9—Pat Carey flew over and didn't see us. Built a smudge, but he kept flying on toward Ft. Smith."

Allen's message had been received in Fort Smith, for all the good it did; the nest hunters gave up waving to the pilot as he disappeared over the trees.

"June 10—Hot, mosquitoes. Silent all day."

That morning, summer hit the area like the opening of a giant oven door, the mercury jumping close to 90 degrees. As if in celebration of the heat, bloodsucking black flies and deer flies joined mosquitoes in declaring open season on all warm-blooded creatures. Before noon the radio

crackled, and they got their message through amidst static and intermittent signals. They did not receive an answer.

"June 11—Our seventh day in this futile location and it is getting
mighty tiresome. The boys are passing the time by setting rodent traps."

At five o'clock, Fuller's radio transmission came through loud and clear.
The news was better than expected. Allen's dear old friend Bob Smith had
landed in Fort Smith on his way to the Arctic. He'd like nothing better
than to delay his trip and look for his "ogema" buddy. Fuller instructed Allen to light a smudge pot to send up smoke signals when he heard Smith's
plane. Less than an hour later, the sound of Smith's Widgeon broke the
air beyond the trees toward the east. When he saw Allen, Smith flashed a
wide grin, stuck his arm out, and waved. Stevens, riding shotgun, dropped
a message down to Allen. Smith buzzed the campsite again, saluted, and
flew off.

Allen unfolded the paper. His suspicions were correct. Ozark's helicopter pilot had flown northeast instead of north. Seems the pilot was
not aware of the 32 degrees compass variation that must be calculated into
the formula in that part of the world. They were more than 12 miles from
their escarpment landmark. Eager to be picked up again and relocated,
hopefully by the following afternoon, Allen was crestfallen when he read
the last of Stevens's note. No helicopter had yet been located. Allen and
the Stewarts would have to wait—for how long, Stevens wasn't sure.

"June 12—Around midnight a couple of timber wolves were howling
their mournful song off to the s.e. [southeast]."

The men vowed to make the best of their situation. The only thing to
do was to stay busy. Bob Stewart took representative samples of bird life
in two 15-acre plots he'd laid out. Allen and Ray took care of business at
camp, staying near the radio for word of their departure.

None came.

Somewhere close by, the whooping crane chicks were about to hatch.
For all the good it did Allen and his team, the cranes might as well have
been nesting on the moon.

"June 13—A hearty breakfast and strong coffee ushered in an optimistic morning. Then the radio squawked to life at one o'clock. Still no helicopter. Further information coming soon."

Again, none came.

"No traffic for us on the 4:45 sked. Black flies are showing up. Sure getting fed up with Camp."

Allen closed his journal, looked up from his notes, and, seeing despair in the faces of his colleagues, he announced a celebration. Having survived another day of oppressive heat and stinging insects, Allen proclaimed five o'clock as cocktail hour and added a nip of rum to their tea.

"June 14—1:30 p.m. No word for us on the 1:00 sked. 5 p.m. No word on this sked either. This is getting bad!"

"June 15—6:00 a.m. New moon showing itself."

"1:00 p.m. Ray spoke to Fort Smith via station at Peace River—No helicopter at Hay River."

"4:45 p.m. Word came to confirm the copter situation—none available. Radio transmission bad. Wait until morning. Will ask him [Ward Stevens] to check with Hay River as to the possibility that another helicopter might soon be there and available. Otherwise, we will have no choice but to head out of here on our own steam, a tough assignment!"

"10 p.m. To bed after much talk. Calm and the [mosquitoes] worse than ever. A perfect fright."

"June 16—Goodbye to Camp!"

Eleven days had passed since Allen called for help. Their supplies were running low. From their constant battle with swarming insects and deadly dehydration, the men were nearing exhaustion. On the morning of the seventeenth, Stevens flew over and dropped another message. The news was not good. There were no helicopters anywhere in that part of Canada. The men would have to make it out on their own. On a straight line, they were only a mile and a half from the Little Buffalo River, but with the river's meandering course, the actual travel distance was at least 7 miles.

"June 17—Really dog tired tonight."

With all the gear packed in their canoe, there was not much room for anything else. Allen squeezed in and attempted to maneuver the heavy craft through the rough current of the Sass while Ray and Bob slogged along the muddy riverbank. Every quarter mile, a logjam barricaded their passage and they stopped to chop their way through. Allen lost count at forty. At 9:00 p.m., their Little Buffalo campsite came into view. Twenty-four days had passed since they had last been here.

"June 18—Another bright, mosquito filled morning."

Ray Stewart (*left*) and Bob Allen after their second attempt down the Sass River, June 19, 1955. Photo by Robert E. Stewart. Courtesy of U.S. Fish & Wildlife Service.

At 11:15 a.m., they reached the Grand Detour location and stopped for a quick lunch of cold beans and hot coffee. Two hours later, they hoisted their gear and portaged for the next seven hours.

"June 19—Heavily o'cast and black in the West this morning. High wind. Later, a little rain and our camp rather miserable."

"June 20—It required all of us until 9:00 p.m. to pack everything to the Slave River and get underway."

The four packers who were supposed to meet them that morning had gotten lost and didn't arrive until 1:00 p.m. When the crew finally reached the banks of the Slave later that evening, the sight of Captain Billy McNeil of the CWS, waiting to motor them back to headquarters, had the men cheering.

"June 21—Ft. Smith at 5 a.m. to Hotel Mackenzie for bath and rest. Mail! Thus we were brought back to Fort Smith, a dirty bearded, and sorry crew, after twenty-nine futile and frustrating days of trying to reach the nesting ground of the whooping crane."

Having gotten word of the nest hunters' arrival, the cook at the Hotel Mackenzie had breakfast ready when Allen and the Stewarts walked in. The eagerness over their mission and the humorous banter that normally accompanied their conversations had waned. Unspoken thoughts of even hotter weather and the inevitable flooding of the search area, making another journey into the already swamp-laden wilderness impossible, hung heavy. Without a helicopter to drop them at the site, there was nothing else that could be done. It was a foregone conclusion—the search of 1955 had failed.

13 ~

They Came through the Twilight

After breakfast, Allen returned to his room and packed for the trip home. His next stop was headquarters. On his way over, he composed the telegram he'd send to Evelyn: "Safe and sound. Stand by for flight connection to Miami. Much Love, Bob." He pushed open the door to the office, prepared to meet the somber faces of his whooping crane team. Together they'd make the final decision to pull the plug on the 1955 search and hope, if all the dominoes fell, they'd have another shot next year. The silence that greeted him when he stepped into the hallway was broken seconds later. Ward Stevens rushed from his office waving a slip of paper, a radiogram, the first of two messages to come in that morning. Another pilot and helicopter had been located in Hay River and was standing by to transport the nest hunters back to the Sass River. If they could make it to the pickup location, the pilot would ferry the crew as close to nesting site as they dared to get. Stevens hesitated. The men had not yet recovered from their twenty-nine-day ordeal. Would they be willing to return immediately?

Silly question. Aching muscles, mosquito-bitten skin, emotional and physical exhaustion be damned, they'd repack their equipment without a moment's hesitation. As the whooping cranes sat on their eggs, some hearing the peeps of the next generation beneath them, Allen was fully aware that he was only days, maybe hours, away from witnessing the event. It was a gamble—one he eagerly took.

"June 22—All set. We will leave here on the *M.V. Buffalo* at midnight tonight."[1]

Returning to the banks of the Sass was bittersweet. Allen was elated over the opportunity, but his understaffed team had decreased by one.

Bob Stewart had been summoned back to Patuxent, Maryland. The US-FWS could not spare his absence from his assignment any longer. He gave his heartfelt blessing to his two teammates and boarded a plane for Edmonton that morning.

"June 23—12:20 a.m. Took off downstream with Ward, Billy McNeil and a crewman named Louie Brown."

The trip back down the Little Buffalo began to look all too familiar. Allen and Ray Stewart arrived at Grand Portage at 4:50 a.m., made coffee, and waited. The morning brightened, the songbirds, having exhausted their repertoire and fed their young, had settled down. For all their rushing to get back to camp, Allen wondered if they were in for another long frustrating stint in the woods, or if the helicopter pilot who had volunteered was as incompetent as the first. When the pilot finally arrived, he was seven hours late.

"12:15 p.m. Holmgren landed his General Air Transport helicopter."

Pilot Holmgren sat his chopper down, climbed out of the cockpit, and,·

General Air Transport helicopter flown by Pilot Holmgren during the second attempt to transport the nest hunters to the correct location, June 23, 1955. Photo by Bob Allen. Courtesy of Alice Allen.

with a smile that brightened the dreary afternoon, shook Allen's hand. When the pilot spoke, Allen liked what he heard. The Mississippi drawl and easygoing attitude reminded him of his pal Bob Smith. This was a good sign, and Allen knew how to properly greet a southerner. He tossed some bacon in a pan, scrambled eggs on the side, and put on a pot of coffee. While they polished off their midday breakfast, Allen learned that his new pilot was a veteran who had flown helicopters off the battleship *Missouri* in the Korean War. If Allen wanted to get close to his whooping cranes, Holmgren was the man who could do it. Allen handed the pilot the map. Less than an hour later, Allen and Stewart were closer than ever to the nests. In the distance, the whooping cranes called, and this time there was no sense of foreboding. Holmgren ferried in the rest of the gear and promised to return between July 8 and 11 to bring them back to Grand Portage.

"1:45—Landed on the edge of crane area (without seeing birds). It has taken us 31 days and a lot of grief, but let it be known that at 2 p.m. on this the 23rd day of June, we are on the ground with the whooping cranes! We have finally made it!"

Allen and Stewart had a little more than two weeks to locate the whooping cranes and document the 1955 hatching season. After Holmgren left, they took stock of their location. It was unlike any terrain they'd ever seen—a no-man's land that had been scarred severely by a forest fire two decades prior and seemed to have given up all hope of sprouting new life. Charred remains of once tall, slender black spruce and the willowy tamarack—one of the few coniferous trees that loses its leaves in the fall—littered a soggy mushy ground. Those trees that hadn't toppled over stood bare, stripped of the branches and needlelike leaves that had once captured the sun's energy and nourished them. Now a mere blanket of rootless vegetation, mosses, algae, lichen, and fungus cloaked the dead, soft wood, sucking out what paltry nutrients remained. The latitude and short growing season made decomposition slow, bringing plant succession to a near standstill. A stratum of moisture hung low, trapping the sun's heat, creating a sauna-like atmosphere. The colorless landscape gave only an illusion of dryness. The burned timber, now saturated with water, cultured mold spores.

Across the Sass, the fire had spared the landscape; patches of birch, willows, black spruce, and tamarack grew among shallow ponds. The air was so laden with moisture that everything—plant life, ground cover, fallen logs—was waterlogged. The temperature hit 92 degrees, the humidity higher. Traversing the area would not be any easier than what they had experienced during the past month. They'd tackle that situation the next morning. Now they set about finding suitable ground to pitch a tent close enough to the river yet far enough away to prevent the wet ground from seeping into their sleeping bags. Their initial concern over not having slept the night before didn't seem to matter. They were a mile away from their cranes, and as far as they were concerned, a mile away from paradise.

The good night's sleep worked its magic, and after a quick, hot breakfast, Allen and Stewart got down to business. With no map to follow from here on, Allen brought out the aerial shots he'd taken of the ponds on the flight more than a month earlier. They headed out across the burn, its mushy surface feeling much like a saturated sponge. Where the burn abruptly ended, a thicket of stubby conifers had braided their branches into a tangle. When the branches became too stubborn to push aside, Allen and Stewart slashed their way through, fighting to keep their boots from being sucked off by the soppy ground. Sweat saturated their clothing before they'd covered 50 yards. Black flies and mosquitoes descended in clouds. Visibility, at best, was no more than 100 feet. Whenever the vegetation gave up its hold on the landscape and a pond came into view, Allen matched it with the photos to give them a modicum of direction.

At precisely 9:25 a.m., they stepped into a clearing, the blinding sun reflecting off the still surface of a small pond. In the distance, a flash of white caught their eye. An adult whooping crane stepped out of the reeds. Moments later, another crane emerged. The two birds stalked away in opposite directions: the one on the left remained on the shoreline, calling in alarm, while the other disappeared in the brush. Allen and Stewart watched, careful not to make a sound. Suddenly, a short-billed gull dove at the crane on the shore, causing him to take flight.

It wasn't until two weeks later that Allen and Stewart would discover what was hidden just beyond their view.

"June 24—Sighted one, then another whooping crane. We had at last met the whooping crane face to face on his Northern nesting grounds!"

Those were the only two cranes spotted that day. At a second pond, Allen photographed several whooping crane tracks against a box of matches, showing the 7-inch-span of their feet. The soft mud on a third pond was heavily pocked with more tracks along with deep holes where the whooping cranes had probed for food. The first day passed with no trace of fledging whoopers. All the same, it was a good start. Over dinner that night, Allen and Stewart made plans to begin early the next day.

"June 25—Both of us seem to be suffering from undue fatigue, possibly because of loss of salt in this hot weather. No salt tablets with us either. No further activity until p.m."

The excitement over their discovery caused the two men to ignore the severity of the elements. Dehydration from the previous day hit them with a severe fatigue, forcing them to postpone the next day's search until the sun had dipped behind the forest wall.

Along with the physical exhaustion, melancholy seemed to creep in after the ordeal of the previous weeks.

"June 26—My 6th Sunday away from home and beginning our 6th week up here. A long haul in many ways. Today we will wash ourselves and a few clothes and prepare collection equipment for this coming week's work."

Cloud cover and a pleasant breeze cooled the afternoon, providing respite from the heat. Allen sent a radio message to Stevens informing him that the work would be completed by the end of the week and to arrange for a helicopter to pick them up any day after July 1.

"June 27—Afternoon at crane pond. Very quiet. Song sparrows singing and soras calling now and then. A rather sad and lonely place."

Pacing their activities from then on, the two men drew survey maps, photographed the birds and the surrounding area, made note of every species of fish, amphibian, reptile, mammal, and insect that made up the marshy food web. Allen was amazed at how similar the habitat was to the Aransas marshes. "It is in truth a lost and unknown place, and the nesting whoopers should continue to prosper here in the spring and summer months, as they have evidently done for so many years. Only man can reach them here and do them harm, and if not permitted to fly low over these ponds or land beside them in a helicopter, even man need not be feared."[2] Allen's joy over finding the nesting area was mixed with apprehension now that the whooping crane's secret was out.

"June 28—No whoopers seen. No confirmation yet of our message to Ward [Stevens] of Sunday last. 10 p.m."[3]

That day, using the aerial photos, Allen and Stewart found Discovery Lake, where Bill Fuller had seen the two whooping cranes on his April 30 flyover. Although the cranes were not visible, their tracks were. Interspersed with the fresh adult prints were smaller ones of their young. Since the water level had dropped, Allen suspected that the cranes were feeding elsewhere and doing their best to avoid the humans who had invaded their territory. Other avian species were not so skittish. Sandpipers, red-winged blackbirds, song sparrows, Pacific loons, and green-winged teals fed along the grassy shore.

"June 29, 10 p.m.—Hot and still. Clear sky. Snipe swimming up river. Still trying to reach Smith [Fort Smith] by radio. No luck."

Stewart sent out the first radio message to Fort Smith at 8:10 a.m., then again that afternoon at 1:15, 3:00, and 6:00. He tried at 8:00 p.m. and once more at 10:00.

The messages went unanswered.

"June 30—Been here a week now. 1:15 Absolutely no results from our transmission."

At 10:10 on Friday morning, July 1, Stewart sent the following message to Fort Resolution with instructions to forward it to Fort Smith: "WORK HERE COMPLETED. WAITING FOR PICK UP."

Finally, at 1:00 p.m., a message from Fort Smith came through. Forest fires were burning in several areas around Great Slave Lake. A crew of twenty firefighters was marooned on Isle du Mort with only one day of rations left. Pilot Holmgren had been dispatched to evacuate them and was unable to pick up Allen and Stewart. The rest of the afternoon and into the evening, they listened to the progress of the evacuation on the radio. Haze from the fires clouded the sky.

Six hours later, Holmgren had most of the firefighters safely back at headquarters. Tomorrow he'd fly to the Sass River for Allen and Stewart. The radio transmission then grew quiet.

Later that evening, snipes and loons began calling, causing the sand-hills to erupt with bugle cry. Finally the whoopers, having the last word, answered back. The clouds drifted off, and a full moon shone over camp.

At 8:00 a.m. on July 2, Allen received a radio message from Ward Stevens, confirming Holmgren's arrival that afternoon. Allen and Stewart had been with the whooping cranes for ten days and were eager to bring information to the thousands who had waited and contributed to the hunt.

They made their last visit to the pond then broke camp at 10:40. At 1:45, Allen lit the smudge pot, sending smoke signals as instructed. At 3:00 they still waited. By 4:00, they grew concerned. Finally, at 5:15, the "wump wump" of the helicopter sounded, and within seconds, it came into view. Then, just as rapidly, Holmgren banked and turned in the opposite direction. The now-thin trail of smoke from the smudge pot dissipated as it rose. Fearing they would be abandoned again, Allen grabbed his shaving mirror and caught the sun's reflection. Holmgren saw the flash, and he was on the ground minutes later.

By 7:00 p.m., Allen and Stewart were back at Grand Detour. A boat and outboard motor supplied by Bill Fuller awaited their arrival. In the stern under the seat were two bottles of beer. Allen and Stewart did not wait until morning to head out. After a quick celebratory toast, they pushed off, making short work of the 45 river miles and arriving on the shore of Fort Smith at 2:00 a.m. No one had expected them to show up in the middle of the night. Allen and Stewart walked into a back room of the Hotel Mackenzie and roused Louie the cook. As he prepared a meal, he informed them that asleep in the room next to theirs was reporter John O'Reilly of the *New York Herald-Tribune*. They woke him and told their tale.

A few days later, the country read the beginning of O'Reilly's three-part story: "They came through the Arctic twilight up the river by the skiff to Fort Smith for the third time. I was there [Fort Smith] to meet them when they came out. In the words of Robert W. Service, Mr. Allen 'looked like a man who had lived in hell.' He was bearded, dirty, and tired, but this time he was grinning."[4]

14 ~

The Bob Allen Keys

The expedition, which was supposed to have taken two weeks, turned into a six-week ordeal. In all the times Allen had been away from home, unaccountable for days, this last month proved the most trying for Evelyn, and for the first time since their marriage, she was frightened for her husband's safety. Ward Stevens kept Evelyn updated via telegraph. Bobby and Alice were away at college. Although they were old enough to know the dangers their father faced, Evelyn did not let on to her children the seriousness of the situation in Canada.

When Allen sent his wife the radiogram on the morning of July 3 with the good news, he also informed her that his work on the Sass River was not yet finished. An aerial survey was needed to determine the extent and range of the whooping crane population and where each family was nesting. As usual, air transportation was not immediately available, and again, Allen would have to wait until a floatplane could be located. Giving Evelyn a definite arrival date to Miami would have to wait. No matter; he was safe.

At 9:10 on the morning of July 6, pilot George Dannemann flew Allen, Fuller, and O'Reilly, who'd been told by the *New York Herald-Tribune* to stick with Allen, over the Sass and Klewi Rivers. An hour later, they spotted the Sass Pair, and standing between the parents were twin whooper chicks. The adults were the first two cranes Allen and Ray Stewart had seen on the morning of June 24—the one standing on the shore sounding the alarm and his mate who disappeared into the brush. Now, from the air, they lain eyes on the nest for the first time and laughed at the cranes' cleverness for evasion. The pair's nest was only a quarter mile away from camp. Soon another set of parents came into view, and with them was another set of twins. A single whooping crane fed on the shore of a marsh pond. Over the Klewi River, the Klewi Pair with two juveniles hunted on the edge of a thicket not far from several shallow ponds. On the first morning of the survey, a total of nine whooping cranes were documented in their summer home, feeding, attending to chicks, and chasing away duck hawks, lesser yellowlegs, herons, and other intruding birds.

Allen couldn't identify all the individual family groups he'd come to know over his years of observing them in Texas, but here they were nonetheless—the Slough, Middle Pond, South Families, glancing up at the plane as it buzzed over. Allen watched as the parents raised their bills, sending out alarm calls and then settling down to continue browsing in the marsh. Discovering the nesting site after nine years was the highlight in Allen's life as an ornithologist; seeing so many whooping cranes from the air that morning was the crowning glory.

O'Reilly completed his crane story and sent it off to his editor with a carbon copy to John Baker and one to Bill Mair. The story entitled, "Four Whooping Crane Offspring Are Sighted," appeared in the July 15 issue of the *New York Herald-Tribune.* O'Reilly began, "American and Canadian researchers let out yells of triumph when the rusty-brown youngsters were sighted from the survey plane."[1]

The nine cranes seen on July 6 represented only a third of the flock. Knowing his time in the wilds of Canada was coming to an end, Allen was eager to complete the job. A few days more, and the remainder of the flock would be located and the survey would be finished.

But those days were not his. When he landed in Fort Smith on Friday, July 8, after an eventful day in the air, a radiogram from Evelyn awaited him. Instead of planning the next day's aerial survey, Allen packed his bags and contacted Pat Carey. On Saturday morning, Carey flew Allen to Edmonton, where he caught a connecting flight back to the United States. The next day, he joined his wife after a six-week absence for what he had hoped would be a celebratory reunion. Instead, he and Evelyn attended her father's funeral. Tom Sedgwick had died while spending the summer with his brother in Massachusetts. Alice met her parents at the airport on their return from the Northeast. "They were carrying my grandpa's ashes, and Dad was wearing all the hair he had grown on that scary trek."[2]

—

Bill Fuller continued with the aerial surveys. Sending updated reports to Allen, the two men analyzed the seven survey flights over the nesting area. Seventeen whooping cranes—eleven adults and six young—had been spotted on September 12, the largest number ever seen in one day. It was determined that twenty cranes were nesting in Wood Buffalo Park that year.

After Allen's discovery that summer, congratulatory letters arrived at the Allen home for weeks to come. One of the first came from Bob Smith, who had read the newspaper stories: he wanted to hear the details directly from Allen. Numerous magazines requested Allen to send an account of his discovery. In the wake of the publicity, the U.S. Air Force, after receiving dozens of calls and letters, canceled their plans to use islands near the Aransas Refuge as bombsites. Kenneth Morrison, Audubon's director of publicity, was eager for another news release directly from the ornithologist. Allen was more than happy to oblige every request.

When Allen sent out his next news release toward the end of the summer, he got to the heart of the matter by describing the young whoopers' vulnerability and asking the public, "Will the five young that have been raised this season be spared, or are they to be thoughtlessly and needlessly destroyed as they attempt to cross the U.S. from Canada to their ancestral winter home on the coast of Texas?"[3]

As the cool fronts began to push their way south, refuge manager Julian Howard spent his days scanning the skies above the Texas coast. On October 27, thirteen whooping cranes came in for a landing, with more arriving daily. After an aerial survey on November 3, Howard determined that the entire flock had come home. With the elation of the discovery was an added bonus. Eight young whoopers had made the 2,500-mile trip, representing the largest number of juveniles to arrive on the Aransas National Wildlife Refuge since record keeping began in 1938. Perhaps it was just luck, or perhaps Bob Allen's efforts of the past nine years had paid off. The hunt was over, the nesting site had been found, and the job of protecting the whooping cranes in their summer home could begin.

Whooping crane Josephine and her egg on the Aransas National Wildlife Refuge, 1949. Photo by Bob Allen. Courtesy of Alice Allen.

In the years that followed the discovery, Bob Allen continued to make strides in his efforts to keep endangered birds from following in the passenger pigeon's footsteps. In 1956, Audubon published his updated monograph *A Report on the Whooping Crane's Northern Breeding Grounds: Supplement to Research Report Number 3*. In this report, Allen reiterated the importance of protecting both the cranes' northern and southern habitats and migration routes, and of continued public education as the best means of saving the species. While attending ornithological conferences, he spoke out against captive-breeding programs and encouraged scientists to focus on protecting cranes in the wild.

Allen continued to visit the Aransas Refuge in the fall as often as possible to watch for the crane families to arrive. He never lost his enthusiasm over the event as is evident in his journal entry on November 1, 1958:

"4:00 a.m. Too excited about those new arrivals of late yesterday to sleep, so am drinking coffee and waiting for daylight." Word that year from Wood Buffalo reported that three families were headed south, bringing with them a nice surprise. The following morning, Allen updated his notes every fifteen minutes. Finally, at 10:20, he noted: "Here they are . . . 3 family groups with 2 young each!"[4] Never before had the arrival of three sets of twins been documented. But more good news was on the horizon: a few days later, a fourth pair flew in with another set of twins in tow.

The public's interest in the whooping cranes had not waned. Almost twenty-eight thousand visitors from forty-four states and nine foreign countries came to the refuge in the winter of 1958–59.

⁓

When Allen returned to Tavernier after that eventful summer in Canada, the flamingo project awaited his attention. As 1956 drew to a close, Audubon published Allen's third monograph, *The Flamingos: Their Life History and Survival*. The 285-page document, detailing the limiting factors that threatened the species and conservation recommendations, still stands as one of the most comprehensive studies of flamingos ever published.

⁓

Allen's days in Tavernier were routine but busy. He resumed his early-morning writing schedule and spent the afternoons in the field, often in a skiff on Florida Bay. The spoonbill colonies had increased sevenfold since his arrival in Florida twenty-one years earlier and had become so numerous that they were a common sight along the roadsides in the winter. More and more tourists were visiting the Keys. Local restaurants, motels, RV parks, and boating and fishing services distributed the Upper Keys Chamber of Commerce new visitor's brochure. On the cover was a picture of the spoonbill; the pink curlew had earned its place in the Keys as the "star attraction."[5]

The Allens were now living in their own home. They'd purchased a small place, and additions were built over the years: an extra room in the back, a second story for Allen's Audubon office, and a small structure on top of that the Allens called "the tower" from which he could see both the Atlantic Ocean and Florida Bay. By 1951, an additional house was built next to the main house for what had been intended to become Evelyn's

Cap Watson, Bob Allen, Charlie Brookfield, and friend on dock in the Florida Keys in the late 1950s. Courtesy of Alice Allen.

parents' retirement home. Instead, Effie Sedgwick moved in that year after developing arteriosclerosis. She died in 1953. In 1960, the house was again used as a convalescence room equipped with a hospital bed, medical supplies, and a wheelchair. Bobby's diabetes had taken its toll. While Evelyn cared for her son, her music students continued their lessons with Alice as their teacher. On November 22, 1962, Thanksgiving Day, at the age of twenty-eight, Bobby succumbed to his illness.

Bob Allen retired from fieldwork in 1960 and devoted his days to writing and publishing articles and updates about his work in *Audubon Magazine*. In 1957, McGraw-Hill published Allen's book *On the Trail of Vanishing Birds*, which won him the John Burroughs Award for outstanding nature book that year. Also in 1957, the American Ornithologists'

Union presented Allen with the Brewster Memorial Award, considered the highest honor for an ornithologist. In 1961, Viking Press published Allen's *Birds of the Caribbean,* and the following year *The Giant Golden Book of Birds: An Introduction to Familiar and Interesting Birds of North America* was released by Golden Press. When the manuscript of *The Giant Golden Book of Birds* was turned in, Allen began researching his most ambitious writing project, a sixteen-volume series entitled *Birds of the World.*

Bob Allen concluded most days in the tower, where he and Evelyn would hash out his writing and then enjoy a well-deserved cocktail as the sun set over Florida Bay. Friends and fellow birders continued to drop in. Around the Christmas holidays, amateur bird-watchers often arrived at Allen's home unannounced, hoping the ornithologist would accompany them on the annual Christmas bird counts. Allen politely declined their offers, explaining that, for him, the holiday time was for the family.

On a muggy summer morning in 1963, Allen laid his notes aside and

Bob Allen at work in his office at his home in Tavernier, Florida, 1950s. Courtesy of Alice Allen.

moved closer to the window. The slight breeze helped, but only momentarily. Alice was visiting and noticed her father's ashen face when she saw him from the kitchen window. That night, he woke with chest pains. In retrospect, Alice felt her father knew something was amiss but kept it to himself so as not to alarm his family. Allen had suffered a heart attack two years earlier. When Alice arrived at her parents' home that morning, Evelyn broke the news.

On June 28, 1963, Robert Porter Allen had died on the way to the hospital. He was fifty-eight. The following year, Evelyn Allen received an official visit from President Johnson's secretary of the interior, Stewart Udall. He presented her with a presidential proclamation containing a map of Florida Bay. What had been three unnamed keys now possess the name of Florida's most renowned ornithologist. The Bob Allen Keys, near Bottlepoint Key, stand in Allen's honor.

Epilogue

Hope on the Wing

Be like the bird that,
pausing on her flight awhile on boughs too slight,
feels them give way beneath her,
and yet sings,
knowing that she hath wings.

Victor Hugo

In the five decades since Robert Porter Allen and his team of nest hunters searched for the whooping crane nesting site, the population has slowly increased. Dozens of organizations see to their protection, and hundreds of scientists and volunteers raise young, document their numbers, lobby for funds, and devote their lives to the white bird's continued survival. Today, whooping cranes number close to four hundred in the wild. That is not a large number, but considering their reproductive challenges and the odds against them, biologists and ornithologists are encouraged by the increase. But the endeavor to save the whooping crane is far from over.

The Whooping Crane Recovery Team (WCRT), made up of American and Canadian scientists, oversees the cranes' recovery and recommends policies to the USFWS and CWS. The WCRT has three primary objectives: (1) protect the Aransas/Wood Buffalo Flock and increase its population to forty breeding pairs; (2) establish a second and even a third flock in the wild, either migratory or nonmigratory, in case trouble befalls the Aransas/Wood Buffalo cranes; and (3) maintain a population in captivity to protect the gene pool. The policies currently in place are resulting in progress, with more than 160 whooping cranes breeding in captivity, but although additional populations have been reintroduced into the wild, as of yet, none of those have been self-sustaining.

The captive-breeding program, which began with Jo, Pete, and, eventually, Crip at the Aransas National Wildlife Refuge and continued at the Audubon Zoo in New Orleans, rocked along with intermittent success. In 1967, a variation on captive breeding proved more successful. To develop a captive-breeding stock, both eggs were taken from the nests of the wild flock in Wood Buffalo and checked for fertility. If both were fertile, one was returned to the nest and the other artificially incubated in a laboratory. If only one was fertile, it remained with the wild flock. If neither was viable, a fertile egg from a different pair was placed in the nest. The fertile eggs taken from the nests were sent to the Patuxent Wildlife Research Center in Maryland, where they were subsequently hatched; the young cranes were used to increase the size of the captive flock and for experimental reintroductions.

One such program, the Rocky Mountain Experimental Program, began in 1975. Fertile whooping crane eggs were placed in the nests of wild sandhill cranes living in Grays Lake National Wildlife Refuge in Idaho. The idea was for the sandhills to hatch the eggs, raise the young whoopers, and teach them to migrate the 850-mile route from Idaho to Bosque Del Apache National Wildlife Refuge in New Mexico. The first phase of the program was a great success. The sandhills proved to be effective surrogate parents. However, when the whooping cranes matured, they did not recognize themselves as a separate species. They had imprinted on the sandhills and did not reproduce. The program was canceled in 1989. Today, no whooping cranes remain in the Rocky Mountain Flock, the last one dying in 2002.

A nonmigratory flock was then established in Kissimmee, Florida, in 1993, but was discontinued after fifteen years. Severe drought conditions and loss of habitat led to a low reproduction rate and a shorter-than-average lifespan. Predation was a recurring problem. Currently, there are fewer than two dozen whooping cranes left in Florida's nonmigratory flock.

The wild Aransas/Wood Buffalo flock is holding its own, but its survival continues to teeter. The refuge in Texas not only provides whooping cranes a suitable climate in which to spend the winter, but during their stay, they spend a majority of their time feeding to build up reserves for their migration in the spring. When these birds are forced to fly daily to find food and freshwater to drink, they use nineteen times more energy than when leisurely wading in the marshes. In 1994, whooping cranes returning to Canada arrived weak and undernourished due to an inadequate food supply that winter in Texas. As a result, the number of nests located in Wood Buffalo decreased from forty-five the previous year to only twenty-eight. When the food supply improved the following winter, the number of nests in Canada subsequently increased.

This wild population took another hard hit starting in the spring migration 2008 and continuing through the following spring. Twenty-one percent of the flock was lost during that twelve-month period, the highest mortality number ever. Of the fifty-seven whooping cranes that died that year, twenty-three died while on the Aransas National Wildlife Refuge. The other thirty-four died between spring and fall, with most losses felt to have occurred between the spring and fall migration periods. The Guadalupe and San Antonio Rivers supply the refuge with freshwater. Overdevelopment and recent severe drought conditions have significantly decreased the rivers' flow into the refuge's marshlands, raising the salinity level and decreasing the whooping cranes' food supply and water source. In the January 2010 whooping crane status report, the population of blue crab and wolfberry was at an all-time low, forcing the cranes to fly to the upland area of the refuge in search of food, putting themselves at higher risk of predation. That winter several reports came in from nearby landowners, noting that the cranes had been feeding at game feeders put out for deer. On one occasion, a crane family was seen feeding at a pond located right next to Highway 35 near Holiday Beach.

To help ameliorate the food shortage, prescribed burns were conducted on more than 14,000 acres, clearing away the brush so the cranes could forage for acorns closer to the marsh. Corn was distributed as a supplement food when the emaciated dead bodies of several young cranes were discovered. Crabbing was closed within the boundary waters of the refuge, and more than twenty-seven thousand abandoned crab traps were removed from Texas coastal waters. When the rains came to Aransas starting in the fall of 2009, breaking a two-year drought, the crane flock responded; the May 2010 count reported a record seventy-four nests in Wood Buffalo National Park.

The lack of freshwater on the Texas refuge, however, is still an issue. In December 2009, the Aransas Project, an alliance of environmentalists and local businesses, sued the Texas Commission on Environmental Quality, the governmental organization responsible for authorizing river-water use, over water diversion along the Guadalupe River. The International Crane Foundation has joined the alliance, and the lawsuit is pending in federal court.

Because of the vulnerability of the Aransas/Wood Buffalo Flock, it was imperative that a second, wild migratory flock be established. With the success of incubating the wild eggs in captivity, the Whooping Crane Recovery Program (WCRP) had the seed for the establishment of this wild flock. What the WCRP needed now was to figure out how to raise and teach the new flock to migrate without them imprinting on another species. The answers lay in the endeavors of two innovative Ontarians.

In 1988, sculpture artist and naturalist Bill Lishman taught a small flock of geese to follow behind as he flew his ultralight around his home in Ontario. Lishman's work later became the inspiration for two major motion pictures, *Fly Away Home* and *Winged Migration*. When scientists working with the WCRP got word of Lishman's success, they contacted him with the proposal that he teach whooping cranes to migrate. Lishman agreed to give it a try, but he wasn't sure if the birds would follow for long distances. Further experiments were needed, and he solicited the help of ultralight pilot and commercial photographer Joe Duff.

Lishman and Duff raised eighteen Canada geese and conducted several successful short trial flights. On October 19, 1993, the two pilots climbed into their ultralight aircrafts and took to the sky. All eighteen geese followed on the wing, flying almost 500 miles from Lishman's home in southern Ontario to Airlie Center in Warrenton, Virginia. When these geese found their way home the following spring, Lishman and Duff knew the same could be done with whooping cranes.

The next phase of the project was to figure out how to raise and train the birds without them imprinting on their handlers. Their idea, which at first seemed laughable, proved successful. Since adult cranes were not available as surrogate parents, Lishman and Duff wore crane costumes to disguise the human form while in contact with the birds. A crane "dummy" was used for imprinting as well as an adult brood model.

With the success of the program, Lishman and Duff founded Operation Migration (OM), a nonprofit organization with a mission to advance the conservation of migratory species and their habitat through innovative research, education, and partnership. The results of their studies were presented to the Whooping Crane Recovery Team, and eventually, OM became a founding member of the Whooping Crane Eastern Partnership (WCEP), a coalition of private and government agencies established to administer the reintroduction of migratory whooping cranes into eastern North America.

After more than a decade of research and trials, OM launched its first human-assisted whooping crane migration in 2001. A team of costumed pilots, biologists, and aviculturists raised, imprinted, and conditioned whooping cranes to follow ultralight aircraft 1,250 miles from the Necedah National Wildlife Refuge in Wisconsin to the Chassahowitzka National Wildlife Refuge in Florida. The following year, the cranes returned to Wisconsin unassisted. The experiment, which many in the field referred to as the wildlife equivalent of putting a man on the moon, was a triumph.

Since then, Operation Migration has been featured on *20/20, 60 Minutes*, Discovery's *Animal Planet*, and numerous other television programs. The Whooping Crane Eastern Partnership has been the subject of more than five hundred media stories annually. OM also participates in the International Migratory Bird Day at Disney's Animal Kingdom. One of OM's ultralights is now on permanent display at the Smithsonian Air and Space Museum in Washington.

At the writing of this book, ten generations of whooping cranes totaling about 100 birds are migrating along the new flyway in the eastern United States. There are close to twenty mating pairs established on the way to reaching the goal of twenty-five set by the Whooping Crane Eastern Partnership's (WCEP).

Each year's project work begins in April, when fertile whooping crane eggs are produced by the captive flock at the Patuxent Wildlife Research Center. Additional eggs had been laid as far away as Calgary and New Orleans and hand-carried by crane caretakers on commercial airlines flights in suitcase incubators to be added to the reintroduction program. The conditioning and imprinting starts while the chicks are still developing inside the egg. A recording of the engine noise of the ground-training vehicle (trike) is played during incubation to acclimate the birds to the sound. When the birds hatch, they are given an identification number. The first numbers indicate the order in which they hatched, and the next two numbers represent the year. For example, chick 6-04 was the sixth crane to hatch in 2004. From then on, they are cared for by a costumed handler who wears a whooping crane puppet head on one hand. The cranes learn to follow the puppet and the trike during individual training exercises. As the birds get older, they begin to socialize with their flock mates and their training continues. At about forty to fifty days of age, they are shipped to the Necedah National Wildlife Refuge, where they begin flight training in preparation for their migration starting in October.

For the OM team, raising a group of young whooping cranes is not much different from raising an extra-large family of children. The birds' personalities emerge immediately upon hatching. There are the dominant ones, the shy ones, the gifted ones, the stubborn ones, the weak ones who require extra care and keep the Patuxent and the OM team up at night, and those who instigate trouble and stand back to watch the outcome.

From the time the young cranes arrive in Wisconsin, they are trained in small groups called cohorts. During training, it's crucial to get each year's young flock in a cooperative frame of mind so the migration can be a success.

The following is a summary of each class of whooping cranes in the Eastern Migratory Flock. On OM's website under "In the Field," you can read daily reports of the progress of the current class of cranes and keep abreast of the entire Eastern Migratory Flock with the status updates. Under "Site Map," you can see the photos of the chicks and read their individual bios. In the class summaries I've compiled, it was difficult not to report on every young whooper since the program began in 2001. Doing so, however, would have added a few hundred more pages to this book.

For me, reading the field notes each year is like reading a page-turning adventure novel. The cranes' stories are fraught with humor, sadness, surprise, and sometimes, tragedy. The dedication of the WCEP team—scientists, ground crew, pilots, bird handlers, coordinators, and volunteers—is unparalleled. My attempt to summarize each year does not hold a candle to reading the actual field notes. The contributors are not only prolific writers but creative and excellent in their craft. By capturing the highlights, I hope to encourage you to log on to OM's website (www. operationmigration.org) and see for yourself. You won't be disappointed.

Class of 2001: The Maiden Voyage

The training over, preparation completed, the weather perfect. The day was October 17, 2001. At 7:15 on this bright, crisp morning, eight whooping crane chicks took to the air behind three ultralight crafts and began their migration south. That first day's takeoff went off without a hitch. It lasted forty-four minutes and covered 29⅓ miles. Only one chick turned back and dropped out, but he was located, crated, and reunited with his flock mates that evening. Forty-eight days and 1,215 miles later, history was made when the first human-assisted migration of wild whooping cranes was completed. Numbers 1-01, 2-01, 5-01, 6-01, 07-01, and 10-01 landed in Chassahowitzka National Wildlife Refuge in Crystal River, Florida, on December 6. This remote refuge, accessible only by water, would become their winter home.

The maiden voyage was not without trouble, however. On the night of October 25, high winds blew through the valley where the birds were penned for the night in Green County, Wisconsin. Team members Deke Clark and Dan Sprague checked on the birds at sunset and were shocked to find their pen overturned and empty. By 2:00 a.m., honing in on radio transmitters attached to the cranes' legs, the team located all but one bird. The body of 3-01 was discovered later that morning; he'd evidently collided with a power line. Later that winter, in Florida, bobcats killed numbers 4-01 and 10-01, and in May 2005, another predator killed 6-01. But along with disappointments came successes.

During training, number 1-01 gained the reputation of a born leader. And once the trip began, he often took the lead position and never fell back. That first year, he paired with number 2-01, an aggressive female, and the following spring, the two cranes returned home to Wisconsin together. That summer, they were often seen hanging around the Class of 2002 during their training. It was as if they visited the rookies to say, "We did it. You can, too."

To this day, four cranes from that first class, numbers 1-01, 2-01, 5-01, and 7-01, are alive and healthy and continue to migrate.

Class of 2002: The Dirty Dozen

The second year saw sixteen whoopers take to the sky on October 13. Due to bad weather, the cranes flew only twenty-one days during the forty-nine-day trip to Crystal River, Florida. On November 23, a week before they reached their destination, the whoopers staged a day of rebellion. Shortly after takeoff, the cranes began falling back from the lead ultralights. The chase pilot flew in to round up the strays that had scattered, but the three pilots had a difficult time keeping up with their wards. One of the cranes, it was not determined which, began leading the others away from the ultralights. After several attempts to wrangle them in, two of the pilots decided to lead the twelve rebels, nicknamed the Dirty Dozen, back to the pen, allowing the well-behaved birds to continue on to the next stop with the other pilot.

The next morning, a heavy fog rolled in, threatening to cancel the flight. But the weather improved, and after several false starts, the Dirty Dozen took off behind the two ultralights to meet up with the rest of the group waiting in Gordon County, Georgia. At first it seemed the birds would cooperate, lining up single file behind pilot Joe Duff's wingtip. Within minutes, they turned and headed back to the pen.

When reluctant cranes return to the previous stop or refuse to leave their pens, the swamp monster—a member of the OM crew dressed in a camouflage tarp—attempts to frighten the cranes into leaving. When the Dirty Dozen returned that morning, the swamp monster was waiting. Wanting no part of this mutant crane, the whoopers rose again and followed the ultralight. Not long after, they fell behind and landed in a field near the pen but far enough from the reaches of the swamp monster. The pilots and birds were up and down several times before Duff and fellow pilot Brooke Pennypacker were forced to land and refuel. Once they were again airborne, Duff radioed that six cranes were following on his left wing. A few minutes later, he radioed Dan Sprague, a member of the ground crew, to report that there were now eight cranes following. Dan radioed back that he had not yet released the other six. Was Duff sure he had counted eight cranes off his wing? Duff counted again. Yep, definitely eight birds! Somewhere along the way, they'd picked up two additional cranes.

The two birds were the curious yearlings 1-01 and 2-01 from the Class of 2001 that had often visited the chicks during their training. They had arrived in the area the evening before on their way south and apparently decided to tag along. The two older birds flew in formation with youngsters before pulling away on their own. In the meantime, Sprague released the other six, but they refused to take to the air. Three of Duff's cranes broke flight and returned. Now Sprague had nine delinquents to deal with. After two days of trying to get the reluctant flyers to leave the Hiwassee Refuge in Tennessee, the crew gave up and crated the birds and transported them by van into Georgia. The week after the cranes' rebellion went smoothly, with the birds covering the remaining distance without incident.

Two cranes from this class went on to make history. Number 11-02, described as a bully and a whacky bird often fighting anything that moved and stomping around as if killing imaginary snakes, mated with 17-02, a small, quiet female. On June 22, 2006, the crane couple hatched twins, making them the First Family of the Eastern Migratory Flock.

Class of 2003: The Flyaway Five

During most of the 2003 trip south, the weather and the birds cooperated, with December 1 turning out to be a record-breaking day. The three ultralights and sixteen whooping cranes left Gordon Country, Georgia, at 7:51 a.m. With a swift tailwind, the pilots skipped the first stop (not unusual—they had done this a few times before), then just as quickly, the second stop fell away and then the third, with the entire group arriving three hours and four minutes later in Terrell Country, Georgia, 200 miles away. Eight smooth-flying days later, on December 8, a crowd of more than a thousand people had gathered at the Crystal River Mall to watch the Class of 2003 glide over to their ultimate stop on the Chassahowitzka National Wildlife Refuge. All sixteen whoopers strutted into their temporary enclosure like their arrival had been an everyday occurrence. In moments, they were digging for snails, splattering their white feathers with mud.

The 2003 migration had taken only fifty-four days.

Number 9-03, the most independent member of the Class of 2003, had no problem making that first voyage to Florida. Getting back to her summer in Wisconsin wasn't so easy. In April 2004, she joined eight of her classmates for the first trip back to Wisconsin. During a stopover in Tennessee, an observer who had gotten too close flushed the cranes from their evening roost, causing them to fly off course. The eight birds ended up in Michigan, but by midsummer three of them had figured out how to get around the southern end of Lake Michigan and return to Necedah. Number 9-03, along with 1-03, 5-03, 18-03, and 19-03, turned and headed west. The Flyaway Five found a suitable marsh in Michigan and stayed until it was time to migrate south. That summer, 19-03 was lost to a predator, and the small group was down to four. On November 7, they left Michigan, and five days later, while roosting on the Cape Romain National Wildlife Refuge in Charleston County, South Carolina, 5-03 was also killed by a predator. It's believed that 5-03 was attacked during the night, causing 9-03, 1-03, and 18-03 to scatter in the aftermath, flying around the Carolinas and settling down on November 20 in Jones County, North Carolina, where they wintered over. The three left on March 30, heading north and following the southern shoreline of Lake Erie into New York, and finally eastward to Ontario.

The last time the wandering three were together was on April 14 in Grey Country, Ontario. On May 8, number 9-03 was reported alone on the shore of the St. Lawrence River east of Lake Ontario. By June 9, she had found her way to Vermont. It was clear she was lost, and all hope that she would find her way back to Wisconsin was dashed. If left alone, her chances of finding a mate, or even surviving, were slim. The tracking team decided to capture her. Easier said than done. She eluded their every attempt. "She's an important bird to the program, and if we leave her where she is, we eliminate any chance there is that this bird will mate," Joe Duff said. "She's a good, wild bird, certainly independent."[1] Number 9-03's migratory instinct must have kicked in. Around August 1, she was in Lewis County, New York. By December 9, she was in Beaufort County, North Carolina. The team captured her on December 16 and crated her back to Florida to join her fellow whoopers for the rest of the winter.

When it came time for the cranes to migrate north in 2006, the WCEP team was encouraged when 9-03 set off in the right direction with the younger bird number 20-05. Then, as the birds neared Tennessee, 9-03 took a turn back to the Northeast. Following her route from the previous spring, she led 20-05 all the way up to Ontario and then back down to Lewis County, New York. They were captured on May 5 and flown to Wisconsin.

After wandering all over the eastern United States for three years, number 9-03 had returned home for the first time since leaving Necedah National Wildlife Refuge. Since then, 9-03 has been on track with the rest of the Eastern Flock and is doing well. Numbers 1-03 and 18-03 made it back to Wisconsin on their own.

On May 31, 2010, number 9-03 and her mate, 3-04, hatched twin whoopers. Although one chick disappeared a week later, the other grew fat and happy.

Class of 2004: The Little Girls

The Cumberland Plateau's eastern edge is marred by a 3,000-foot rocky uplift called Walden Ridge. The dreaded 176-mile long rise, running southwest to northeast across Tennessee, has earned the nickname "the Beast" from the OM Team. For a young, inexperienced whooping crane migrating across the country for the first time, this flyover is a daunting obstacle. For an ultralight, it can be dangerous. The crackerjack pilots have braved the altitude safely, but not always swiftly, and managed to coax three generations of cranes up and over the Beast. In 2003, this leg of the journey proved harrowing. On November 20, all sixteen cranes lifted off smoothly. As they approached the ridge and began to rise, the entire flock broke off, turned around, and headed back to the previous night's stopover. The swamp monster performed its monster dance and kept the birds from landing.

The flock approached the ridge a second time and again turned back. Deciding that the swamp monster was less frightening then the Beast, all sixteen landed. It was evident they were going nowhere. The crew gave up and returned the birds to the pen. Bad weather grounded them for the next three days. On November 25, they gave it another shot. Thirty-eight minutes after takeoff, two birds made it over the ridge, easily following OM pilot Richard van Heuvelen. When the other fourteen turned back, pilots Joe Duff and Brooke Pennypacker coaxed six more over. The eight remaining cranes scattered. At the end of the harrowing day, these weary eight were located, crated, and driven to the next location to join their flock mates.

In 2004, a new strategy for tackling the Beast was put to the test. Rather than stop below Walden Ridge and fly directly over it, the OM team located a spot 15 miles north, giving the pilots a longer but more gradual incline to climb. On November 18, all fourteen members of the Class of 2004 flew north toward the Appalachian Mountains, then over the Beast. One hour and fifteen minutes later, they landed safely at the Hiwassee State Wildlife Refuge. From that day forward, all future voyages would follow this route.

Scaling the big mountain that year were the two youngest birds, referred to by the OM team as the "little girls."[2] These two had proven that, despite their size and age, they did not fly like girls. Number 19-04 copped an attitude early on and had earned a reputation as one not to be messed with. The brave, independent chick rose to the top of the pecking order in her cohort. Her buddy, number 20-04, was not only the youngest, but the smallest. When left alone she would often scrunch down into a small puffball, but while slumming around with number 19-04, she would suddenly puff up like a big bird ready for trouble. After a day of exercise, she'd often rush into the field to hunt mice, earning the nickname "little dirtball."[3] Troublemaker number 14-04 took notice of the two gals and began hanging around.

During flight training, numbers 19-04 and 20-04 had learned quickly, but the first day of migration proved difficult for them. The chicks persistently turned back along with four others and number 14-04. After several attempts to get them to follow the ultralight, the reluctant birds were crated to the first stop.

Bad weather resulted in eleven down days during the next two weeks. Finally, on October 24, the day looked promising, and the pilots took off at 7:14 a.m. It was clear from the get-go that the cranes would not cooperate, flying in all four directions, causing the pilots to wrangle them up every few minutes. Toward the end of the day's journey, three birds were missing, the two little girls and the troublemaker. The crew located them and crated them to the next stop. The reminder of the journey was troublesome, but the two "little girls" with attitude hung in there.

In the spring of 2006, number 20-04 took up with a flock of sandhill cranes in Rusk County, Wisconsin. Number 19-04 paired with number 12-02, and in June 2010, the couple hatched a chick.

Class of 2005: Jonathan Livingston Whooping Crane

During number 6-05's first two months, numbers 5-05 and 7-05 often challenged him for the dominant position. The three cranes engaged in several mild skirmishes, with number 6-05 often the instigator but rarely the cleanup guy. On June 15, all three were shipped to Wisconsin as part of Cohort One. There, number 6-05's dominance quickly withered, and his status fell. His flight training was difficult due to a recurring respiratory problem, resulting in occasional coughs and a weak-sounding peep.

On August 10, during a flight training exercise on the refuge, the noise of nearby highway traffic spooked Cohort One. Rather than cause additional stress to the inexperienced flyers, the pilots guided the birds over a wooded area and back to the pen. Unable to quickly gain altitude, 6-05 fell back and got lost.

Pilot Richard van Heuvelen circled over the area several times and was unable to locate the chick. An emergency call went out, and a full-scale search began, complete with GPS, crate, first-aid kit, vocalizer, waders, binoculars, and, most important, birdie treats. Under rainy skies, van Heuvelen searched from the air while several others combed the woods. Six hours later, a call came in from a refuge employee. He spotted number 6-05 strolling down the Headquarters Road toward the entrance. Piecing things together, it was most likely that 6-05 heard the vocalizer, but its radio signal was too weak for the receiver to hear. Since the little guy loved to forage, it was suspected that he had probably been nearby the entire time, enjoying a bountiful buffet in the woods, and when he was sufficiently satiated, the tired chick decided it was time to head home.

On the first day of migration, 6-05 refused to follow the ultralight and had to be crated to the first stop. He held his own until November 25, when it was time to cross the Appalachians. That morning as Joe Duff gained altitude, all twenty chicks followed. Soon 6-05 dropped away. On the other side of the mountain, Duff landed with nine birds. Ten others were on their way down, and one lone bird—a mere white speck in the sky hundreds of feet up—was still flying. Thinking the high flyer was an older bird from a previous year's flock, the team was surprised to learn it was 6-05, who had obviously found his wings and was having too much fun to land. The remainder of the migration went well for 6-05. He is still flying today.

Class of 2006: The Best Was Not to Be

The Class of 2006 offered great hopes for the WCEP. Their genetic viability was better than that of all previous classes. Dr. Ken Jones, the geneticist for WCEP, reported that this group's genetic diversity would enhance the flock's strength in the future. Except for a brief scare over one errant crane, all eighteen cranes arrived in Florida without much trouble. The migration, although a long one due to inclement weather, went smoothly, with fewer birds than ever requiring crating along the way.

Two days before the cranes completed their journey, they had a short but tough flight. Warm temperatures and turbulent conditions exhausted the birds shortly after takeoff. Some of the chicks fell behind. One clipped a tree limb upon landing, and another touched down 3 miles from the stopping place. Number 15-06 was nowhere in sight. A search began immediately and continued late into the night before it was called off. The next morning, only seventeen birds flew to the next-to-last stopover.

During training, number 15-06 had gained a reputation as being an obstinate bird, often frustrating his handlers and later challenging the ultralights while migrating. But when a bird goes missing, such negative characteristics are quickly forgotten.

Richard van Heuvelen drove the tracking van along the back roads to the place where 15-06 had last been seen. Cover pilots Don and Paula Lounsbury, who helped with the migration in Indiana, volunteered to search for the bird from the air. About two hours into the search, the Lounsburys picked up a faint beep and radioed van Heuvelen, who was 30 miles away. As he raced to the area, the pilots reported that the signal was growing stronger. When van Heuvelen got close, his signal came in loud and clear. The Lounsburys spotted the bird from the air and directed van Heuvelen to the location, a small pond off the road.

Number 15-06 was standing on a mound in the pond chirping loudly and surveying the area as if looking for his rescuers. Richard van Heuvelen pulled over, donned his crane costume, and trekked to the pond, but the young crane became frightened and was reluctant to follow. Richard van Heuvelen, using the puppet head, probed the dirt and tossed pieces of wood in 15-06's direction. The crane calmed and allowed himself to be picked up and crated for his trip to join his classmates in Marion County, Florida.

For the first five migrations, the young whooping cranes were acclimated to their new home in Florida by placing them in a 4-acre pen without a top cover. Once the cranes realized they could fly out, they left the pen to forage the area on their own. At night they were called back into their pen, where they were protected from predators. After five years, new challenges arose. Because whooping cranes are territorial, older birds would fly into the pen and chase the youngsters from the feeding and roosting stations. Aggressive encounters often resulted. If the young, inexperienced whoopers are chased from their pen out into the open, they could easily fall victim to predators. To prevent the Class of 2006 from harassment by older birds, a top cover was added to a portion of the pen, and the chicks were placed inside. It would be removed after the older birds departed and had moved on to their normal wintering areas.

On the night of February 1, the weather forecast warned of a storm brewing in central Florida. The chicks were checked before sunset, their feeders filled and freshwater provided. The monitoring team was not concerned. The chicks were used to bad weather. One of the refuge employees was out later that evening in his airboat and reported the conditions were calm, with no indication of severe weather.

The storm blew in around midnight and grew to an intensity no one expected.

The news the next morning reported the storm as the second-worst non-hurricane storm in Florida history; twenty people had died. When the monitoring team went out to check on the cranes, they were happy to see the pen intact but grew uneasy when the cranes were not visible.

On February 2, the annual Whooping Crane Recovery Team meeting was under way in Louisiana. Members of the Whooping Crane Eastern Partnership and the Whooping Crane Conservation Association were in attendance. Joe Duff received a call from the monitoring team and had to interrupt the meeting to report that the entire Class of 2006 had died in the storm. Lightning had struck, hitting the water close to the pen, electrocuting the birds.

The Operation Migration Class of 2006 was gone in an instant; gone were the hundreds of hours of raising and training the chicks to follow the ultralights, gone were the thousands of dollars used to fund the migration project. But for the dozens of staff members and volunteers of the Whooping Crane Eastern Partnership who had cared for and grown attached to birds, the emotional loss was immeasurable.

When the bodies of the birds were collected, only seventeen were found. The troublemaker number 15-06 was not in the enclosure. A search ensued, but there was not much hope of finding him alive. The next day, a slight beep of his radio transmitter was heard near the pen site. At first, it was assumed that his body had been overlooked. Then a day later, another signal was heard a few miles away. Number 15-06 was alive! He was found with two sandhill cranes some distance away. In the aftermath of the disaster, this tenacious little bird, for the first time in his life, was a cause for celebration.

Over the next few days, the tragic story of the Class of 2006 was reported by all the major news networks across the country and was picked up by more than five hundred media agencies internationally. Thousands of e-mails, letters, and phone calls came in offering sympathy and support. Monetary donations were given to offset the financial setbacks caused by the disaster. In a media release, John Christian, co-chair of the Whooping Crane Eastern Partnership, said: "My heart is aching both for the young birds we lost and for the dedicated people who have devoted so much of themselves to this project, only to see the lives of these cranes end in this devastating manner. These birds were the start of a new generation of life for the species, but we will recover and continue our work. Our thoughts also go out to those in central Florida who suffered personal losses as a result of these storms."[4]

For the next week, number 15-06 was active on the refuge, flying with sandhills and older whooping cranes. He was seen at the nearby Halpata Nature Preserve, the location of an alternate pen site, but roosting outside the enclosure where predators were often spotted. For his safely, he was captured and placed with another crane that had also begun roosting in a less than favorable location. Once a suitable location was selected, 15-06 was released and monitored for several days. As the spring migration began and the Eastern Flock headed back to Wisconsin, the OM team waited anxiously for news that the sole survivor of the Class of 2006 had joined a group and was on his way. On April 30, his body was found near the Halpata pen site. A necropsy was unable to determine the cause of death of number 15-06, a stubborn little trooper who, for a few short weeks, offered the only smidgen of hope for the Class of 2006.

Class of 2007: One Tough Little Bird

The youngest chicks, number 33-07 and the small female number 35-07, were two of the last birds to arrive from Patuxent. Number 33-07, despite his age, had no problem displaying aggression toward older chicks. Whenever 33-07 was removed for his swimming exercises while in Patuxent, a collective sigh of relief seemed to come from his four group mates. Number 33-07 and 35-07 had been trained with older whoopers, and when they joined the cohort containing 23-07, 26-07, and 27-07, number 33-07 upset the social order and proclaimed himself in charge. The others learned to stay out of his way, and the group settled down.

On the forty-second day of migration after a week on the ground due to bad weather, the Class of 2007 set off again. The morning was bitter cold as they left Muscatatuck National Wildlife Refuge in Jackson City, Indiana, on the way to the next stop in Shelby County, Kentucky. About 15 miles into the flight, 33-07 dropped out. A tracking van was sent to locate the bird, but was unable to pick up a radio signal. The next day, top-cover pilots, a tracking van, and the rest of the crew traveling in various vehicles, backtracked north hoping to hone in on a signal. It was a great day for flying, and the team hoped 33-07 would take to the air of his own volition, but when the sun set, the missing whooper was still out there. The next day's search led the crew back to Muscatatuck NWR, thinking 33-07 might have returned to the last stop. The other sixteen cranes were led south while the hunt for the missing bird continued.

The next day, the search crew returned to Morgan County. Frustration levels rose. OM had never lost a bird on migration; a few had separated from the flock but had always been found. November 24 and 25 came and went with no success. There was the possibility number 33-07 could have joined a flock of sandhill cranes heading south. If that were the case, capturing him among a large flock would be difficult. Leaving him with the sandhills would lessen the likelihood he would ever mate in the future. He was too valuable for the team to consider releasing him directly into the wild. Because he had dropped out several times and missed flying certain sections of the route, chances were he would not find his way back to Wisconsin in the spring. He needed to be reunited with his class to ensure his survival.

With thunderstorms on the horizon, the team did not fly on November 26, allowing all manpower to focus on finding number 33-07. The media in the area were alerted, and a missing-bird poster of the five-month-old whooping crane was circulated. That day the team received several calls from locals who said they had spotted the bird, only to discover one sighting was a great blue heron and several others were white plastic bags. For the next two days, the OM team and several volunteers thoroughly

combed southeastern Indiana and most of Kentucky. WHAS-TV in Louisville broadcast news of the missing bird, and the *Louisville Courier News*
ran the story in their local news section, prompting more than six thousand e-mails and phone calls from folks concerned about the lost bird.

On the morning of November 29, Arthur Mayer was out surveying
his property when he spotted a lone white bird with black wing tips. He
snapped a photo and e-mailed it to OM. A tracker confirmed that the bird
on Mayer's property was indeed 33-07. The wandering whooper didn't
stay long, but at least they had a lead on his location. He then flew off
and was spotted again at Muscatatuck NWR. He landed on a dairy farm
near Big Springs, Kentucky. When the trackers found him, he was peeping loudly in a cattle pasture. After the six-day ordeal, the whooper, now
a bit humble, was back with his classmates. Except for dropping out on
December 29, he behaved himself the rest of the way.

The remainder of the migration was not without difficulties. Bad
weather resulted in the team covering only 10 miles between December
6 and 17. Joe Duff had engine trouble along the way, and 3-07, the most
dominant bird in the flock, challenged the ultralights almost daily. The
2007 migration was the longest yet, but despite the difficulties, all seventeen birds arrived safely, with 33-07 crated the last few miles due to an
injury.

Class of 2008: Good Luck!

It could have been abandonment issues, an aggressive gene, or a loose
screw, but when number 10-08 pecked away his shell and entered the
world, he was a force to be reckoned with. His parents were from the
Class of 2003 nesting for the first time at Necedah. In their inexperience,
they abandoned the nest. Their two eggs were collected and transported
to the Patuxent Wildlife Research Center. Number 10-08 and his sister, 11-
08, were incubated and added to the ultralight cohort. When number 11-
08 was shipped to the Necedah NWR, printed on the side of his box were
the words, GOOD LUCK. The team isolated him for a couple of days to
observe his behavior. Feeling that he'd adjusted to his new home after a
few days, they introduced him to the members of his cohort. Within three
hours, he had fatally injured one crane and seriously injured two others,
including his sister, 11-08. Number 11-08 experienced mental and physical

stress, resulting in her feathers developing improperly. Sadly, she had to be removed from training and was sent to the Milwaukee Zoo. The other injured crane was removed as well.

Number 10-08 was isolated again and then placed in Cohort One with the older chicks, who the team hoped would keep 10-08 in line. The strategy worked until it was time to combine Cohorts One and Two. The aggressive crane wasted no time in grabbing the beak of number 13-08 through a chain-link fence. The younger bird was rescued before any serious injury resulted. The next morning, 10-08 attacked several other youngsters from Cohort Two. He was again placed in confinement.

The WCEP team held a conference to decide what to do with the rebel crane. He was too genetically valuable to remove from the flock, but too aggressive to continue to train with the other chicks. The Class of 2008 had already dwindled to fourteen and could not afford another loss. Ten days before the scheduled migration, the WCEP team decided to release the five-month-old chick on the Necedah NWR, hoping he would take up with older cranes and follow them south.

On the evening of October 22, number 10-08 was given his freedom. His flock mates had left on their maiden voyage five days earlier. The training crew left a pumpkin as a good-bye treat, gave the bird a pat on the back, and walked away. A few days later, as if knowing exactly what he was doing, he had taken up with two older cranes, numbers 18-03 and 13-03, who just happened to be his natural parents.

Class of 2009: Water Rat

At first it seemed that number 18-09 preferred to muck around in the muddy water rather than fly. He was independent-minded, and his fascination with the nearby swamp during flight training had become a problem. He was the last to come out of the pen, probably hoping no one would notice him so he could play in the water. As the other birds took to the runway to follow the trike, 18-09 would run to the fence and hop over into the marsh. An adult pair, 13-02 and 18-02, took a liking to the little bird and challenged the trainers whenever they tried to lure him back to the group.

One day toward the end of July, number 18-09 hung back and chose not to follow the trike. When the training pilot and the good little birds came around on the second lap, 18-09 leaped over the fence and fled into the swamp. Numbers 8-09 and 14-09 seemed to think the endeavor looked like fun and followed. The swamp monster came out of hiding and frightened 8-09 and 14-09 back over the fence to the runway. But it would take more than the swamp monster to get 18-09 away from the water.

At the end of the day's training, two team members, one playing the bad guy (swamp monster) and the other, the good guy (sweet-talking human "bird" in costume), tried to scare and coax 18-09 back over the fence where he belonged. All of a sudden, the two older cranes appeared with the intention of keeping their ward from returning to the pen with the odd-looking crane with baggy cloth "skin." After an aggressive display by both parties, the human cranes, now covered with mud, managed to wrangle 18-09 home.

The idea of releasing 18-09 to the two adults who seemed to want to adopt him was discussed, but with insufficient data on how well wild adults raise a chick they did not hatch, the move was considered too risky. Over the next several days, 18-09 made progress. Lured out of the pen and onto the runway with grapes, he began to fly with the other chicks on the way out. Returning from flight training, however, he habitually hopped the fence and joined 13-02 and 18-02, who had, in the meantime, established the marsh near the pen as their territory, making it even more difficult for the team to regain possession of 18-09.

As training continued, 18-09's behavior improved. Except for a few incidents, he performed well during migration. In the spring, he found his way back home, no doubt stopping at a few mud puddles on the way.

Year 2009 was one to celebrate. OM had crossed the 10,000-mile mark in leading whooping crane chicks on their first migrations south. On January 20, after eighty-nine days on the road, ten of the eleven chicks in the Class of 2009 arrived safely in Florida.

Class of 2010

The Class of 2010 will always hold a special place in my heart. One foggy morning in August of that year, while visiting the Necedah National Wildlife Refuge, I had the opportunity to watch an early-morning training flight of Cohort Two. I had been reading the daily field notes since the chicks were hatched and was delighted to learned that number 10-10, one of my favorite birds, was one of the five in Cohort Two running along the runway, flapping her wings, and doing her thing.

The scientists and handlers who raise and train the chicks avoid referring to their wards by anything but their assigned number. This year, however, several 2010 chicks earned nicknames, some more than one. Number 16-10 was a slow learner, often needing extra-long lessons during training, but as she grew, she became aggressive and feisty, earning the name "Frances." Another late bloomer, number 6-10, was shy and introverted during ground school. Life on the wing was a completely different story from life on turf. Once in the air, she flew like a daredevil aviator, often getting in front of the ultralight in an attempt to overtake it. She earned the moniker "acrobatic queen." At times her antics caused her to lose control and fall below the aircraft. Once she gained her wings back, she'd try again to take the lead position. One morning, pilot Richard van Heuvelen reported seeing her flying inverted and suggested she might be proficient enough to star in her own air show. Being confident in the air, she was the last to land at the end of a day's fight. No surprise that 6-10 flew the entire migration trip.

Number 15-10, curious, happy, and eager, was given the names "the optimist" and "Champ" because he consistently gave it his all during training. He was one of the first to leave the pen and didn't need to be coaxed to take to the air. For some unknown reason, one of his handlers named him "Louis." During migration he took to following number 10-10, who had also earned three nicknames. Her favorite food on the Patuxent National Wildlife Refuge, where she was hatched, was the purple clover. She couldn't resist gulping down as many blossoms as she could get her beak on. Intern Trish Gallagher reported seeing the large flower buds traveling down the chick's esophagus after she swallowed and named her Flower Child. On mornings when 10-10 refused to leave her pen for training, Brooke Pennypacker picked wild flowers and used them to lure her out. Pennypacker named her Woodstock. And another intern, Geoff Tarbox, named her Zoey after a spacey character in a video game. Even though 10-10 was content to settle down among the flowers and gaze off into space during training, she proved a trooper on migration and completed the journey successfully.

Eleven chicks took off on October 10, 2010, and landed in Florida in only seventy-three days. Due to a torn tendon, number 2-10 was removed from the flock and returned to Patuxent Wildlife Research Center. Once in Florida, the flock was split into two groups, five going to St. Mark's National Wildlife Refuge and five to Chassahowitzka National Wildlife Refuge. The acrobatic queen, Louis, Frances, and the others are all doing well, and Zoey "Flower Child" Woodstock need not worry—the marsh of her winter home has its share of flowers.

At the writing of this book, ten classes of captive-raised whooping cranes have been migrating from Wisconsin to Florida. It is estimated that there are thirteen or fourteen breeding pairs in this Eastern Migratory Population (EMP). Like the wild Wood Buffalo/Aransas Flock, the cranes face dangers along the way. The WCEP attempts to keep tabs on the birds as well as they can. Current status reports are given periodically on the Operation Migration website. But with all the innovative new programs and efforts to protect this bird, the problem that most concerned Robert Porter Allen more than fifty years ago still exists. On December 30, 2010, three juvenile whooping cranes from Direct Autumn Release (a program operated by the International Crane Foundation in Baraboo, Wisconsin) were intentionally shot and killed in Calhoun County, Georgia, on their first migration. The bodies of numbers 20-10, 24-10, and 28-10 were discovered on private property by the owner. Then, in February 2011, two more whooping cranes, numbers 22-10 and 12-04, were killed by gunshot, their bodies discovered in Cherokee Country, Alabama. The USFWS and the Georgia Department of Natural Resources Board are conducting an investigation and have offered rewards of more than twenty thousand dollars for information leading to the arrest and prosecution of those responsible. These mortalities have decreased the number of adult whooping cranes in the EMP to ninety-four, the lowest number in three years.

As the investigation continues, the chicks of OM's eleventh year were in Necedah training for their first migration. Whooping crane fans and OM followers from across the globe wished the young birds and the pilots Godspeed on their maiden and future journeys.

Acknowledgments

Robert Porter Allen died forty-three years before I decided to write this book. There was plenty of reference material from which to tell his story as an ornithologist, but without contacting those who actually knew him, this biography would lack the personal, intimate details necessary to also portray Allen as a friend, neighbor, husband, and father. Phil Kahl, who as a young man studying wood storks in Florida under Allen's tutelage, was grateful to Bob Allen for making sure the National Audubon Society president, John Baker, kept Kahl on the payroll. Carlton Hopper Jr. and his mother, Flora, fondly remembered the Allen family from when they lived in Austwell, Texas. Donna Sprunt, the wife of Sandy Sprunt, who succeeded as Audubon Research Director in Florida when Allen retired, shared her remembrances. And Katharine Picard, a friend of the Allen family, remembered Bob Allen as a kind and generous man who loved spending time with the neighborhood kids.

Meeting Bob Allen's daughter Alice Allen was truly a delight and blessing. Without her kind willingness to assist me in my research, this book would never have been possible. She opened her home and heart to me and gave me the complete picture of her father that no other source could ever provide. As we sat and talked in the Allen Music Studio surrounded by mementoes of her talented, remarkable parents, Alice made the early days of Tavernier, Florida, when the Allens settled there as vivid as those of my own childhood. She listened to and answered all of my questions with candor and humor, and later she reviewed the manuscript for inaccuracies, providing further necessary details.

The dedicated staff of the Tavernier Science Center and Florida Audubon Office, where Allen's documents are kept, welcomed me and graciously turned over their library and copy machine for my use during my visits. Dr. Jerry Lorenz, Florida Audubon's current Research Director, who is continuing Allen's spoonbill studies, provided Allen's actual journals, which were priceless in adding depth to Allen's story. I am forever grateful to Pete Frezza, Florida Audubon's biologist, who helped me locate Allen's correspondence files, photographs, and maps, made additional copies when I needed them, and took time out of his busy schedule to motor me out to Florida Bay, where we visited Bottlepoint Key and a nearby key where the spoonbills nest. Thanks also to Lucille Canavan, the backbone of the office, who shared her work space with me.

The many individuals who are united in their devotion to successfully establishing a second wild flock of whooping cranes, the Eastern Migratory Flock, answered numerous questions and allowed me to watch the training of Operation Migration's (OM's) Class of 2010: Dan Peterson, Education and Outreach Coordinator at the Necedah National Wildlife Refuge; ultralight pilots Richard van Heuvelen and Brooke Pennypacker; lead technician and trainer Barb Clauss; Liz Condie, OM's Director of Communications; and OM's cofounder and ultralight pilot Joe Duff. Also helpful was Joan Garland of the International Crane Foundation.

Thanks also to Tom Stehn, Whooping Crane Coordinator at the Aransas National Wildlife Refuge, for his detailed statistics on the Texas flock from 1938 to the present, and Rhona Kindopp, Ecosystem Scientist at the Wood Buffalo National Park, who provided me with information on the geology and climate of the whooping crane nesting area in Canada.

Thanks to those who read all or part of the manuscript and gave their suggestions: Mary Kalbert, Pam and Mike Herber, Mike Staring, Jim Devaney, Ruth Biblo, Jennifer Sherin, and my sisters, Karen Stanford, Karla Klyng, and Krisann Price. A special thanks to copy editor Susan Murray, who did such a wonderful job helping me with the details.

And finally to my husband, Lloyd, who supported me through the entire process. His patience and willingness to listen to my concerns and offer insightful advice were invaluable. The mosquito infestation that occurred during our five days and nights in Necedah, Wisconsin, didn't bother him at all.

Notes

Chapter 1. By Some Strange Miracle

"By some strange miracle" is taken from Robert Porter Allen, *On the Trail of Vanishing Birds* (New York: McGraw-Hill, 1957).

1. Allen, *Trail*, 7.
2. Ibid., 8.
3. Quoted ibid., 244.
4. Teddy Roosevelt, *Bird-Lore*, June 1899.
5. Quoted in Frank Graham Jr. and Carl Buchheister, *The Audubon Ark: A History of the National Audubon Society* (Austin: University of Texas Press, 1990), 58.
6. Alice Allen, interview by author, Tavernier, Fla., April 4, 2007.
7. Allen, *Trail*, 11.
8. Evelyn Allen, DVD oral history video, Tavernier, Fla., 1988.
9. Ibid.
10. "K" Wilkinson, *It Had to Be You* (Key Largo: Sunshine Press, 1996), 51.
11. Robert Porter Allen, *The Flame Birds* (New York: Dodd, Mead, 1947), 20.
12. Ibid., 44.
13. Ibid., 46.

Chapter 2. The Decision

1. Wilkinson, *It Had to Be You*, 49.
2. Evelyn Allen, DVD oral history video, Tavernier, Fla., 1988.
3. Wilkinson, *It Had to Be You*, 50.
4. Allen, *Flame Birds*, 172.
5. Ibid., 180.
6. Ibid., 218.
7. Ibid., 29.
8. Ibid., 230.
9. Ibid., 233.
10. Robert Porter Allen, *A Report on the Whooping Crane's Northern Breeding Grounds* (New York: National Audubon Society, 1956), xv.

11. Edward Howe Forbush, *A History of the Game Birds, Wild-Fowl and Shore-Birds of Massachusetts and Adjacent States* (Boston: Wright and Potter, 1912), 476.

12. Hal G. Evarts, "The Last Straggler," *Saturday Evening Post*, July 14, 1923.

Chapter 3. The Clang of a Bell

"The Clang of a Bell" is taken from Robert Porter Allen's letter of August 29, 1946.

1. Baker to Allen, January 18, 1946.

2. Baker to Allen, June 11, 1946.

3. Allen to Baker, August 29, 1946.

4. Ibid.

5. Ibid.

6. Allen, *Trail*, 35.

7. Ibid.

8. Karen Harden McCracken, *The Life History of a Texas Birdwatcher: Connie Hagar of Rockport* (College Station: Texas A&M University Press, 1986), 105.

9. Ibid., 105.

10. Allen, *Trail*, 41.

11. Baker to Allen, November 13, 1946.

12. Allen, journal entry, January 10, 1947.

13. Allen, *Trail*, 50.

14. Allen, *Whooping Crane: Research Report No. 3*, 170.

15. Ibid., 170.

16. Baker to Allen, January 10, 1947.

Chapter 4. Things of Value

"Things of Value" is taken from Robert Porter Allen's *On the Trail of Vanishing Birds*.

1. Allen, *Trail*, 38.

2. Allen, *Breeding Grounds*, 8.

3. Ibid., 8.

4. Jimmy Kirkman, "Allen Here, Awaits Flight of Crane," *Telegraph Bulletin*, March 24, 1947.

5. Ibid.

6. Allen, *Whooping Crane: Research Report No. 3*, 89.

7. Allen, *Trail*, 70.

8. Ibid., 71.

9. Ibid., 75.

10. Ibid.

11. Ibid., 76.

Chapter 5. Unforgettable Days

1. Allen to Baker, August 29, 1946.

2. Ibid.

3. Walkinshaw to Bard, May 15, 1947.

4. Allen, *Trail*, 84.

5. Walkinshaw to Baker, May 24, 1947.

6. Larry Walkinshaw, report to National Audubon Society, June 1947.

7. Ibid.

8. Alice Allen to author, June 23, 2010.

9. Smith to Allen, May 23, 1947.

10. Walkinshaw, report to Audubon, June 1947.

11. Allen, *Trail*, 87.

12. Allen, journal entry, June 5, 1947.

13. Smith to Allen, June 2, 1947.

14. Allen, *Trail*, 84.

15. Walkinshaw to Allen, June 12, 1947.

16. Ibid.

17. Walkinshaw, report to Audubon, June 1947.

18. Allen, journal entry, June 20, 1947.

19. Ibid., June 25, 1947.

20. Ibid.

Chapter 6. Small Families

1. Peterson to Allen, August 24, 1947.

2. Allen, *Breeding Grounds*, 8.

3. Pettingill to Allen, July 18, 1947.

4. Peterson to Allen, January 21, 1948.

5. Bond to Allen, April 10, 1947.

6. Smith to Allen, August 22, 1947.

7. Ibid.

8. Allen, *Whooping Crane: Research Report No. 3*, 142.

9. Dr. Glover's medical report, September 1947.

10. Allen, journal entry, December 19, 1947.

11. Peterson to Allen, December 13, 1947.

12. Allen, journal entry, December 13, 1947.

13. Baker to Gustav Swanson, August 6, 1947.

14. Allen, *Breeding Grounds*, 9.

15. Ibid.

Chapter 7. Vanished

1. Pat Stockton, "The Whooping Crane," *Saskatoon Star-Phoenix*, May 1, 1948.

2. Allen, *Breeding Grounds*, 9.

3. Allen, *Whooping Crane: Research Report No. 3*, 208.

4. Allen, journal entry, May 30, 1948.

5. Ibid., June 4, 1948.

6. Allen, *Trail*, 91.

7. wwww.greatcanadianrivers.com/rivers/mack/mack-home.html.

8. Allen, *Trail*, 92–93.

9. Ibid.

10. Allen, journal entry, June 9, 1947.

11. Ibid., June 12, 1947.

12. Allen, *Trail*, 105.

13. Ibid., 106.

14. Ibid., 107.

15. Ibid., 98.

16. www.oldcrow.ca/index2.htm.

17. Allen, *Trail*, 99.

18. Ibid., 102.

19. Ibid., 111.

20. Ibid., 118.

Chapter 8. The Story of Rusty

1. Allen, *Trail*, 125.

2. Ibid., 120.

3. Ibid., 121.

4. Allen, *Whooping Crane: Research Report No. 3*, 184.

5. Ibid., 183.

6. Allen, *Trail*, 131.

7. Allen, *Whooping Crane: Research Report No. 3*, 190.

8. Ibid.

9. Ibid., 182.

10. Allen, "The Whooping Crane and Its Environment," *Audubon Magazine*, March-April 1950, 92.

11. Allen, *Trail*, 132.

12. *Life*, May 8, 1950.

13. Allen, *Trail*, 132.

14. Ibid., 133.

15. Allen, *Whooping Crane: Research Report No. 3*, 203.

16. Allen, *Trail*, 134.

Chapter 9. A Sudden Change of Plans

1. "Fate of Cranes Stirs Two States," *Racine Journal Times*, December 12, 1951.

2. Baker to Hickey, August 11, 1954.

3. Allen, *Trail*, 139.

4. Ibid.

5. Ibid., 141.

6. Ibid., 144.

7. Alfred Lord Tennyson, "Crossing the Bar."

8. Allen, *Trail*, 145.

9. Ibid., 146.

10. Ibid.

11. Ibid., 147.

12. Ibid., 148.

Chapter 10. A Different Kind of Revolution

1. Allen, *Trail*, 163.

2. Ibid., 168.

3. Ibid., 169.

4. Ibid., 170.

5. Ibid.

6. Ibid.

7. Ibid., 171.

8. Ibid., 177.

9. Ibid., 178.

10. Ibid., 179.

11. Ibid., 180–81.

12. Ibid., 186.

13. Ibid., 190.

14. Smith to Allen, July 1, 1952.

15. *New York Herald-Tribune*, August 6, 1952.

16. Allen to Smith, June 25, 1953.

17. Allen, *Trail*, 196.

18. Ibid., 201.

19. Ibid., 202.

Chapter 11. Empty Nest

1. Mair to Baker, July 7, 1954.

2. Allen, *Breeding Grounds*, 6.

3. Allen to Baker, July 12, 1954.

4. Mair to Baker, August 4, 1954.

5. Baker to Mair, August 12, 1954.

6. Robert Porter Allen, "Whooping Cranes Face Another Test," *Audubon Magazine*, September-October 1954, 221.

Chapter 12. Cards on the Table

1. Mair to Farley, November 26, 1954.

2. Fuller to Allen, March 28, 1955.

3. Allen to Baker, April 4, 1955.

4. Baker to Allen, Western Union telegram, May 5, 1955.

5. Allen, *Trail*, 216.

6. Allen to Baker, May 22, 1955.

7. Allen, *Breeding Grounds*, 21.

8. Allen, journal entry, May 24, 1955.

9. Allen, *Trail*, 219.

10. Allen, journal entry, May 28, 1955.

11. Allen to Baker, May 31, 1955.

12. Allen to Baker, June 4, 1955.

13. Allen, journal entry, June 5, 1955.

14. Ibid., June 7–21, 1955.

Chapter 13. They Came through the Twilight

"They Came through the Twilight" is from John O'Reilly's "The Whooping Cranes' Nest Discovered," *New York Herald-Tribune*, July 13, 1955.

1. Allen, journal entry, June 22–27, 1955.

2. Allen, *Breeding Grounds*, 31

3. Allen, journal entry, June 28–30, 1955.

4. O'Reilly, "Whooping Cranes' Nest Discovered."

Chapter 14. The Bob Allen Keys

1. John O'Reilly, "Four Whooping Crane Offspring Are Sighted," *New York Herald-Tribune*, July 15, 1955.

2. Alice Allen to author, July 8, 2010.

3. Robert Porter Allen, National Audubon Society news release, September 9, 1955.

4. Allen, journal entry, November 1, 1958.

5. Allen, *Trail*, 28.

Epilogue: Hope on the Wing

1. http://operationmigration.org/meet_2003_flock.html, Bird Bios, Class of 2003.

2. http://operationmigration.org/meet_2004_flock.html, Bird Bios Class of 2004.

3. Ibid.

4. http://operationmigration.orgFJ2007_Winter1.html, In the Field, February 3, 2007.

Bibliography

I relied mainly on Robert Porter Allen's personal field journals, correspondence, scientific reports, and interviews with his daughter Alice Allen. I read and reread his eloquently written books *The Flame Birds* (1947) and *On the Trail of Vanishing Birds* (1957).

Listed below are other important or especially significant resources and publications that have been of use in the making of this book.

Allen, Robert Porter. *The Roseate Spoonbill* (monograph). New York: Dover, 1942.

———. *The Flame Birds.* New York: Dodd, Mead, 1947.

———. "The Whooping Cranes Still Dance." *Audubon Magazine*, May-June 1947, 136–39.

———. "An Editorial Comment." *Audubon Magazine*, July-August 1948, 231.

———. "Field Notes." *Audubon Magazine*, September-October 1948, 296–28.

———. "The Whooping Crane and Its Environment." *Audubon Magazine*, March-April 1950, 92–95.

———. "The Unique Drama of a Wild Whooper." *Audubon Magazine*, May-June 1950, 194–195.

———. "The Flamingos." *Audubon Magazine*, July-August 1951, 264–65.

———. *The Whooping Crane: Research Report No. 3 of the National Audubon Society.* New York: National Audubon Society, June 1952.

———. "Bird Colonies along the Texas Coast." *Audubon Magazine*, July-August 1952, 270–72.

———. "A Night on the Tongue of Ocean." *Blackwood's Magazine*, May 1953, 462–71.

———. "Help Wanted for the Whooping Crane." *Audubon Magazine*, September-October 1953, 210–13, 224–25.

———. "A Report on the Flamingo." *Audubon Magazine*, January-February 1954, 24–28.

———. "Whooping Cranes Face Another Test." *Audubon Magazine*, September-October, 1954, 221.

———. *The Flamingos: Their Life History and Survival.* New York: National Audubon Society, 1956.

———. *A Report on the Whooping Crane's Northern Breeding Grounds*. New York: National Audubon Society, 1956.

———. *On the Trail of Vanishing Birds*. New York: McGraw-Hill, 1957.

———. *Our Vanishing Wildlife*. Garden City: Nelson Doubleday, 1957.

———. *Birds of the Caribbean*. New York: Viking, 1961.

———. *The Giant Golden Book of Birds: An Introduction to Familiar and Interesting Birds of the World*. New York: Golden Press, 1962.

"Baby Whooping Cranes Are Big Birds Now." *Reading Eagle* (Associated Press), July 12, 1957.

Baker, John. "Search for the Whooping Cranes: The President Reports to You." *Audubon Magazine*, July-August 1945, 245.

———. "Bob Allen Looks for Whooping Cranes: The President Reports to You." *Audubon Magazine*, January-February 1947, 55–56.

———. "On the Trail of the Whooper: The President Reports to You." *Audubon Magazine*, May-June 1947, 173–75.

———. "The Mystery Deepens: The President Reports to You." *Audubon Magazine*, September-October 1948, 303.

———. "The President Reports to You." *Audubon Magazine*, May-June 1949, 178–80.

———. "The President Reports to You." *Audubon Magazine*, July-August 1949, 251–53.

———. "News of Wildlife and Conservation." *Audubon Magazine*, January-February 1950, 52.

———. "News of Wildlife and Conservation." *Audubon Magazine*, July-August 1950, 256.

———. "Cranes Move East: The President Reports to You." *Audubon Magazine*, January-February 1952, 29, 50.

———. "Whooping Cranes Sighted in Canada: The President Reports to You." *Audubon Magazine*, September-October 1954, 220.

———. "Progress for Whooping Cranes: The President Reports to You." *Audubon Magazine*, January-February 1956, 22.

"Crane No. 38?" *Life*, May 8, 1950.

"Cranes to Be Mated." *Hutchinson News-Herald* (Associated Press), July 15, 1948.

"Death of Whooping Crane Reduces North America Total to 109." *Galveston Daily News* (United Press International), March 29, 1979, 49.

Derby, Stafford. "A White, Shining, Superb Creature." *Christian Science Monitor*, September 26, 1955.

"Don't Shoot White Birds (Whooping Crane)." *Milwaukee Sentinel*, September 23, 1953, 16.

Evarts, Hal. "The Last Straggler." *Saturday Evening Post*, July 14, 1923.

"Fate of Cranes Stirs Two States." *Racine Journal Times* (Associated Press), December 12, 1951.

"First Whooping Crane Born in Captivity." *Port Angeles Evening News* (Associated Press), May 31, 1956.

Forbush, Edward Howe. *A History of the Game Birds, Wild-Fowl and Short-Birds of Massachusetts and Adjacent States.* Boston: Wright and Potter, 1912.

"Fresh Hope in Two Eggs." *Life*, May 21, 1956, 131–32.

Furmansky, Dyana F. *Rosalie Edge, Hawk of Mercy: The Activist Who Saved Nature from the Conservationists.* Athens: University of Georgia Press, 2009.

Graham, Frank Jr., and Carl Buchheister. *The Audubon Ark: A History of the National Audubon Society.* Austin: University of Texas Press, 1990.

Hoose, Phillip. *The Race to Save the Lord God Bird.* New York: Farrar, Straus and Giroux, 2004.

Kirkman, Jimmy. "Allen Here, Awaits Flight of Crane." *Telegraph Bulletin*, March 24, 1947.

McCoy, J. J. *The Hunt for the Whooping Cranes: A Natural History Detective Story.* New York: Lothrop, Lee and Shepard, 1966.

McCracken, Karen Harden. *The Life History of a Texas Birdwatcher: Connie Hagar of Rockport.* College Station: Texas A&M University Press, 1986.

McIver, Stuart B. *Death in the Everglades: The Murder of Guy Bradley, America's First Martyr to Environmentalism.* Gainesville: University Press of Florida, 2003.

Nichols, Harman. "Another Whooping Crane Missing from Dwindling Flock of Just 28." *Holland (Mich.) Evening Sentinel*, March 14, 1956.

Operation Migration. "Bird Bios Class of 2003." http://operationmigration.org/meet_2003_flock.html.

———. "Bird Bios Class of 2004," http://operationmigration.org/meet_2004_flock.html.

O'Reilly, John. "Here Come the Cranes." *Sports Illustrated*, September 20, 1954.

———. "Whooping Cranes' Nest Discovered." *New York Herald-Tribune*, July 13, 1955.

———. "Crane Habitat Reached after Month's Failure." *New York Herald-Tribune*, July 14, 1955.

———. "Four Whooping Crane Offspring Are Sighted." *New York Herald-Tribune*, July 15, 1955.

Peterson, Roger Tory, to Bob Allen, August 24, 1947. Tavernier Science Center, Tavernier, Fla.

———, to Bob Allen, December 13, 1947. Tavernier Science Center, Tavernier, Fla.

———, to Bob Allen, January 21, 1948. Tavernier Science Center, Tavernier, Fla.

Picard, Katharine. Telephone interview by author. May 1, 2010.

"Whooping Crane Dies at 33." *Reading Eagle* (United Press International), March 29, 1979.

"Whooping Crane Is Born in Texas." *Sarasota Herald-Tribune* (Associated Press), July 10, 1967.

Sprunt, Donna. Interview by author. March 4, 2010.

Stockton, Pat. "The Whooping Crane." *Saskatoon Star-Phoenix*, May 1, 1948.

"Texas Defies Louisiana to Separate Cranes." *Abilene Reporter-News* (Associated Press), December 12, 1951.

Viele, John. *The Florida Keys: A History of the Pioneers.* Sarasota: Pineapple Press, 1996.

Wagner, Robert. "Life with the Captive Whooping Cranes." *Audubon Magazine,* September-October 1956, 222–24.

"Whooping Crane Eggs Touch off Big Hassle." *Ogden Standard-Examiner* (Associated Press), May 12, 1957.

Wilkinson, Jerry. E-mail interview by author. October 8, 2010.

Wilkinson, "K." *It Had to Be You.* Key Largo: Sunshine Press, 1996.

Wing, Joe. "Experts to Fly North with Last of Whooping Cranes to Seek Mystery Nests." *Milwaukee Journal,* April 3, 1948.

———. "Whooper: Here's the Life History of One of the Last of Whooping Cranes." *Austin (Minn.) Daily Herald,* January 12, 1953.

Index

Kathleen Kaska, an award-winning author of books, short stories, articles, and stage plays, taught middle-school science for twenty-five years. Her passion for whooping cranes led her to write this book.

When she is not writing, Kathleen spends much of her time traveling back roads and byways with her husband, her laptop stowed in her bag, and a bird-reference book and binoculars always on the front seat. They divide their time between their two favorite places, the Pacific Northwest and the Texas Coast.

Kathleen is also a published mystery writer and a frequent contributor to *Texas Highways* magazine.